DEDICATED TO THE MEMORY OF
MY PARENTS
BLOD AND GEORGE PENLINGTON

THEY GAVE ME THE WORLD

"I can't tell where the journey will end

But I know where to start."

Avicii – Wake Me Up

Around The World In Wonder Socks

Travels Of A Nony
(Not old, not young – somewhere in the middle)

Arthur Penlington

ISBN-13: 978-1514758861

INTRODUCTION

Ah, middle age. Those magical years when we get to prise open the bursting piggy bank of our lives. Stuffed full of wealth, health and wisdom this is the bit where we start to cash it all in.

Welcome to Nirvana, a land of milk and honey. The mystical destination that kept us going through toiling years of blood, sweat and tears.

Middle age is a time of choices and finally we have the will and the wherewithal to act on them. Our lives are increasingly a heady mixture of freedom and flexibility all topped off with a fine veneer of knowledge and experience. This is our moment.

Or there again, perhaps not. Best you don't pop open the champagne corks just yet for there are pessimists out there who see it slightly differently. For them the middle years are a time of sagging, spreading, stiffening and settling. This is only the bad stuff beginning with the letter 'S'. You should see what they can do with the 'F' words (and no, I don't think they have that particular one in mind).

'F' has its own litany of middle age baggage. There's flab, flatulence, fallen arches and funerals. Although, truth be told, I've laughed my socks off at several final send-offs. Then there's that killer 'F' word, 'Failed'. In middle age it's often butted up against many of life's biggies - failed marriage, failed business and the ultimate nightmare, failed breathalyser.

The point is that middle age can be saddled with seriously bad connotations. The wonder and vigour of youth has often given way to weariness. We work long and hard and settle easily; into routines, habits, life choices and armchairs, although at the end of a hard day that's less of a settle and more a total collapse.

What we do and what we are have been framed by years of conventions and rituals. Life has become increasingly defined by the concepts of less and more. We take less risk, we become more conservative; we have less hair, we take more pills – spell check tried to replace 'pills' with 'piles', perhaps it's smarter than I thought.

So take your pick. In middle age you can either have your cake and eat it or chuck it in the bin because it's absolutely forbidden by the latest fascist diet you're slaving through.

Trying to pin down a definition for middle age can also be a little tricky. In the film, 'On Golden Pond', Ethel (Katherine Hepburn) is trying to convince her curmudgeonly husband Norman (Henry Fonda) that despite being in their late 60s and 70s, respectively, they're still middle-aged. Norman will have none of it.

"Middle age Ethel means the middle, middle of life. We're not middle-aged. People don't live to be 150."

"Well, we're at the far edge of middle age, that's all," replies Ethel.

"We're not you know. We're not middle aged. You're old and I'm ancient."

Women born around 1960 have an average life expectancy in the mid-70s, for men it's a few years less. However, these figures are rapidly changing. The current crop of newborns is predicted to live on average for another 10 years. In percentage terms that's a whopper, so don't let the little buggers grow into bleating teenagers who complain about their lot. Truth is their 'lot' is actually a lot more than our lot, if you see what I mean.

Age is obviously crucial in determining our middle years but it's equally about health, fitness and especially attitude. We are not our parents' generation, life is way easier. So, for the purposes of this book, I've defined middle age as ranging from early 40s to mid-60s. I'll admit my definition is totally unscientific but having a random stab in the dark saved me a heck of a lot of time on research.

The middle years' drift towards conservatism can be particularly true of travel. Many of us stray from the road less travelled to one well and truly trampled down. We often have more money so destinations become a little more exotic but we are generally less ambitious and our holidays are more planned and packaged. Resorts and cruises increase in their appeal. We're met at airports by people holding up our names on clapperboards. We're catered for and cocooned in coaches and tour groups.

But these are actually our peak travel years. Recent figures show the prime age for getting away is now 50-54, an upward shift from the 45-49 age bracket. This suggests we have more opportunities, more time and money. Kids are old enough to fend for themselves or to have flown or fled the nest entirely. Although one of modern life's great ironies is that we're now often the ones doing the fleeing.

There's a scary graph showing a horrible upwards curve in the number of grown up offspring staying or, worse still, returning home. They bring with them bad habits and big demands. It's us that now need to get away. But do we really need to be less ambitious in our travel or are we surrendering too early to the easy life?

There's never been a better opportunity to slip the tight fitting corset of packages. Doing it yourself is comparatively simple. Lonely Planet, Google and TripAdvisor mean you never have to make a total leap into the unknown. Forums, blogs and reviews allow us to make fully informed decisions on flights, hotels and much more. Want to know whether the guesthouse is on a busy road? Just click on Google Maps for a street level tour of your destination. Keen to find out if the breakfast waiter has halitosis? Load up TripAdvisor and read the reviews. There's an absolute mine of information from people who've been there, done that, got the virus.

This is how I've been travelling for years. A little smug that it was DIY and unpackaged but also increasingly aware that it was, nonetheless, fairly regimented. Flight, tick; hotel, tick; recommended restaurants, tick; quaint little hidden coffee shop, tick. It hadn't dawned on me I was living off guidebooks and just doing the packaging myself. I was independently doing the same as the rest of the herd who'd bought Lonely Planet. It meant I was often planning out the unexpected, I was denying myself truly authentic, unscripted, travel experiences.

I began questioning whether it would be very different if I just did it all ad hoc, unplanned. Literally tossing a coin and wandering down the different paths it sent me. So, after plenty of thought and even more hesitation, that's what I set out to do. I sold my home, put all my worldly possessions in storage and took a deep breath. I booked a one-way flight to Bali and four nights in a small hotel. The rest would be left to fate.

One year later I stopped tossing and finally returned home. The intervening 12 months were crammed full of remarkable people, places, and incidents. I learned a hell of lot about myself and more than anything I recaptured my life and set free my spirit. I'd unbuckled the straightjacket which had been unknowingly strapped around my ambitions. And I did it all on my own terms.

This book is the story of that year. It's not a diary, chronology nor even a step by step guide. It's a series of stories and snapshots of my experiences, the amazing characters I bumped into along the way and the remarkable places I discovered. It's all in here, the good, the bad and the toilets (sometimes way beyond ugly).

It's also a rallying call to pretty much everybody out there who feels their travelling has become a little predictable or lacking a spark. But fear not, this isn't one of those jaw dropping tales of macho travel which is realistically beyond the pale for most of us mere mortals. You know the ones; first person to climb Everest backwards in a pair of open toed sandals or swimming the length of the Amazon underwater on one gulp of air per day.

I have no special skills, the premise is that if I can you can. I didn't set out to do anything particularly wild but in the space of a year I drove a passenger train, ate ice cream with the most beautiful woman in the world, hunted with Borneo tribesmen and had lovemaking tips from a gigolo. You'd be amazed what can happen with a willingness to travel a little differently.

#

1

THE PLAN - NO PLAN

Just what is the etiquette for politely declining the sexual advances of a headhunter? It was another one of those ticklish 'cultural issues' my half-hearted research had missed. But now, in the dead of night, deep in the Borneo jungle, I had an urgent need for an answer which would leave his pride and my bottom intact.

Two tribesmen, my guide and I were sandwiched together for the night on the achingly hard, wooden floor of the longhouse. The lusty tribesman next to me was well within stroking and groping distance. For the fifth time in an hour his leg had snaked around mine and gripped me vice-like. His warm breath moistened my neck and his spittle dripped in my hair.

Panic was rising on my side and I sensed something entirely different was rising on his. I wondered if he was wide awake and amorous or hard asleep and having a frisky dream. If he was away with the fairies I suspected I was there with him, the star attraction in his fantasy. None of the answers brought me any comfort.

My only relief was the knowledge his tribe, like most in Borneo, had given up headhunting around 60 years ago. My skull would be leaving the encounter untouched. Unfortunately, other more sensitive parts of my anatomy were in peril of faring a little less well.

I'd been tolerant and gentle the first four times I'd had to remove his lecherous leg. By the fifth my patience had gone and I jabbed him sharply in his ribs. It did the trick, he grunted and his grip immediately slackened.

Although his lusting limb may have relaxed, my brain was still in turmoil as I lay waiting for the next advance. Only the snoring from our two dead-to-the-world companions muffled the wild drum beat of my pounding heart. Fear, the jungle and a randy headhunter can be a devil of a concoction when it comes to trying to sleep.

I lay there wide awake, wondering if I'd have to fight off another attempted clinch. Finally, I reached the point where I just had to know whether he was sleeping or simply biding his time. Cautiously, I inched myself over onto my other side to check him out. His face loomed monstrously large in mine. After a hard day and night downing rice wine his mouth was half open and twisted in a grotesque homage to 'The Scream' but, thankfully, his eyes were firmly shut. Mine, on the other hand, almost leapt from their sockets. Hanging just above his head was his tribal knife, 18 inches of lethal menace. I'd watched him use it to devastating effect throughout the day. The terrifying sight spurred me into inaction. If he came back a sixth time there would be no more resistance from me, bugger that! I'd happily trade my life for whatever prize he sought, my body is hardly a temple anyway.

Fortunately this proved to be his last onslaught, he was done for the night. Despite the bone-aching discomfort of the floor and the transfixing fear of his weaponry my mind slowly relaxed. Gradually it cleared enough to address a fundamental question. What the hell was I doing there?

Eleven months ago I had been quietly under-preparing for my trip. The thought of being a headhunter's sexual playmate had taken up precious little of my time. How on earth had I got from there to here?

There was, of course, a box full of reasons, good and bad. A couple of years earlier my marriage had hit some hitherto unnoticed rocks and been fatally holed below the waterline. It sank, taking with it half of my wealth and most of my energy, but not, for some strange reason, Gonga, a pint-sized, thumb-sucking cuddly gorilla who had been my wife's confidant during youthful traumas.

Fast forward past all the emotional stuff and two and a half years later I had re-emerged with my life back on an even keel. I'd been wrapped in the care of good friends and the embrace of a gorgeous Japanese lover. And throughout it all there was Gonga, who had quietly switched jerseys and been valiantly batting away for team Arthur.

But with all this came the realisation that I was lacking a spark. I'd lost some vitality. It was probably down the side of the sofa along with four dollars of loose change I'd recently discovered. Strictly speaking, under the terms of our separation, I was only entitled to half, but I cunningly kept that one quiet.

I began to think of the best way forward and a holiday seemed to be the answer. A change of scenery, a chance to meet some fascinating people and a few adventures. Nothing too wild.

From the sanctuary of my study I roamed the globe looking for the perfect spot. Destinations leapt off the computer screen. So many places to visit, so many things to see. Southeast Asia, exotic, spiritual, vibrant and mostly unknown to me. Europe would also be a good bet. I know much of it, I can just get by in French and there are a lot of old buildings and ruins I could drool over.

The longer I looked the more the list of must-sees grew. It was all so exciting and enticing. But gradually over days my attitude began to change. I became a little frustrated at all the incredible sights I knew I wouldn't be seeing, simply too many to pack into a single holiday. Then came the Hallelujah moment, a blinding flash of insight. I realised I was thinking too conventionally, I was planning a holiday when I could be making a journey. Instead of being a tourist I could be a traveller. The key difference was time and that was something I didn't lack. I'd finished my career with BBC TV News years earlier and apart from some casual university lecturing and a little web writing, my life was my own. It was one of the perks of my middle age.

Now the questions flowed. What would be the ideal duration? Would solo travel be lonely? How much would I need to pack? If Harrison Ford looked cool in 'Raiders Of The Lost Ark' jungle gear, could I? That was easy to answer and was promptly crossed off the list.

It all seemed a little daunting but slowly it also began to make sense. I'm one of life's researchers so I set to work. Destination guidebooks, flight schedules, train timetables and hotel reviews were pored over. Next came climate charts to check temperatures and rainfall. Since moving from the UK to Australia I don't do cold, a little skiing excepted, this would be a hot trip.

A basic plan began to emerge and I somehow became set on the idea of three months away. It seemed a long time. I launched myself into the detail, checking specific dates for hotel availability, making connections work from planes to ferries.

Preparation for three months of travel is no small matter and there was a lot of head scratching when parts of the itinerary defied my planning. My files grew bigger by the hour. Then came the inevitable spanner in the works. I'd discover some overlooked gem, an amazing festival, a pristine landscape or beaches of white, dreamy sand. My route was constantly amended and once or twice entirely ripped up.

Somewhere in this process my travel adventure began to move from pleasure to pain in the arse, it was becoming a chore. My enthusiasm waned and drooped and trust me, droopy is not my best look.

Then came the real moment of clarity, a radical thought. If I was looking for a jump-start to my life, I should remove the straightjacket of a plan and let fate and circumstance be my guide. Why not just make it up as I went along, not be tied to timetables and reservations. Just do it on the hoof.

Initially it seemed a step too far but gradually I warmed to the idea. My boldness and enthusiasm began to surge. Why put a timescale on it at all? I could just travel and keep going, only stopping when I decided I'd had enough. I wouldn't bring it to a halt because of some arbitrary deadline. I could travel in a way I'd never managed before, utterly without restraint. What a liberating idea.

Now I really was on a roll. My imagination kept firing and I could feel myself slipping free of the bonds of my life. Finally I hit upon the biggest idea of all, I should sell the house. I was living there on my own but my ex still owned half of it. To be fair she wasn't demanding the place be sold, she wasn't desperate for her equity. But I was at the point of no return, in for a penny in for a pound. I decided to get rid of it. I'd gather up all my furniture and possessions and put them in storage. My life and my travels would be completely without restraint. Gulp!

Once the decision was taken everything took on a momentum of its own. It all just seemed to happen around me and I became an interested but slightly bemused onlooker on my own life.

All of the complex travel plans I'd been making were binned. Now everything boiled down to just one simple question. Where should I start? And that was relatively easy. Nothing would be more certain to kill my thirst for adventure than a 12-hour plane journey. I wanted something close, somewhere a little ethereal but not too much of a leap into the dark. Somewhere to gingerly put my toe in the water of travel. Boldness could wait a week.

The shortlist started and ended with Bali. A little exotic but in many parts modernised with hotels and infrastructure. In other words a very safe bet. The flight would be a short hop from Brisbane to Darwin and then a little skip over to Denpasar. Done, booked, sorted. It was as simple as that.

Next I booked four nights in a small, cheap boutique hotel and that was that. My new principles of travel dictated that I shut down the computer and abandon all other destination research. After week one it would be time to simply play it as it comes. My gulps kept getting bigger.

The next few weeks were lost in frenetic activity. The house was sold, possessions packed and stored, admin half-heartedly sorted. Before I knew it I was sitting on the bedroom floor of my empty home, the only objects left my 50 litre BlackWolf backpack (that means small) and all the clothes and gear I'd decided would be necessary for cheap, unencumbered travel. And here I might have overdone it.... actually, underdone it would probably be more appropriate.

#

The online world is packed to its giga gunnels with warnings of hell, fury, plague and pestilence for those who screw up their packing. Blogs, tweets, and factoids urge virgin travellers to 'go light'. The patriarchs of the backpacking tribe post videos sharing the intimate secrets of their sacks. Packing is earnestly debated in dozens of travel forums. The correct number of T-shirts, trousers, socks and hats; hiking boots or trail shoes; one pair of shorts or two? A guy who suggested three was cyber bullied for his profligacy and is currently undergoing re-education at a Peruvian youth hostel.

But backpackers have reached a surprising consensus on an area close to my heart, actually a rather more delicate organ. They are united on undies. A very clear line is drawn and there is absolutely no room for manoeuvre in underwear. Girls are explicitly told to pack seven sets of knicks, for men the magic number of jocks is three.

Now this got me thinking, and this is dangerous territory. I understand the concept of seven for ladies, one for each day of the week, then it's soapy suds time. Completely logical. But why do blokes only get three? Nowhere on the net is there an explanation, it's an off-limits kind of conversation. The issue is the backpackers' equivalent of Bill Clinton's gays in the military policy of Don't Ask, Don't Tell. And we all know what a cock up that was, or wasn't as it turned out.

So I remained dumbfounded by the disparity. Certainly I'm old enough to appreciate that men and women are different. Men are from Mars and women are from..... somewhere else. I've also been around long enough to know guys will happily forego a bit of personal hygiene. But a ratio of 2.33 clean undies to 1 for the girls? Anyway, I digress, this is neither the time nor the place for me to be getting into ladies' knickers.

What became very clear was I'd gone too far. I'd taken all the advice to heart and there was next to nothing to pack. A couple of splittable long pants, one long and two short sleeved shirts, a few small accessories, a first aid kit I knew I'd never need and not much else, not even any socks. It was the first mistake of my travels.

Avoiding the second mistake was easier. I opted for seven sets of jocks – bugger the backpacker etiquette, I'm neither a fan of chafing nor hand-washing.

#

2

THE BIRTH OF A NONY

Convincing people that I hadn't lost my sanity wasn't easy. "No plan, no bookings?" That was a regular reaction. It was less of a question and more of a statement whose unsubtle and unsaid subtext was "you've gone off the deep end mate!"

"On your own?" That was another frequent comeback. It was closely followed by my own favourite, a kind of double take. "Backpacking did you say?" This kind of stunned incredulity happened a lot, most memorably from a doctors' receptionist during a phone conversation to book my travel jabs. She was certainly not the first to use the 'B' word so sceptically.

Some people tell me my voice is my best feature. It's not necessarily got a lot to compete with and it's probably far from being a real compliment. But I've fooled myself into thinking my phone manner is an exotic mix of youthful, virile and sophisticated. The receptionist's tone implied otherwise.

"You wouldn't get me doing that at your age", she said.
This was a hammer blow to my ego as she hadn't even asked my age. Without pause she continued her assault on my sensitivities.

"Isn't backpacking what we all did a long time ago before we discovered nice hotels?"

Sad to say she's not alone. Many friends choked on their Sauvignon Blancs when first hearing of the plan, or lack thereof. I/they tend to lead comfortable lives. Admittedly some camp but the closest they get to hardship is when the croissants are frozen not fresh.

Partly, I suspect, it's a problem of pigeonholes. We like to categorise things, it makes the world fit our need for certainty. Selling my home and heading off to who knows where for God knows how long, in my early 50s to boot, didn't lend itself to a world of stability. It was a little outside the norm.

I began wondering where I fitted in the grand scheme of things. What societal label could I attach to myself to make people a little more comfortable with my scheme? I was too old to be a typical world travelling backpacker. Of course there are people of all ages out there but late teens or early 20s is generally the norm. Nor am I a grey nomad - too young for that, they're retirees of a slightly more advanced age and yanking a backpack around isn't generally what they're about.

Could I be a flashpacker? These are backpackers who enjoy the odd upmarket escape from roughing it and stay in half decent guest houses and lodgings. I'll confess it sounded plausibly me or at least it did until I found an article suggesting flashpackers are mostly in their 30s and early 40s.

So here I was, I didn't really fit any easy traveller category and the idea of being a 'middle-aged backpacker' sounded a little boring. In a world obsessed with labels and niches I thought it best to invent my own. So welcome to the world of the NONY, Not Old, Not Young, somewhere in between. It's uncomfortably close to the Italian word for grandfather, 'nonno', which really wasn't the image I was after, but it would have to do.

I currently live in Noosa, Queensland, where the average age is in the high Nonys. It's beautiful, a backpackers' beach and surfing destination in its own right, although if truth be told I take it somewhat for granted. It's a lovely place to live, not an easy place to leave, but the world was calling. The seductive, siren voices of travel had been cooing in my direction for a while and now it was time to coo back.

After a blur of last minute arrangements my final farewell was to my friend Rod who had kindly given me a lift to the airport. Half way to our destination there was a brief panic as I realised I still didn't have a crucial part of my cargo. A last minute detour was made to an outdoor specialist shop where I hastily bought two pairs of socks. A week earlier I'd splashed out on some Oboz multi-terrain shoes, they were to prove a very smart investment. But socks had slipped my mind entirely.

Now time was against me so I grabbed the first ones to hand and went to pay. As I stood waiting for the cashier I read the label. It turned out that what I had in my hands were 'the ultimate walking socks'. Excellent news, although the reasons why weren't immediately obvious. To me the ultimate socks would be ones that never get separated from each other and never require washing. This pair didn't seem to hold out any promises on either count.

I hadn't checked the price, after all I was only buying socks. At the checkout up flashed the price, $60. I stood open jawed in shock. Had they been hand woven by maidens using silk thread? There were no telltale signs of handcrafting, my only description would be short and black with no other obvious discernible selling point. But it was too late to argue and we set off once more for Brisbane airport.

When Rod pulled his car up outside the departure hall there was a brief, slightly uncomfortable moment of silence. But then he turned and looked me in the eye.

"Good luck mate. Have a fantastic time and look after yourself. You know you're always welcome to come back and stay with us any time."

I knew it was a genuine offer and it probably masked the serious concerns of a number of friends. On the golf course a couple of days earlier Rod had grabbed my arm and with evident concern asked, "What happens if something goes wrong or you don't like this kind of travel?"

It seemed a fair question and it was easy enough to answer. "I'll just come home," I said.

His reply stopped me in my tracks.

"But you don't have a home!"

He was right. All I had was a storage unit packed to the roof with 'stuff'. Selling up had felt so liberating and exciting at the time but with one simple question it suddenly seemed at best an enormous undertaking and at worst the stupidest idea on earth. I'd been a homeowner for a long time but now, I realised, I wasn't just out on a limb I was effectively out on the street. Excuse me while I take another gulp.

The horror of this exchange had consumed my final couple of days in Oz but I'd slowly reconciled myself to the idea. After all, I'd taken my own grown up decision and I had money in the bank, all I really lacked was a building with my name on the deeds. No big deal.

But now sitting with Rod at the airport drop-off zone the strangest thing happened, words deserted me. All I could manage were a few choked breaths. Finally I forced out a reply, "Thanks for everything Rod, I.... I...."

It's all I could manage before my throat convulsed. I got out, shut the door and walked off, no real farewell, no goodbye waves. And so there I was on the verge of the greatest journey of my life with a small backpack, two new pairs of wonder socks and emotions I never saw coming. I'd expected heroic fanfares in my head as I strode straight-backed into the awesome arena of adventure. Instead, I was welling up and wondering, not for the first time nor the last, what the hell am I doing?

#

3

DESPAIR IN DARWIN

By take-off I'd recaptured a little of my fragile spirit. Sitting next to me on the plane were Sam and Andrew Lythgo who were heading out to Bali for some fishing and brotherly fun. Andrew, it turned out, was a published author, his book 'Confessions of a Futures Trader' had apparently sold rather well. Both he and Sam were natural storytellers and perfect travelling companions for a few short hours.

Generally, when I board a plane, I say a silent prayer for two things, no babies anywhere in earshot and an empty seat next to mine. But I was having a change of heart, not where babies were concerned, that's 100% totally non-negotiable. Actually, make that 101% just so we all know where we stand. But the empty seat idea needed a reappraisal.

I knew of friends of friends who'd actually met on a plane a few years ago, fallen in love and married. Remember that next time you're on a flight. Have a crafty peek at the person in the adjacent seat and consider whether you might be sitting with your future life partner. If you're actually reading this on a plane you might want a stiff drink first before taking a look. The object of your interest might be a dribbling, overweight buffoon with bad breath and a comb over - and I'm not just talking about men here. Hence the need for a fortifying drink.

But the idea of romance and the realization that I was out on my own in the world prompted a change of mindset. Travelling alone, you quickly work out that talking to people is generally way more satisfying than ignoring them. There'd be more than enough time on my own so I decided to become that bloke sitting next to you who insists on chatting throughout the flight. This, despite knowing you were almost certainly hoping for an empty seat. Sorry.

It had been an entertaining and encouraging start and by the time we landed in Darwin I felt genuinely excited to be on my way. I'd have a couple of easy hours at the airport before my next flight to foreign shores.

Darwin airport is perfectly neat and tidy but hardly over endowed with distractions so I headed straight to the check-in desk. Ahead of me were about 30 people. I wondered which lucky one would be sitting next to me on the flight to Bali.

The queue shuffled forward at the usual snail's pace. Check-in is normally one of travel's dull necessities but I became aware of a growing ripple of excitement and people pricking up their ears. A young couple had been led away from the counter and were deep in conversation with an officious looking airline rep. Actually it looked less of a chat and more a withering lecture. Heads were being shaken and the couple began to look more and more frantic.

The queue continued to snake slowly forward while necks craned to the side to eavesdrop. A few minutes later the supervisor was called back to the counter. Another couple were clearly having check-in woes of their own. After the briefest of chats they too were led to the side. Both young couples looked crestfallen and one of the girls began to wipe tears from her eyes. The queue became alive with whispering. It turned out the unfortunates held only one-way tickets to Bali and had no proof of any onwards travel plans.

"Apparently that's against the rules," said the woman in front of me to her husband. "I've never heard of that before."

They simultaneously turned to me and with a quizzical look on her face the woman asked, "Have you ever heard of a rule like that?"

"It's news to me," I said.

That wasn't exactly the truth. I'd stumbled across this particular rule just a week or so earlier.

In the final days before departure I'd started reading online travel blogs. I wasn't after the 'go here, go there' type of destination advice, I'd banned myself from that, but I was searching for nuggets on how to make travel easier.

There are so many blogs out there it's surprising the net doesn't collapse in on itself. Amid the general 'got up, made breakfast, weather hot, showers not, blah, blah blah', there are plenty of gems. One in particular had set alarm bells ringing. It mentioned a requirement for travellers on one-way tickets to have proof of onwards travel from the country they're about to enter. Whether you leave by air, sea or land is irrelevant as long as you have proof that you won't be overstaying.

Most people travel with return flight tickets so this isn't usually an issue to be considered. Plenty of airlines I've since come across don't even bother checking. But not all. Carriers are deemed liable if a passenger arrives in a country without proof of confirmed onward travel. If the traveller is refused entry the airlines are obliged to return them from whence they came and at their own cost. After a little research it turns out there are a fair few tales of people, backpackers in particular, being refused onto flights because they didn't have the necessary evidence.

And so I stood in the Darwin queue with my heart sinking, stomach churning and my bladder suddenly feeling overly full. All down to the simple fact that I too was clutching a one way ticket to Bali. I had no onwards travel plans, I didn't even know where I'd be at the weekend.

I glanced nervously at the two young couples as they stood leper-like off to one side. I'm sure their arrangements were at best vague and at worst deliberately non-existent. They were almost certainly spontaneous travellers with a wide-eyed and carefree wonder for the world. In other words, younger versions of me.

I had the required 30-day visa for Indonesia and had absolutely no intention of overstaying, I just didn't want to restrict myself to a plan laid out a month in advance. This rigidity was exactly what my travel aimed to overcome. Sometimes the world can screw you around with its rules.

I pictured the scene five minutes into the future where I would suffer the indignity of being marched over to join the helpless couples. My self-image had been of a fearless global traveller, a risk-taker on the cusp of a brave new world, ballsy and free. But now I felt worried, impotent and potentially screwed!

The queue shuffled relentlessly on until finally I stood at its head. I scanned the three check-in staff and hoped for the smiling one off to my right. But even as I made my earnest wish a voice called out from my left.

"Next please."

It was the sour looking assistant who'd just rejected the second couple. My only tactic was to ignore her hoping to buy a few seconds so young Ms Smiley would be free to check me in.

"You're up mate," said an annoyingly helpful guy behind me. I blanked him as well.

"Nexxxt!"

This time it was shrill and loud enough to pierce eardrums and, more worryingly, the word 'please' had been dropped. Almost simultaneously the friendly guy in the queue prodded me and pointed in the direction of the voice. I was doomed.

With a deep breath I summoned up a cheery smile and walked to the counter. I put on my finest charming and disarming act to distract the assistant. Hopefully she wouldn't even notice my one way ticket. In my deepest and most virile voice I gushed and gabbled and, although I say so myself, she was soon putty in my hands.

Thirty seconds later the putty turned to mush.

"This is a one-way ticket," she said. "I need to see proof of your onward travel plans."

I was screwed. My bladder expanded a little more.

Fortunately I did have one shot at bucking the system. The blog I'd stumbled across had made me a little alarmed but also a lot forewarned.

It also suggested a couple of ways around the onwards travel requirement. Option one was to buy a fully flexible return ticket. After arriving at destination just cancel the unused return section and get the appropriate refund. Useful, but flexible fares can be hugely expensive. Option two was much cheaper and more.... interesting. Now this may get you into a little bother with the airlines or immigration - if you get caught - so obviously I can't recommend it. Just mentioning it in passing, that's all.

The suggested trick is to go through the full online process of booking an onwards flight up until the point of putting in credit card details. Use your smart phone, iPad or whatever to take a screen grab of the page which shows all the flight details. To all intents and purposes it looks just like an e-ticket. If you're asked for an onwards travel booking just show this page. Ultra attentive check-in counter staff may spot what you've done, for others it might just go unnoticed. I was about to find out.

With my confidence fraying at the edges I reached for my iPad, opened up my photos page and showed a screen grab. Mrs Check-in gave it the once over while I stood passive and silent. I'd ceased the charm act, my brain was fighting on too many fronts. All its efforts were now focused on preventing bodily functions from happening at an inappropriate time and an especially inappropriate place.

The assistant seemed to take forever. Her eyes scanned what appeared to be an onwards flight ticket from Bali, Indonesia, to Kuala Lumpur in Malaysia. Finally, she turned away, hit a couple of buttons on her keyboard and I heard the blissful sound of a boarding card being printed.

Bali here I come! It was a huge relief. I suspect that having a little grey hair, a few years on my body clock and a pair of respectable glasses, gave me an air of middle age honesty and respectability which, on this occasion, was not entirely deserved. One up to the Nonys! Over the next 12 months the middle age thing helped me out in a couple of tight spots.

I left the counter and quietly slipped over to the stranded couples.

After making them promise they wouldn't dob me in I gave them a quick tip for their future one-way travels.

The first unexpected drama of my journey was over. Little did I know that scrape number two was waiting patiently in a holding pattern overhead and was about to come literally crashing down on top of me.

But for now I happily offered up a silent thanks to the helpful blogger and smugly congratulated myself for my research. For the first time, and certainly not the last, a little bit of time invested in research had saved my bacon.

Three hours later I was in Bali walking through the arrivals door of adventure and a big, bright, brave new world. I felt utterly fabulous, I was riding high.

#

4

DISASTER STRIKES

Week 1; Seminyak, Bali; 4,650 kms travelled,
1 pair of broken thongs;
7 undies all worn - good call by me ☺

I was falling. Not in slow motion like people always tell you. If anything it was fast, furious and bloody painful. My big, bright, brave adventure was slithering to hell.

Now, I'm well aware that you can't travel the world without some bumps along the way, life, incidents and imbeciles happen. But even by my own accident prone standards this one was a record. Just eighteen hours after arriving in Bali disaster struck.

I'd rented a motorbike for $5 a day, a bargain, even if the beast was less a motorbike and more a putt putt scooter. It was painted in wild pink and for some unfathomable reason was emblazoned in large capital letters with the word B***ARD.

To add to my humiliation the rental guy handed me a helmet Biggles would have rejected as being a little too foppish. It was round, made of brown leather and had two huge, hanging ear flaps which dangled down to my shoulders. The flaps were lifeless until I reached 5 miles an hour, at which point they suddenly took on a life of their own and frenziedly whipped me across the face. I was trying for a biker-cool kind of feel but with a mere 50cc of bright pink machinery under me and Mutley and Dastardly headgear on top, it wasn't even close to happening.

I reconciled myself to the fact nobody in Bali knew me and by the time I recounted the tale to my friends the scene would be wildly embellished. In alternative Arthur world I'd be riding a 500cc machine of raging, throbbing chrome and black, a babe magnet between my legs and a Darth Vader helmet on my head. A kind of brutal cool was the look I'd be cultivating in my homecoming stories

An hour after hiring the scooter I was on a narrow stretch of potholed bitumen crammed with other bikers, mostly teenagers looking way cooler in a brief moment than I'd mustered in half a century of life. On the periphery of my vision I saw one of the oncoming scooters begin to wobble. A moment later it turned into a wild, bucking bronco and I saw terror on the rider's face. She was squeezing both brakes but fatally her right hand was also twisting the accelerator. The bike jerked and lurched violently forward and with one final turn of the handle the scooter surged and snaked off to her right. She scythed down one rider, smacked into a second, and next in her crosshairs was me. With bikes all around me there was nowhere to go and she clipped my rear wheel, hurling me from the seat. I scraped along the ground, my hands, knees, arms and elbows shredding skin as I went. Other motorbikes screeched around me and I flailed around in a sea of wheels before finally coming to a face-down halt. Like an ever-faithful horse the pink B***ARD dutifully followed and finally came to a stop on top of me.

There was the briefest of pauses and then all hell broke loose. Wobbly turned out to be a young Aussie girl 10 minutes into her first ever scooter ride. She was in hysterics even though she had no obvious signs of injury. Remember John Hurt's terrifying death scene in the film 'Alien' when a monster burst out of his chest cavity? This was way worse.

Not be outdone, one of the Balinese riders she'd tried to decapitate had jumped to his feet and was screaming as if Armageddon was upon us. In moments a crowd was on site and the place became a cauldron of shouting and pointing.

Off to one side there was me, momentarily stunned and trying to take it all in. Five or six Balinese men and women gathered around me, picked up the B***ARD and began asking if I was ok. Yes and no. Everything still working, nothing broken, but I sat painting the road red with my blood. Dozens of black chippings were stuck on and in my knees, arms, elbows and hands. Some protruded from under my blackened skin like little nuggets of coal. The dirt from the road was already congealing with the blood and I could almost feel the infection seeping maliciously into me.

I was led to the side of the road and sat on the kerb where I tried to make sense of what had happened. Wobbly's shock was slowly eased by her friends who in turn were doing their best to calm her tormentors. Wallets and purses opened as on-the-spot compensation was demanded. This was justice Balinese style, cops and documents were irrelevant.

My bike was terribly scratched along its front and right hand side and a large crack ran down the rear mudguard. I wasn't faring too much better myself, chunks of skin were missing and my limbs were hideously grazed.

Despite the concerns of some locals I eventually got back on the B***ARD and rode warily back to my hotel. I wasn't in a great state but in adversity you find the best in humanity. A United Nations of people set about putting me back together again.

Fortunately I'd met an English couple, Debbie and Paul, from Port Sunlight, Merseyside. Debbie was a nurse and she examined my wounds. Lots of TLC and advice was offered along with bandages and anti-septic wipes from the first aid kit which just two days earlier I'd almost dumped in the near certainty it would never get used.

Later, with Debbie's prompting, I went to the pharmacy and bought several creams and sprays, principally to keep infection at bay. Norina, the receptionist at Uma Karan, my small hotel, wasn't satisfied. She abandoned her post, marched off to another store and returned with a Chinese healing potion. This was the bees' knees she said, or something sounding remarkably like it. She'd paid for it herself and absolutely refused to take a cent for it.

A Singaporean couple staying at the hotel offered me much sympathy and their contact details if I needed some post injury recovery time at their home. Amazing really as I'd only met them for 45 minutes or so while they waited to leave for the airport. And that generosity of spirit kept coming.

That evening I met up with Marie-France, originally from Mauritius but living in Bali since the mid-2000s. She ran a hair and beauty business on the island. Her name and contact details had been given to me by my hairdresser, Debbie, back in Noosa. It was the first of many "I have a friend you should meet" type conversations that would open countless doors through the coming year. She was full of empathy, sympathy and dozens of fascinating stories.

Over some delicious local food and drink she painted a picture of Bali that went a long way to reinvigorating me. To cap it all the Greek restaurant manager, and later the French owner, sent over free drinks in sympathy for my less than ideal introduction to the Indonesian island. It was a wonderful evening to finish off a bitter sweet 24 hours

By the end of the night I was almost perversely glad that I'd gone sliding off my bike along that gravel road. Nothing to do with masochism (pain and I are not happy bedfellows) but rather because it led me to so many decent and caring people from all over the globe. That night I went to bed bandaged on every limb but content that I was in the warm and caring embrace of humanity.

The next morning it was time to front up to the bike hire company, to confess my sins and face a potentially hefty bill. Both Marie-France and Norina had offered to call and negotiate damage costs but I decided to do my own dirty work.

At first there were seriously deep frowns and heads that shook like they were spring loaded. The owner wanted to take the bike to a repair shop for a quote but I knew that would mean time and hassle. With blood seeping through the bandage on my left knee I wasn't in my most patient mood. Bali turns out to be the world capital of motorbike crashes so I convinced them they were experienced enough to name a fair price. I braced myself for the outcome fearing a price tag of a few hundred dollars. The owner finally stopped his shaking head long enough to open his mouth. The cost would be 500,000. Rupiahs that is, and it worked out at the princely sum of $50. It seemed a fair price but I was under instructions to haggle.

Marie-France had given me a quick rundown on how much I should pay. Her rules were never settle for the first or second quote, be polite, patient and firm. The business owner was no poker player and his sheepish grin suggested I was being ripped off. I huffed a little, puffed some more and even tried a touch of male strutting. Bit of a failure this one as my newly acquired limp deprived it of a little authority. It looked like a lame interpretation of the hunchbacked King Richard III.

However, the owner began lowering his price. Twenty minutes later we agreed a deal and shook hands. The bill would come in at 120,000 - $12 to you and me. He seemed happy and so was I. Could you imagine Mr Hertz or Mrs Avis being so accommodating? Bali Radiance will forever be my scooter hire company of choice in Seminyak.

I kicked my heels for a few days, they at least weren't scraped to hell, and although my knees and elbows weren't looking any better I resisted going to the hospital emergency room. Apparently it's always busy, crammed full of stupid foreigners who've been in motorbike accidents.

Accurate and up to date figures are a little difficult to come by but in the first quarter of 2011 there were 173 recorded road fatalities in Bali, with a further 482 people seriously injured. Most of these involve motorbikes. Across a year that would probably work out at about 650-700 road deaths. With a population of just about four million it's a frightening statistic. To put it in context, in 2010 Britain had 2900 deaths from a population of 62 million. Bali's death rate is well over three times that of Britain and when you drive on the island's roads it's not hard to see why. The busy areas around Denpasar, Kuta and Legian seethe with motorbikes. Red lights and signs are routinely ignored, unlike pavements and walkways which are regularly and ruthlessly pressed into action as shortcuts. Those Hollywood movies featuring wild car chases along sidewalks look like a gentle scene from 'Driving Miss Daisy' compared to Bali in the rush hour.

Alcohol is a big factor in accidents, as is inexperience and testosterone. Drunken young guys on holiday are heavily over-represented in the casualty figures. Many don't even wear helmets, in violation of the law, but the cops are mostly uninterested, at least until late afternoon when it's time to earn a little cash. In Bali and other parts of Southeast Asia it's referred to as tea money - as in, time to get some money to buy tea. Impromptu roadside checks suddenly appear and the targets are mostly the comparatively well-off foreign tourists not wearing helmets and usually without a relevant driving licence. Just having your own Australian or British licence isn't enough. If you drive a vehicle here (and in many other countries) and don't have an international licence, you're breaking the law. Fines of up three hundred dollars are demanded on the spot, it's far from clear whether the money is going into police coffers or policemen's pockets. Perhaps 'far from clear' is overstating it, corruption makes this place tick.

Tourists can rent motorbikes for as little as $5 a day, unsurprisingly many of the dirt cheap hire shops don't include insurance and scooters aren't always officially registered. Licences are sometimes requested by these stores and other times not. It all means that even with your own holiday insurance cover you may be out on a battered limb. Many policies specifically exclude accidents on motorbikes. There are stories of families remortgaging or even selling homes to pay hospital bills. Seriously injured people are regularly airlifted from the island. The golden rule is check before you hire. Biker beware!

After a few days recuperating, it was time to move on. The south coast around Legian is extremely busy and it's not an ideal place for recovery. I was still bandaged up and a little sore but able to ride. Marie-France had told me of a perfect place to heal, Ubud, ancient, highly spiritual and the setting for much of Elizabeth Gilbert's book 'Eat, Pray, Love'. This, she said, was a place high on meditation and healing. It also turned out to be home of the five dollar massage. Actually, there are dozens of seriously smart spas where you'll need to fork out a fair bit more but with my travel cheaply plan I would be going down market.

With the pink B***ARD in dry dock I switched to a more sedate black, white and red machine and headed off, cautiously but almost certainly still uninsured. The thing about middle age is that we get older but not necessarily smarter.

#

5

THE EYES OF A HOLY MAN

Week 2; Ubud, Bali; 4,750 kms travelled; laundry bill – 90cents ;
1 shirt lost ; first aid kit ravaged

I am sitting cross-legged in awed and silent contemplation. Only the soft rhythms of a Holy Man's handbell filter through the silence. When the ringing stops I clasp my hands prayer-like and raise them slowly above my head. In my palms I gently rub flower petals and make my humble gesture to the gods.

The Holy Man makes his way through the faithful and stops before me. His stern eyes bore down and take in my sarong, sash and the udeng on my head. With sombre purpose he drops sacred water in my hands and commands me to drink. More water is splashed on my head and as the trickles ease down my face the Holy Man places rice on my damp forehead. Grains are also placed in my hands and I am told to eat. I chew a couple and glance penitently up into his eyes.

His stare shocks me with its raw and ferocious intensity and I sit transfixed, unable to turn away. I have an awful sensation that the Holy Man has looked deep into the murky depths of my soul. My mind begins to fret over what he's seen and then I have the weirdest feeling that he also knows exactly what I'm thinking. It feels like he's reading my mind. Bloody hell, that's not good. But abruptly he stops, turns and walks away. This is the signal that the temple ceremony is over and with it my day as a Hindu.

The invitation to the Full Moon Ceremony came from a Balinese family who lived 25 minutes outside Ubud. I'd been staying with them a few days, my first real taste of doing things a little differently. I'd arrived in Ubud and been immediately attracted to the town but these days it's getting pretty busy and commercialised. I wasn't going to get a real insight into the Balinese by staying in a guesthouse or hotel teeming with foreign tourists.

I'd been alerted through travel blogs to the idea of homestays. Essentially, it's staying and living for a short time with a host family. Bed and breakfast in a way. But the difference is you get to spend time with the family and have an opportunity to get a look under the skin of local culture and customs.

Finding them was fairly straightforward. I'd arrived in Ubud in time for lunch, sought out free wifi, opened up my iPad and began my search. There are dozens of listings for homestays in the area, most of them are really just regular B&Bs with lots of foreign guests. But a little digging soon produced what I wanted. For $20 a night I'd have a one bedroom building of my own plus breakfast in a family compound out in a rural area. Maximum number of guests was just three.

Finding the place wasn't easy but eventually I arrived in the village. The early signs were not encouraging. Mounds of rubbish tossed mindlessly and at random pockmarked the place, like so much of the island. The Balinese are not enthusiastic about waste management. You'll never see the recycling bin outside on a Tuesday.... or any other day for that matter. But driving into the family property was like entering a new world. Everything meticulously clean, nothing out of place. My quarters were newly built with incredibly ornate doors and beautiful tiles. The large, extended family who owned it had apparently sunk all their money into the building.

Over four days the two brothers, their wives, children and other friends and relations took me into their family and I took them into my heart. Their English was almost non-existent, which was still way better than my Indonesian, but they were desperate to improve. At nights we would gather on my verandah. There were no chairs, all of us sat on the floor passing away easy hours with attempted talk and much laughter.

They loved my iPad, particularly the camera app that created freaky images. Their real favourite was the 'Speak Indonesian' programme I'd uploaded. Really useful phrases like "Get the pink B***ARD off my leg" or "That Aussie girl's a motorbiking clown", are never included in these apps. But the family would be in howls of laughter at some of the stuff that was there. I'd regularly point to myself as the computer generated voice announced in Indonesian, "I am 30 years old". Their shrieks were further hammer blows to my fading sense of youthfulness. "Do you have an English menu" was another favourite to get them going.

Through the course of these evenings other people would come and go, some practising their English others just sitting and being part of a gentle family evening in the warm caress of a Bali night. Communication was difficult but the generosity and kindness of their collective embrace touched me deeply.

After a couple of days came the real advantage of a homestay. I was invited to join them for more meals and taken to watch as they worked in the rice fields. More people would show up and take me around the village to see the temples and school.

Somehow the family also managed to explain that in a week's time there would be a major Hindu festival, Purnama, to mark the full moon. It was one of their favourites and they invited me to join them.

I headed back to Ubud for a few days and the following weekend returned to stay once more with the family. In my room traditional Balinese clothes were neatly arranged for me to wear at the ceremony. There was a choice of sarongs, a sash for my waist, an udeng for my head and a shirt. It took a fair bit of fiddling around and the decision between which one of the two patterned sarongs to wear was tough. I now have renewed tolerance for the female mind.

I finally made my choice and checked myself in the mirror. I'll admit to some vanity here because I was very pleasantly surprised. David

Beckham had famously caused a storm in the 90s by wearing a sarong and I secretly thought he looked pretty cool, now it was my turn. I checked the mirror one more time, looking gooood!

I knew the family was waiting outside along with a few of the villagers, all keen to see me in my fineries. Out I went to strut my stuff catwalk style.

The screams and shrieks almost burst my eardrums. The women in particular were in hysterics, their natural politeness gone. One moment they were howling their heads off, the next they buried their faces in the hands so as not to show disrespect to their honoured guest. But it was hopeless. I was clearly the new village idiot dressed in a clown costume.

Apart from the dreadful embarrassment it was also very baffling. I thought I looked quite the guy. After a minute or two Made, the family head, came to my rescue, took me inside, shook his head, and with one of his few English phrases nailed his intended sentiment.

"Not good", he said.

Judging by the excited chatter still going on outside this was clearly Balinese understatement. I took off my gear and under Made's guidance began again.

It turned out the choice of sarongs wasn't actually a choice at all, both were to be worn, layered and in a specific style. The sash I'd used as a cummerbund around my waist should have been folded in half and worn under the shirt. As for the udeng, it's best nothing is said.

Suitably re-arranged we set off for the ceremony. Throughout the journey the children and the women would suddenly burst into uncontrollable laughter at the memory of my faux-pas. It would bring a semi-stern rebuke from Made until he himself couldn't control himself.

An hour later we were at Gunung Kawi Temple in the town of Tampaksiring. The 11th century complex houses one of only two holy water spring temples in Bali. The family went off to change from their Sunday best into casual but modest clothing and then we joined a throng at a small gate waiting to enter the purification area. It was all a little chaotic but after 20 minutes we were in.

Hundreds of people stood waist deep in cool water in a kind of ornate bath the size of an Olympic size pool. Along one side a dozen spouts sent water gushing over the heads of the faithful. I stood on the edge while the family, young and old, entered the water and joined a semi-orderly line which snaked backwards and forwards towards the spouts. The pouring water is considered to be holy and standing under it is believed to cleanse the sins of the past month. It is a way for Hindus to purify themselves.

After thirty minutes the family was tightly packed in a heaving mass of bodies. The children and elderly often disappeared from view and the intensity ratcheted up as they inched towards the gushing water. It looked frantic but as each finally reached their goal and submerged themselves they reappeared with total joy on their faces. Their spirits were immediately purified and their souls alight with happiness. It was an amazing spectacle. The same followed in two smaller pools before the family finally left the water, cold but exuberant.

After drying and once more changing into their finest clothes we all headed to the temple. The few tourists wearing temporary sarongs for modesty stood just behind a rope where a sign sombrely instructed, "Prayers only allowed beyond here". I dutifully stopped.

The family walked off but moments later Agung and Made returned. They guided me past the rope and into the inner prayer area. I really wasn't sure I belonged there. The women and children were already kneeling along with sixty or so others. The brothers joined them and the Holy Man began ringing his bell. Prayers had started.

I stood solemnly and respectfully at the back but soon the two women, Puta and Ari, turned and beckoned me. At first I pretended not to notice them but they were insistent. I moved with a little trepidation and sat on the floor behind them. Within a minute the women and daughter, Ita, parted and signalled me to join them. I was frozen to the spot, sure that I was committing heresy. But they were adamant and I moved forward. I had barely settled uncomfortably into my new spot when the men, a little further forward, also moved aside and instructed me to sit with them. I was desperately hoping the Holy Man hadn't seen the advance of a non-believing heathen through the ranks.

Moments later there was not a chance in hell he could miss me. The brothers began to push me forward. I dug my buttocks into the stone in resistance but it was a losing battle and I slid involuntarily forward. I was out front at the head of the faithful, alone and isolated.

The Holy Man began his prayer instructions and behind me I heard the devoted start to chant and make movements. I was at a total loss. There was nobody ahead or besides to copy. Balinese Hindus have a range of deities and at this moment I feared that up in Swarga, their heaven, I wasn't being looked upon too favourably. After what seemed like an eternity Agung and Isma saw me floundering and slid forwards to guide me through the ceremony.

Gratefully I mimicked them, placing a petal behind my ear and more in my palms. On their cue I offered up my hands to the gods and, like them, said a silent prayer.

My prayer was quickly followed with an earnest wish that the Holy Man, who was now heading towards me, was not about to punish my intrusion by casting me down to Naraka, or hell. This is where the demons live. Hindus believe our spirits are sent there as punishment for misdeeds on earth. At this point I was sure I was misdeeding myself to an eternity of unpleasantness.

Of course, the Holy Man did nothing of the kind. He definitely did a double-take when he got to me and his eyes really did bore way inside the feeble fabric of my mind. But I meekly followed his instructions and made it through to the end of the ceremony.

Many strict Hindus fast on full moon day, my family didn't and we headed off for a Balinese picnic by the river. We sat around in our finest clothes, ate simple food and delighted in the day and each other. As I quietly observed the family I envied them their ease with each other and their contentment with the world. They were warm, generous and gentle people. I quietly said a prayer and asked their gods to send them every ounce of health and happiness they had to spare, and a little more besides.

#

6

STARING DEATH IN THE FACE

In death we are all equal. But there is a place in northern Bali where what follows sets it apart from the world. A dark place, home to an ancient people with an equally dark reputation, where you can literally stare death in the face.

In Trunyan there is neither burial nor cremation. The dead are taken from the village by boat to a small clearing around the cove. Bodies are partially covered with a thin white cloth, placed under a fragile bamboo cage and simply left. The cadaver is at the mercy of nature and the elements. It is ravaged, rots and decomposes until just the skeleton remains.

Only 11 bodies can lie there. When the space is needed skulls are removed and placed trophy-like on stone shelves. The rest of the bones are discarded, often just casually tossed on the fringes of the clearing. To the Bali Aga, the original Balinese, all that matters is the soul and that has long since departed.

The people are the aborigines of Bali but now they account for only two percent of the population. They were usurped by the Hindu-Javanese who came to the island in the 13th century and flourished. The Bali Aga retreated physically and mentally into isolated communities and remain a breed apart.

Trunyan itself sits on the eastern side of a mighty crater lake across from Mount Batur, an active volcano. A rock wall rises sheer behind the village condemning it to large periods in dark shadows. Beyond is Mount Agung, Bali's highest mountain and a home to the gods. The setting gives the village an air of surly, nebulous gloom.

The Batur caldera, or crater lake, is understandably popular with tourists but only a few venture around to Trunyan. The village's contradiction is to have an ugly reputation while all around is great natural beauty.

Until comparatively recently travellers' only way in was to hire oarsmen to row them across the lake. There are legendary tales of the boatmen stopping mid way and threatening startled tourists if they didn't pay a suddenly hugely inflated price. For those who made it to Trunyan they were often confronted by an intimidating atmosphere, aggressive begging and exorbitant prices.

A couple of years ago the Bali Aga asked the Indonesian authorities for help in alleviating their poverty. An offer was made to build a road to the village to help attract tourist dollars. But there were conditions. Strict commitments were demanded for the Bali Aga to change their ways. Prices were to be fixed and transparent and visitors were not to be harmed or threatened. The people of Trunyan agreed.

I'd heard about the village from a sixty something American trekker who was staying at my small guesthouse in Ubud. He mentioned the unique death ritual and told me of the new 'road'. But he couldn't really vouch for it as he hadn't actually made the journey. It was exactly the kind of scenario I'd envisaged for my unplanned trip. Nuggets of gold passed by word of mouth.

So it was I rode the B***ARD, mark two, along the newly constructed highway to the village. In reality large parts were no more than a rutted, twisting, potholed dirt track. After a few hairy moments I made it and I soon met Daro, a young man with good English and a desperate desire to promote his birthplace. He explained that Trunyan actually has three cemeteries. The first, Sema Bantas, is for people who died unnatural deaths. For the Bali Aga this is not a good way to leave this life. The bodies are buried in unmarked shallow graves without ceremony.

The second was the 'baby cemetery', Sema Nguda. It is not what its name implies. This is the epithet given to both children and adults of any age who die unmarried.

Finally, there is Sema Wayah, the cemetery for which Trunyan is known.

I was shown a chalkboard price list for the boat to the main cemetery, proof that everything was transparent and above board. At more than $20 it was expensive for Bali but at least there would be no hidden rip off. I paid up but my cash had barely disappeared into somebody's pocket when I was immediately told I must also make a 'donation' for the upkeep of the cemetery. I tried to debate the matter but was forcefully told it was compulsory. The people of Trunyan hadn't quite fully changed their ways.

After handing over some rupiahs the oarsman set off on our quiet journey. I mentally prepared myself for what might lie ahead. They rowed for fifteen minutes around a headland and finally pointed out the path leading into dense growth, darkness and my date with the dead.

The cemetery is in a small clearing, stillness sits heavy in the air. I was all alone and took a few reverential paces towards the bamboo tombs. I peered cautiously inside the first and there above a decaying tangle of cloth was a skull. Its mouth wide open in a kind of petrified trance. No other bones were visible. There was a similar sight in the next couple of bamboo chambers. But at the far end was the latest body. It had been there three months and time had already taken its toll. The flesh had mercifully gone. Only a few parts of the skeleton were visible along with the sandals that were once on its feet.

Mounds of rubbish lay on the fringes of the main cemetery and here and there a bone or two. It sounds unsettling but for the Bali Aga the body is nothing. Sentimentality is for the soul.

For all the expectation of what the cemetery experience would be like the anticipation was more disturbing than the reality. I had a feeling of almost indifference. This may have been due to an acceptance of the villagers' belief in animism. The absence of a recent corpse with decaying flesh also helped. As did the remarkable fact that the cemetery never has the smell of death. A giant Taru Menyan tree, from which the village takes its name, stands in the corner. Its sweet fragrance and thick, spreading roots are believed to counter the odours. Around the cove the 'baby cemetery' is not blessed with a similar tree. I am told I cannot see it.

"We do not go ourselves except to take bodies," Daro had told me. "The smell is terrible. It is too much."

As I left the cemetery three villagers sat at a table and asked me to sign a shiny new visitors' book. On the table was a large, empty jar. As I wrote I noticed from the corner of my eye that one man was surreptitiously pointing out to another that the jar was empty. They feared I wouldn't understand the jar's purpose. With a slight of hand befitting the world's dodgiest magician he reached into his pocket, took out a note and dropped it into the jar. As I got up to leave one of the men indicated towards the jar. To ensure I understood the message he helpfully pointed out a sign stating 'donation'.

I refused and reminded him that I had paid $20 and already made one donation. The men spoke no English but got my drift and were not happy. The already heavy air took on an even surlier feel.

After 15 minutes I was rowed silently back to the village. One hundred metres from the shore the two oarsmen stopped and uttered a single word of English, 'donation'. I said no. Technically, I'm not sure you can have a Mexican stand-off while sitting in a canoe in Bali but that's what happened. The men muttered darkly to each other and again demanded a donation. I shook my head and there was an uneasy silence. Thirty seconds or so later they sulkily rowed me back to land.

On the road out of Trunyan I considered my experience and began to comprehend my ambiguity to the death show. The Bali Aga in their understandable wish to earn the tourist dollar are clumsily trying to create what marketeers would call 'an experience'.

The old rickety cemetery landing stage at the cemetery had recently been replaced by a new structure including a toilet block. As I was being rowed in a villager, on cue, began playing some traditional but bizarrely upbeat music. At the cemetery skulls had been placed on either side of the entrance and for some unfathomable reason cigarettes placed around them. And while bones are discarded as rubbish around the edges of the graveyard the most prominent, a pair of femurs, were nicely laid out so tourists couldn't miss them.

Trunyan is a fascinating place and the Bali Aga are truly different. But I was left with a sense that their ancient culture is now being melded into the early makings of a tourist show. The villagers have realised that their traditions play directly to our Western fears of death and the macabre. They know we are fearful yet intrigued. But in their naivety there is a danger that they will turn Trunyan into a kind of dark, Disney of death.

\#

7

HARRY THE CROCODILE

Week 3; Gili Islands, Indonesia; 4,900 kms travelled;
1 wonder sock missing, presumed lost

It's a slow night in paradise and the prospects aren't looking good. So poor in fact that the waiter gives up, sits down at my table and starts to talk.

He is young, fit and has the smile and swagger of a loveable rogue.

I ask about his job. He is 28 years old and has been a waiter for seven years. When I learn he earns just $80 a month I give him my most sincere sympathetic look.

The rogue dismissively waves it away. He tells me that he is doing fine, courtesy of his 'other work.'

I give him a questioning look and he leans in a little towards me, drops his voice to a conspiratorial whisper and tells me, "I am a crocodile."

He pronounces it trocodile but when he uses his arms to mimic the closing jaws of a croc I get his meaning, although I am still none the wiser.

Seeing my perplexed look he

smiles, drops his voice still further and proudly says to me, "You call it gigolo."

Harry, the name he uses for the ladies, begins his story.

He was born and raised on Gili Air, one of three small islands off the coast of Lombok in Indonesia and a short boat ride from Bali. As a young man he realised many female tourists were looking for a holiday romance and were happy to splash the cash on local guys who made them feel good.

Harry saw a chance to improve his lot and undertook two years of what he calls self-training.

"I had to learn to speak good English, develop my body and work out how to treat the ladies in a special way." Since then his income has rocketed.

"They pay for everything. Food, drink, parties and we have a very good time. When their holiday is finished they never leave without giving me something."

"Never?" I ask. "Never," he insists and his chest thrusts out with male pride. One thousand Euros is his best gift and he assures me that "gift" is the correct word. He never demands money, doesn't need too, that's for the amateurs.

"I give them lots of fun. I say very special things to them and it makes them feel great. They are always grateful."

He has his rules. No girls in their early 20s, "they have no money." Late 20s sometimes but women in their 30s and 40s are the best. He's also not averse to female Nonys.

I ask how he meets them. He calls it "fishing". He does a slow fisherman's cast into the restaurant and his eyes work the room. This is his territory and he oozes confidence. He will spend hours flirting. If any ladies take his bait he tells them to meet him at midnight, when his restaurant work is done, and he will take them to see turtles.

Does that line really work? I let him know I am a little doubtful. Harry repeats his strongest clamping jaws action shouts "SNAP" and lets out his roguish laugh.

But Harry's not alone, he tells me there are 25 crocodiles on the island. Competition is strong and he points out two other crocs in his restaurant with a couple of 30-something American women.

I decide, in the interests of research you understand, to delve into murky waters. I ask Harry if he sleeps with many of the women. He snorts at my innocence and says, "All of them."

I can't resist and ask him for numbers. Heading toward 30 this year, he tells me. We are in the death throes of April, I am stunned and highly sceptical but later I see the evidence before my very eyes. The American women are leaving but their crocs stay by the bar. One of the ladies turns and pleads with the gigolo,

"Will you please come and dance with me later? Pleeeease."

The croc plays a little hard to get but after a little more pleading and a touch of mild teasing he turns to her.

"For you I will try to move the moon", he says and her face lights up. In that brief exchange is all the proof I need.

It's far from clear whether the women Harry meets are part of a growing trend of female sex tourism, or just travellers merely open to a holiday romance and happy at the end to show their gratitude. I ask The Crocodile about their intent and he rocks his shoulders in a "bit of both" kind of answer.

Just over the water in Bali a 2010 documentary film called 'Cowboys In Paradise' followed the so-called 'Kuta cowboys', young guys who make a living through female sex tourism. The authorities were angered and embarrassed by the movie and arrested 28 of the beach boys, although all were later released. In Bali it is a sizeable and growing business.

Back in the restaurant Harry The Crocodile is in full flow. He takes me through his repertoire. Flowers and massages are high on his list. Then come the gigolo's pearls of wisdom. "Take it slow. Start at number ten and work your way very slowly to number one. No rushing. That's why young men are no good. Too quick."

Wham, bang, thank you ma'am, I ask him? He doesn't know the phrase but he likes it and repeats it mantra style. I point out that he is saying "man" instead of ma'am and that does rather make a difference.

He is shocked when he realises the implication of his misused language.

I eventually thank Harry for the most unexpected night of my journey so far. I also apologise for keeping him talking for an hour and hope he hasn't missed a catch. "No good tonight. I don't feel strong. You have to be strong for the ladies." In the interest of taste and decency I don't ask him to elaborate.

Travel throws up many amazing characters. This encounter is high up on the memorable list. It will be a long time before I forget how I got up close and very personal with the awesome power of Harry The Crocodile.

#

8

PEACEFUL BLISS ON PARTY ISLAND

Harry's island is the third in the chain of the Gilis, an hour by fast boat from Bali and just off the Lombok coast. Walking around the entire island can be done in 45 minutes. Small groups of beach huts and guesthouses and a few little bars and restaurants crowd in close to the beach, it's all very laid back.

Next to it is Gili Meno. Quieter still with a few places to stay, chill and drink in the serenity.

Drinking is also the name of the game on the third of the islands, Gili Trawangan. But here it comes in shots and buckets. Gili T's reputation is as far removed from Meno as you can get. This is party central, a mecca for young backpackers who want to let their inhibitions go.

I went there on a word of mouth recommendation. Actually, the recommendation was not to go there. I'd met a couple in Ubud who told me about the beautiful Gilis. They said I would enjoy the tranquillity and the beautiful beaches. But they told me Gili Trawangan should be avoided, it wasn't for a Nony like myself. They told me mid 20s was the upper age bracket for enjoying the delights of the place. At first I decided to follow their advice. At second I thought bugger it. I'm supposed to be out there experiencing life and avoiding stereotyping my middle age. So I went.

Jumping off the boat and wading through the clear water with my fellow travellers was a fun way to arrive, even if I was the oldest person by a century or two.

The island, although small, was full of bars, cafes, shops and cheap places to stay. Horse drawn buggies raced up and down the narrow Main Street, no cars are allowed in the Gili islands. You very quickly get a sense of what the place is all about. There are always guys offering cheap rooms, cheap bikes, cheap drugs.

That was the first real shock. Indonesia has no tolerance for drugs. Lengthy jail sentences are the penalty for buyers, for traffickers it can be death. Yet on Gili T you can't walk 100 metres along its main drag without being offered marijuana, cocaine or magic mushrooms.

Then there are the adverts for cheap drink and late night parties. It's what this place is about and after dark it is a home of hedonism, if you're young enough to want it. I have to confess it didn't light my fire.

But the setting is gorgeous, the water is dreamlike in its turquoise tinged transparency and the sand is a blinding white. After taking a while to understand the extremes of the island I set off to find a bed. I would be looking away from the nightlife noise which I am told is all night, every night.

I hired a bike for a mere a $2 a day. I set off to cycle around party paradise and quickly discovered why the bike was so cheap. Its brakes were more concept than reality and its suspension a mere notion. Every cobble or rut was like a whack on the arse with a cricket bat. The bike turned out to be one of the better ones on the island, it fell the wrong side of safe but marginally the right side of death trap.

At the southern tip of the Main Street there are, surprisingly, a couple of rather swish resorts, they are clearly not catering for backpackers. More surprising is that after this point the island becomes almost empty. Trees and bushes on one side and the stunning sea on the other. After ten minutes of wild shaking I came to a group of chalets, two storeys high, thatched roofs and low slung hammocks. They were thirty metres from a beautiful beach and surrounded by nature. Not even the merest hint of party noise.

The setting was heavenly, a hundred postcards of paradise rolled into one. Breakfast and dinner were served in a couple of little Bali huts on the beach with the water lazily falling and rising at my feet. The sand was honeyed and the shades of blue water and flawless sky framed the green island of Lombok in the distance.

At night the setting sun dropped trance-like into the sea. Its shimmering decline painting pastel pink shades over the heavens. It was a blissful anomaly. Instead of parties I'd unearthed a little paradise. And it was costing me $30 a night. There were moments when I wondered whether I would ever be able to prise myself away.

In the evening Gili T can also tease with surprises. At the bottom of party street I came across an outdoor cinema. The movies and I have had a love affair dating back to my early years and exotic locations only add to the appeal.

A hand chalked board listed the week's forthcoming attractions. In testosterone filled Trawangan I expected some kind of kick ass action movie full of adrenalin and car chases. But as I looked down the week's schedule there was a treat. That night's movie was due to begin in 15 minutes. It was the 1957 black and white classic '12 Angry Men' starring Henry Fonda. And so I found myself lying on a double width beach bed next to the gentle lap of the sea with waiters bringing drinks and food at my leisure.

On the big screen Henry fought against injustice and intolerance and under the stars I sipped and slurped on the amber nectar of a mango shake. A couple of hundred metres away the party wouldn't really get going for a few hours. I wouldn't be going. I'd already reached a state of ecstasy, no tablets nor magic mushrooms required.

#

9

THE LAND THAT TIME FORGOT

Week 4; 5,500 kms travelled; 4 wonder socks
1 delayed flight; 1 lost hat, 1 new hat

Sumba is an island adrift, a castaway from the modern world. Here, priests predict the fate of sick children through the entrails of slaughtered chickens, colossal megaliths house the dead and headhunting is remembered by the living.

It is a place that stuns the senses. Soaring and spectacular homes built of bamboo and grass; ancient rituals untouched by the outside world; endless and empty white beaches. It is a rich travel experience, yet very few tourists make it here. The numbers each year are counted in the hundreds.

Sumba is one of the Lesser Sunda Islands of Indonesia, just an hour by plane from Bali. But it might as well be in a different galaxy as far as the 3.3 million tourists who visit Bali each year are concerned. Even the Balinese ignore it.

I'd discovered it after returning to Bali from the Gilis. During a quick visit to the airport I hunted down the schedules of small airlines which flew to destinations I never knew existed. I'd decided to randomly select a destination, buy a ticket and fly into the unknown. Sumba was one option, Flores another. I knew nothing of either so I reached into my pocket and fished out a 1000 rupiah coin. I selected my heads and tails and tossed. Sumba it was.

I checked the net for information, there's not much out there but what there is whetted my appetite. The place was effectively free of tourism but with fascinating lifestyles and customs. By now I was comfortable with the idea of just making it all up as I went along. It really was a fun and easy way of travelling. Sumba, however, felt like the first big spur of the moment decision I'd made and I was exhilarated when I booked my ticket for the next day.

There aren't too many flights to the island and it turns out there can be delays, mine was one of them. When I turned up at the airport I couldn't actually find it listed anywhere, not a good sign.

After struggling to find anybody even mildly involved with the airline it was confirmed that the plane was 'delayed'. It happens and when it does you have to be a little stoic. I calmly produced my stoic look. Next came my book, it was a slim thriller. I had a feeling I'd be getting through a fair chunk of it while waiting at the airport.

"So what time is the plane expected to leave?" I asked somebody who owned up to being with the airline.

He made a slight tilt of the head with an accompanying shrug of the shoulders and then a long drawn out thought.

"Maybe tomorrow."

"Maybe tomorrow?"

My stoicism vanished. "Tomorrow" sounded bad but "maybe" was the killer word when it came to retaining my inner calm. I was hoping I'd misheard but I knew I hadn't. A long conversation followed and by the end of it I'd been told 24 hours wasn't too bad, nothing to get excited about. Sometimes it's a week. That hit home hard but the airline rep explained it was not typical. He was sure I'd be fine.

"So will it definitely be leaving tomorrow?"

"Maybe," he repeated.

It had come from nowhere to become my number one hated word

in the English language. We would become well acquainted over the next few months and over time I learned to take it with my own philosophical shrug. But not yet.

"In that case I'll cancel and fly with another airline," I righteously replied.

Fat chance. He didn't say it but he sure as hell was thinking it. I knew in my heart that this was not a route other airlines would be fighting over. I contemplated finding some other place but decided I'd stick with Sumba. I considered how much reading I could do in 24 hours. Then I wondered what I could get through in a week.

I had one final thought to share with the airline rep.

"So will your airline be putting me up in a hotel until the plane is ready?" It was in hindsight a pathetic and pompous western attitude but I hadn't yet warmed into my new persona of laid-back world traveller.

The answer wasn't 'no' but only because he didn't think such a stupid question warranted any answer at all. In the end he gave me his personal mobile number so I could check a new departure time with him in the morning.

I headed off to Sanur, found a hotel and hunkered down for a day and a night. Next morning I called the mobile and found myself in Groundhog Day.

"Hello. We spoke yesterday. I was supposed to fly to Sumba. I'm checking what time the plane will be leaving today?"

I couldn't see him but I could feel he was back in shrugging and tilting mode again. There was another long pause.

"Maybe later."

"Maybe later?"

That damned word "maybe" again, a small vessel for a large amount of uncertainty.

"When will you know?"

I should have seen his answer coming.

"Maybe this morning."

Later never happened, or at least not that day. Later turned out to be the next morning. So the delay turned out to be 48 hours. At least I didn't have to wait at the airport, a couple of phone calls each day was enough.

No tourists I spoke to in Bali had heard of Sumba, a big tick in its favour. Even when it came up in conversation with the Balinese I got the same reaction. "You mean Sumbawa".

But no, actually, I didn't. Easy enough mistake to make. Sumbawa is a large island just east of Lombok, and is used as a stopping off point for Komodo and Flores, it's fairly well known. Sumba is further along, still quite a size but none of the locals knew a thing about it. To be fair to the Indonesians that's understandable. The country is not short of an island or two.

In Australia children quickly master the names of the small handful of states and territories. Likewise in the USA schoolkids are taught at a young age to memorise the names of the 50 states. In Indonesia it doesn't quite work like that. Little Hertanto and Verawati would be hard pressed to name even point one of one per cent of the country's staggering 17,508 islands. No wonder nobody had heard of Sumba. I was hoping the pilot flying me there knew which chunk of rock to set us down on. He was spoilt for choice.

It may have only been one hour by plane but in reality it was light years away from Bali. There were no taxis, nowhere to eat, not even food stalls that I could see.

I found an old man with an even older motorbike and he dropped me at my 'hotel'. I won't bother with a description but let's just say there was no other option.

The next issue was transport. Unsurprisingly Hertz and Avis didn't appear to have an office on Sumba. I managed to convince a young guy at the hotel to let me hire his motorbike, there were no alternatives. I headed out but it was hard going. Five or six roads were good, most weren't, many were just rough tracks. Signs were non-existent and finding traditional villages without basic Indonesian was extremely difficult. The island has five other languages, not mere dialects, and very few people spoke English. A guide was going to be necessary and, as it turned out, saved my neck a couple of times.

The hotel managed to find a local schoolteacher who was happy to guide me. So the next day Peter and I headed off in a small 4x4. On our journey we stopped to buy some gifts for the village heads we'd be meeting. Peter explained that even with these there were no guarantees we'd be welcome.

Ratenggarro was the first traditional Sumbanese village we visited and on arrival I was stunned. The homes were towering pinnacles of wood and straw, some rising more than 20 metres vertically up to the sky. The village's position was also breathtaking. The settlement stood above a tidal inlet leading to the wild waves of the Indian Ocean. To its east and west were glorious but deserted white sand beaches. The village was clearly built with defence in mind.

Arrival in a Sumbanese village is a surreal experience, a journey far back in time. Some children scream and wave others stand in mummified silence, slack-jawed by the rare sight of a western tourist.

The adults were generally cautious and some a little unwelcoming, even with a guide from the region. Gifts of betel nuts, a Sumbanese favourite, were handed over to the village elder along with a few cigarettes and a little cash. Peter and I were expected to sit and talk and show respect to the village head. Nothing happened in a hurry. Slowly, in each village, the atmosphere eased and the people became friendly and inquisitive.

The homes were built on three levels, animals on the ground floor, humans the next and finally the Marapu, or ancestral spirits, in the cathedral like spires.

Marapu is the island's ancient religious belief system and is fundamental to the way they live. Ratos, village priests, still predict the future through dead animals or by talking to rocks. Some innocuous looking stones are at the heart of Marapu beliefs and are sacred. Standing on one of these can have very serious consequences. The spirits sometimes also occupy corners of the buildings and for the unwary venturing too close is not a trivial event. Twice Peter barked at me to stop as I headed unknowingly into a sacrosanct spot.

The houses are based around four pillars of wood, each intricately carved. Status symbols of buffalo horns and the jaw bones of pigs lined some of the walls.

The homes and the lives of the villagers are defined by the dark. Little light penetrates the bamboo walls. In the centre of the huge houses are open fireplaces for cooking. The smell of smoke infects everything. Bedrooms are small, semi-partitioned with a basic rush mat on the uneven bamboo floor for sleeping. There are no pieces of furniture. Food and water are often short and government aid is crucial. Malnutrition and malaria are both fatal here. It is akin to Stone Age living.

Outside the homes are the megaliths. Mammoth rocks weighing many tons which are mausoleums for the dead. Each carries carvings of spiritual symbols. In ancient days when members of the royal families died servants would also be sacrificed to continue their roles in the afterlife. The megaliths are immense and it is not uncommon for more than a hundred men to be required to haul them into position.

Villages also feature an andung, a ceremonial tree where the heads of enemies were hung. Headhunting officially ceased about 50 years ago, although some darkly suggest 30 years is more accurate. Violence between clans does still erupt and can be fierce. Just over a decade ago 3000 men stormed one town in a dispute and dozens of people died horrific deaths.

In these traditional areas most Sumbanese men still carry long sword-like knives. They are essentially for working in crop fields but they are also lethal weapons. Arguments which end in extreme violence do still happen. Land disputes are apparently a particular problem. But for tourists Sumba is safe and at just over an hour from Bali it is an accessible yet unique place that offers a window into a distant past.

Back at my base the 'hotel' also offered me a glimpse into the past, its best days were clearly behind it. The present and the future held little to recommend it. Actually, if I'm being honest I should replace the word 'little' with 'nothing' but it's time for a 'little' charity.

The one thing it did have was a restaurant. One of the finest in all of western Sumba. It also happened to be the only one I found during my stay. I had no choice but to eat there. The first meal I ordered was chicken. It turned out to be from the street fighting thug gene of poultry. Tough as old boots and stringier than Rastafarian hair. A knife and fork were of no use and I asked the waitress for a pneumatic drill and an industrial pulper. Fortunately she had no English and nor, I suspect, the tools needed to cut the prizefighter into edible chunks. After 20 minutes I gave up. All I'd accomplished in that time was to discover that chicken skin sticks better to its meat than any ultra-strength, new formula glue. I went to bed on a diet.

The next evening I was forewarned. Although nobody spoke a word of English I had sort of worked out that the back page of the menu was vegetarian. Tonight I would avoid tangling with meat. But without a clue as to what the menu items were I decided to cover the bases and over order, it was hardly going to break the bank. I randomly selected four separate veggie dishes, sat back and waited to be surprised.

Ten minutes later I was. Out came an egg which lay somewhere between soft and hard boiled. Not quite what I had in mind when I'd ordered vegetarian but I ate it. Strike one but I waited expectantly for the second course and the promise of some much needed greens.

It didn't happen. Next up was a single fried egg. Oh dear, rather a lot of egg going on here. Still it was food and it was edible. I laughed again at my minor misfortune and with strike two I knew my chances were improving all the time. The third course would nail it, I was confident.

After a short break the waitress reappeared. She carried with her a plate full of disappointment also known to you and me as an omelette. Time to face the truth. I waded through my third egg dish and decided whoever invented the phrase 'three strikes and you're out' had probably eaten in the same restaurant. I left some cash and headed to my room. In the dingy dump that was more cell than boudoir my mind turned back to eggs. I suppressed the urge to race back to the restaurant to discover whether the final course had been a rather nice soufflé.

#

10

TOP TEN SCARY PLANE LANDING

Week 5; Tioman, Malaysia; 8,500 kms travelled;
1 expired visa; 6 flights, 2 leather wrist bands (cool)

Life and food in Sumba did eventually get more comfortable when I stumbled across Oro Beach Hotel. It was a lovely little lodgings with a handful of thatched villas perched just by the beach. I contentedly lost track of time. This turned out to be not such a good thing. In a quiet moment sitting in the gardens I had an idle thought about my passport. It soon turned from idle to frenzy when I realized my Indonesian visa would expire soon. Very soon. That day in fact. Trying to get an extension on Sumba would be a fruitless exercise. Oh dear.

I scrambled and managed to get on a flight back to Bali, amazing considering how difficult getting to Sumba had been. With just half a day remaining on the visa and no idea of where to head next I was soon standing once again in Denpasar airport scanning the departures board. My choice basically boiled down to Singapore or Kuala Lumpur. I tossed the 1000 Rupiah coin again and KL it was. I'd been there before so I'd just use it for a short stay and look for somewhere else in the country as my next destination. The beach was my preference.

I knew nothing of Tioman, not even of its anonymous existence. But in a quest to discover a beautiful stretch of Malaysian coastline its name had come up. The small island, 32 kilometres off the country's east coast, wasn't as picture perfect as some but it was a contender.

And then I found its X factor.

Apparently Tioman has one of the most perilous plane take off and landings in the world. It appears in numerous 'top tens' for scary. That did it for me. It went from invisible to irresistible.

I found a flight with Berjaya. Not being one of aviation's premier carriers I checked the company website. The picture of a sleek new flying machine in its shimmering livery oozed safety and quality. I knew the pilots' abilities would be unimpeachable. There would be no greenhorns on this run.

Suitably comforted I bought a ticket and arrived at the airport carrying a backpack and a very bullish attitude. But as the flight was called and I walked onto the tarmac my bulls dropped. It was an old bucket and looked in very dodgy health. Its engine casings a mish mash of faded colours. In some places no colour at all, the paint had peeled off. Above the cockpit were a few wild lashings of grey, the work of a Do It Yourself amateur who'd run out of time, patience and paint.

I decided the only flight about to happen would be mine on foot in a frenzied escape from the airport. But it was too late. I was whisked up half a dozen steps and into the bowels of the beast. The interior of the plane matched the outside. It looked old and a little tatty. The signs were not promising.

I'd checked in early to get a great view and had bagged seat 1A. It shouldn't have surprised me to find the seat faced backwards down the plane. Everybody would be able to see the terror in my eyes and the whimpering on my lips.

I've seen way too many emergency briefings in my time but this one had my full attention. I even took notes, just in case. I also gave a forensic once over of the hostie doing the drill. She had no visible scars, broken bones or nervous twitches that would have been telltale signs of previous crash landings at Tioman.

Briefing done it was time for take off. The bucket seemed ominously slow gaining height and I cursed the carrot cake I'd eaten at the airport.

On this old dame a few ounces here and there could mean the difference between life and death. But after an eternity we finally made it above head height and the flight was underway.

Half way through the journey I went for a nervous pee. I walked tentatively down the exact middle of the plane. My footsteps were featherlike for fear the slightest movement would unbalance the old crate. I eased the toilet seat smoothly up and down to avoid creating turbulence. Although the way my knotted stomach was feeling I'd probably be making some of my own very soon.

Forty or so minutes into the flight the Captain gave the traditional 'we're about to start our approach' speech. This sounded rather more grave than normal and finished with the words, "I hope to see you again". It may just have been me but I'm sure he put extra stress on the word 'hope'. Something a little more definite would have eased my growing anxiety.

Oh dear, could I fit in a second toilet trip? I decided against it. I'd made it once without bringing us down, rolling the dice a second time on this tub seemed a little risky.

Here goes, we started out descent. Very soon it mutated into a full on dive and we lost height rapidly. Jungled hills appeared. They soon began to tower above us and fill the left hand side windows. I craned my neck trying to search for the runway ahead. Suddenly it appeared, but not where I expected. It was way off to the side, a crazy right angle from our current course and we were already very, very low. How the hell?

This was clearly a one shot deal, there would be no second attempts. I gripped the armrests as the trees crowded in on us, closer and closer. The water below was rising up. The angle of approach went from extreme to bloody ridiculous. As we arrowed in to a wall of jungle the bucket suddenly banked sharply right. Trees and roof tops hustled the plane for room. At the moment of imminent death the captain suddenly flipped it back left. We straightened momentarily and a nano second later hit the runway. Hallelujah.

Only after I left the plane did the full, daunting scenario reveal itself and I stared frozen in astonished disbelief. The airstrip pointed straight at the hillside, a steep, impenetrable wall just a brief distance away. There was no way over, only around at the proverbial right angle.

Barely out of my stupor I heard the engines roar and watched the plane hurtle headlong at the hill. It hardly left the ground before wheeling away in another street level twist. I vowed there and then to find the ferry times for the journey home.

Tioman, it turned out, had played a starring role in the film South Pacific as Bali Hai. At its best it's a photographer's dream with jungle spilling down hillsides to white sand and beautifully blue water. But a few parts, such as Air Batang Bay where I stayed, were a little careworn. It felt untidy and unloved. Salang, just a short boat ride up the coast was much easier on the eye but it suffered from the curse of sandflies. Most of the island is impassable jungle and I confess to seeing little of the place.

On one of the days I did go wandering I met Asram, a fireman at the landing strip. He assured me that in the four years he'd been there Berjaya had a flawless flying record. However, he advised against coming during the monsoon. Lots of circling waiting for the torrential rains to ease, he says. Advice noted.

I asked him what happened if pilots had to abort a landing at the last moment. He shook his head and said, "one go only". He may or may not have been pulling my leg but sheer hills rise up astonishingly close to each end of the runway.

I laughed nervously at Asram's words and ambled as nonchalantly as possible to the ferry office to recheck the timetable.

(Note: Given the madly litigious world we now live in I probably should point out that Berjaya's planes meet all necessary aviation standards that I'm aware of. Their planes and pilots get the job done. And in the interest of a good yarn I have obviously exaggerated the hell out of the story. But it is a corker of a landing.

#

While Tioman was part paradise, part careworn it did throw up some memorable characters.

My arrival at ABC beach was a little unusual. Across from the airstrip is a small harbour. There I paid for a ride as the only passenger in a speedboat which thundered me ten minutes up the coast to my lodgings. Because of rocks it was once more time to strap on the backpack, jump over the side and wade 30 metres ashore.

Not having a clue where I was headed I interrupted a sunbathing late 60-something tourist. It turned out he knew the accommodation I was after and was staying there himself. He told me to turn right, keep walking and I couldn't miss it. He was wrong on both counts. Hardly ideal but when I bumped into him later that night he overflowed with apologies. Over the next week we became firm friends.

Tony was a lover of life, an incisive thinker and great fun. Hours were spent debating various issues, chief amongst which was the question of at what point enthusiastic wooing of a potential lover becomes stalking. The starting point for this was a documentary I haphazardly remembered about the former ABBA singer Agnetha Faltskog (apologies for the political incorrectness but she was the blonde). The documentary examined the bizarre relationship formed by Agnetha and Gert van der Graaf, a Dutch obsessive who had stalked the singer for years. They later became lovers. All very bizarre. Almost as odd as two men of a certain age sitting in would-be paradise having this kind of left-of-centre conversation in the first place.

Tony also introduced me to the fascinating world of Swedish communication. He'd lived in the country, married there, set up business there then left there. This gave him time to learn the language (he speaks several) and observe the ways of the Swedes.

One memorable morning he and I spent an hour or so at breakfast. On the next table were half a dozen young Swedish backpackers. Conversation was almost non-existent and food ordering was an exercise in meditation. To each and every Swede at the table the impatient waitress would ask the same question, "What would you like?" The same pattern was repeated by all, lengthy silence until the question was re-put with even less patience. Everything the youngsters did was at snail's pace and with an outward show of enthusiasm to match. The few comments from within the group were generally met with silence, contemplation and sometime far off in the future a nod of the head or even a 'Jaaaa' in response. Italian they are not.

Tony shared with me a story from remote northern Sweden which, he said, would give insight. One day a young girl was visiting her grandmother in late autumn when the door flew open. In from the snow walked a huge man. He took off his skis, walked to a chair near the stove and sat down. Not a word was said by anyone. After an eternity the grandmother finally asked the man if she could get him anything. He thought for a while and then gave a lengthy and considered 'Jaaaa'.

The grandmother went to work and returned with some coffee and homemade cake. As the man ate the grandmother carried on with her regular chores.

For 30 minutes the three sat in silence, the granddaughter increasingly perplexed by the scene. Finally, the man stood up, put on his coat and grabbed his skis. As he was about to open the door he turned to the grandmother, said, "Thanks for your company," and left.

The utterly bemused girl asked her grandmother who the man was.

"That's Gunnar, my next door neighbour. He lives ten kilometres away and likes to pop in occasionally for a chat."

For neither grandmother nor neighbour was this uncomfortable.

Tony then told me of some research into the communications of Swedish babies. Apparently French babies were found to gurgle at twice the speed of their Swedish equivalents. The pace and the pattern of their speech determined in the womb and the first few weeks of life.

Aside from Swede-watching Tony and I also spent time with a remarkable English couple, Phyllis and Roger. They were late NONYs, cycling enthusiasts and had pretty much pedalled around every spare inch of the globe. They were intrepid to their core and yet looked and sounded every inch a conventional couple. Roger was particularly inspiring as he had only one arm, the other lost in a workplace accident years earlier. He made no concessions to the disability and had continued cycling and backpacking here, there and everywhere without any fuss but with the aid of a prosthesis.

The couple spent several days with us and then moved further up the island. Towards the end of the week Tony and I decided to seek them out. A short boat journey to Salang on the north west coast brought us to a beautiful bay with a dozen or so hotels. Not knowing where they were staying we decided to sit and have a cooling drink, hoping to spot them walk past.

When that yielded no result plan B was put into operation. This was a small place so we'd start inquiring at hotel receptions. I walked to the nearest one and spoke to the receptionist.

"Hello, do you have an English couple staying here? Their names are Phyllis and Roger. I don't have their surnames."

My vague question was met by an equally blank facial expression. I overcame my reluctance and decided to state the obvious.

"The man only has one arm. Have you seen him?"

The receptionist curled his lip up, frowned and shook his head.

"We have many people like that here," he said. "Is there anything else you can tell me about him?"

Dumbfounded, I stood mute and rooted to the spot. Was this tiny cove hosting a convention for one armed travellers? Were sharks terrorising the bay ripping limbs from the swimmers? It was the most unexpected answer of my life. Was there anything else to describe the one armed traveller from England? Not that came to mind, no.

Tony and I decided against asking more questions and retreated to survey the beach half expecting to see an army of the limbless.

That didn't happen but we did eventually find Phyllis and Roger. They enjoyed the story and Roger had one to match.

He and Phyllis were out on their bikes one day and were involved in a crash. Bikes, bodies and backpacks flew in all directions. Kind-hearted locals quickly went to their aid and began collecting the debris from the road. One young man went into the ditch to look for their scattered possessions. He was confronted by the ghastly sight of an arm. It had been ripped straight off one of the poor foreign bikers so he did the only decent thing and immediately fainted. Only when he came too was he given the good news it was just Roger's prosthesis.

Tony, Phyllis and Roger were living proof of the power of a true Nony. The idea of a package holiday was complete anathema; no settling, just spirit and undying wanderlust.

#

11

CHASING THE DRAGON

Week 6; 9,100 kms travelled; 4 lots of laundry to date;
no actual dates; 2nd pair of thongs broken;
lost – the will to live ☹

George Town, Penang. The fabled Pearl Of The Orient. Rich in history, layered in exoticism, a fusion of kaleidoscopic cultures. It is a thing of beauty. But it has a dirty little secret. George Town was built on drugs.

The town was founded as a British trading post. Its merchant fleet used the port as a staging centre between opium growers in India and their whacked out consumers in China.

At the start of the 20th century it's estimated a mind-blowing 25% of adult men in China were literally having their minds blown by opium. That's a staggering proportion of the population. In those days the Brits, the Japanese and any other marauding invaders were militarily kicking the Chinese here there and everywhere. It's not surprising when you think a large chunk of the army and navy were out of their brains on heroin.

"Hey man, peace. Wanna take part of our country? Cooool. Have a puff of this good stuff when you're done, bro."

The British were quickest to see the chance of making a fast buck and in the early nineteenth century the trade accounted for a third of all Penang's imports and exports. It was a massive source of revenue.

The authorities saw a further chance to swell their coffers and began licensing poppy farms in Penang itself. Opium dens soon followed. They were legal and loved by many, particularly the Chinese, who flourished in Malaysia.

In George Town, as in China, users would lie on opium beds, suck long, thin pipes full of the poppy latex, infuse their lungs with smoke and their brains with vivid and wild highs. Chasing the dragon, as it's called.

A hundred years on from the opium trade's heyday it was my turn to sample the Penang drug experience.

I found myself on a George Town bed, vague glimpses of The Pearl drifting through the window. Weird, unformed images swirled through my mind and a numbing fog clouded my head. For the umpteenth time I felt myself lapse back into unconsciousness.

I had lost a night and a day. Gone, but God knows where. The drugs had made time meaningless. Every half an hour or so would bring a brief moment of consciousness. I would will myself to grip reality but nothing could overcome the overwhelming effects.

The colonial addicts smoked opium, my drug of choice was a little different. In fact it wasn't a choice at all. I was a victim of an accidental overdose of cough syrup.

I'd had a rough cold and hacking cough for days and it was spreading to my chest. For $5 I was told I could see a Malaysian doctor and get all the necessary drugs. What a deal. After a thorough examination the news was good, my chest was fine. I was given a prescription, went to the pharmacy and given cough syrup and a decongestant. The syrup was clearly labelled. I was to take 15mls three times a day.

My first dose was just before the return flight from Tioman to Kuala Lumpur. The impact was immediate and I calmly sleepwalked up the stairs into the plane. The remainder of the day disappeared in naps at airports, on planes and in buses. Somehow I made it to my Penang hotel. I was a little perplexed by my desperate tiredness but at eight o'clock it was time for another dose of the syrup.

Much of the next 36 hours was lost to lapses in and out of consciousness. Every time I tried to get out of bed I fell back into a trance. I had no dinner and the next morning slept through breakfast. At about 2pm I managed to stay awake long enough to pick up the bedside phone and call room service.

Sometime later in the mellow muddle of my mind came a tapping noise. Slow and rhythmic, it formed a gentle soundtrack to my dreams. Gradually I became aware of it getting louder and louder until finally it crashed through my sleep, ripped open my mind and woke me with the realisation somebody was knocking at my hotel door.

I staggered out of bed and was met by a man with a tray. I was a little surprised, he, on the other hand, was absolutely startled by the crazed sight that confronted him. A dishevelled and clearly drugged up man, with a bath towel held weakly over his modesty, was leering at him. I suspect the towel was positioned a little immodestly, at this point I barely had control of any of my limbs.

"Is this for me?" I managed to drool in a deeply confused state. That really caught him off guard.

"Didn't you order it? Room 728."

By now I had no real recollection of having made an order and I sure as hell had no idea of my room number. Name, age and sexual orientation would have been beyond me at this point.

The waiter brought in the food and asked for cash. I muttered the words 'credit card', which he firmly declined. No credit card allowed, he said, apparently I hadn't let them swipe a copy when I'd checked in. Again, news to me.

"I don't have money," I said. I had no idea whether I did or didn't but my mouth was moving independently of my brain.

"You have to pay cash or I can't leave the food."

"Ok. Goodbye." It was no concern of mine. I didn't even know if I'd ordered the food or was even hungry. No idea at all.

The poor, startled waiter backed out of the room and left. With my eyelids barely apart I headed back to bed and the sanctuary of sleep. But just as my coma reclaimed me a loud knocking roused me once again. Another stagger, the towel even less limply held, and there he was again.

"The manager will put it on your account." He marched in and marched out with fast, fearful footsteps. I set languidly to work on the sandwiches and chips. I remember little except it took an almighty effort to eat anything.

Sometime far off into the future I resurfaced submarine-like from my sleep. Scarcely breaking through the waves of consciousness for a minute or two, I vaguely wondered why there were chips on my bed and bits of bread and cucumber actually in it. Barely had the thought crossed my mind before I dived once more into the murky depths of my coma.

Eventually through the waking haze came a brief moment of clarity. I really shouldn't be in a borderline comatose condition for yet another day. Something was going on and I finally had enough brainpower to search for a culprit.

I managed to turn on my iPad and searched for the name of the medicine. There was the answer to my listlessness. Take between 2.5 and 5mls three times a day. It was accompanied by a clear warning, "May cause drowsiness".

It should have read "May induce a catatonic state if an idiot pharmacist has screwed up and massively over-prescribed it". He'd trebled the dose as a minimum and possibly hit the jackpot at the high end with up to six times the recommended measure.

Late in the afternoon I finally made it out of bed, intent on food to give me energy. The room service food had mostly failed to find my stomach, although bits of it were attached to various parts of my body. Some I picked off but others actually had to be combed out. Best I stop here, chances are you have an innocent but entirely inaccurate picture in your head.

Like a punch drunk prizefighter I sluggishly made it to the end of the road, entered a restaurant, slumped into a seat and ordered the first thing on the menu, Wonton soup, then promptly fell asleep.

I was woken by a waitress with a worried look on her face and a bowl of soup in her hands. Here was my potential salvation and I began to eat. The rest of the meal gets a little hazy from this moment on. At some uncertain later point I awoke from another sleep, a tiny dew drop falling silently from my nose sending the merest of faint ripples into an ocean of soup. Alarmingly, it was just one inch below my face. I had fallen asleep mid slurp and almost drowned in Wonton. I have had numerous romanticised visions of my death, often it comes while defending the honour of dozens of vestal virgins, whatever the hell they might be. But death by soup is not a heroic way to die and definitely not how I pictured it.

As I fought off the urge to sleep again I began to think. Was it the cough syrup causing this or possibly something worse? Could I have malaria? Oh yes, malaria, quite likely. Bloody mosquitos. The next one I come across will feel my vengeful wrath. My confused thoughts carried on in this rambling manner for a little while. But on the outer edge of my existence I became aware of the other diners and they were all looking at me. The restaurant was silent. It dawned on me that I hadn't been 'thinking' at all. I'd actually been speaking to myself, OUT LOUD! The entire cafe had been treated to what I thought were my internal thought processes. Needless to say I made my sheepish excuses, paid the bill and left, slowly, for yet another appointment with my bed.

#

The following day I had finally recovered consciousness from my drugs overdose. I still felt a little numbed and my cough was making an irritating comeback. Every ten seconds or so was another hacking rasp. It all combined to leave me feeling a little low.

Being ill on your own is never great but when you're alone in a foreign land, away from friends and family, it adds another dispiriting layer. My loneliness was starting to get to me.

At night I wandered over to a large food hall, ordered a couple of dishes and sat on my own at a large table. Around me were probably 150 or so people, mostly Malaysians but also some foreign tourists. They seemed to be enjoying the moment. When you're feeling a little low the rest of the world always appears to be having a good time. I, on the other hand, was utterly devoid of fun and contact. My exchange with the startled room service waiter had been the most in-depth connection I'd had in days.

As I waited for my food a guy began playing pub style music on a large electric organ. Some nights it would have been entertainingly bad but this night it added to the air of depression. I tried my best to block out his first couple of numbers but then his singing hit a nerve. He launched into a seriously off-key version of Ralph McTell's 'Streets of London', a classic observation on homelessness in the city.

The organ man's stand-out weakness, aside from tirelessly hitting the wrong note, was an inability to pronounce consonants. To be fair he was singing in a foreign language. But this night fairness was missing from my mindset.

"*Have you seen the ol ma....*"

Moments after his opening my dinner arrived. The first slurp of hokkien mee made me wince and I burned my tongue.

The entertainer's singing seeped through my ears and into my brain.

"*....sitting there on his own lookin' at the worl.*"

A few more tentative mouthfuls and a prawn slid from my spoon down my T shirt. F**k! Everything felt like it was going wrong. I couldn't catch a break and I sure as hell couldn't find a positive thought. I was spiralling into self-pity.

"*....So how can you tell me you're lo-o-ly, an' say for you that the sun don' shi.*"

The line, sung in a grotesque Bob Dylan sneer, hit home. It melded perfectly with my lonely, miserable mood and I felt my spirits sink yet lower. I desperately fought the urge to shout "It's lonely, you clown. LONELY. Pronounce the bloody N"

The waiter returned with a side dish. Malaysian food is generally very good, this was very goo.

"So how ca' you tell me you're lo-o-o-ly, an' say for you that the sun don' shi'."

Laughter from the couple behind, lousy food in front of me, I'd had enough. I dropped some cash on the table, got up and began to trudge back to my hotel, just able to catch his parting last line,

"...an' he wanders home alone."

The song is part kick up the arse for when we, who live easy lives, feel sorry for ourselves. Compared to the wretched lives of the homeless there's nothing to moan about. I know it. I've even quoted it in my time. But now I wandered home alone and lonely, my spirits at rock bottom after days of illness and grogginess. When I got back to my room I lay down on my bed and felt a warm tear trickle down my face.

#

12

THE TEMPLE OF BOOM

You're not supposed to talk ill of the dead.... but I'm sure Buddha has broad shoulders.

In his name and honour Penang hosts one of the most unforgettable temple complexes in the world, Kek Lok Si. It is magnificent yet monstrous, awe inspiring but appalling, grandiose but.....you get the drift. By turns it takes your breath away and then leaves you nauseous.

From a distance it is stunning. The largest Buddhist temple complex in the country sits high atop a hill and it's all presided over by an immense figure, Kuan Yin, Goddess of Mercy. Standing a colossal 30 metres in height under a giant canopy, the bronze statue imposes magisterial command over the area for miles around.

When I first saw it I was instantly uplifted by its sheer scale. My illness was well and truly in retreat, my self-pity banished and the sight energized me. It felt good to be back out and about seeing what surprises the world had to offer.

Kuan Yin dwarfs the physical world of mankind, her spiritual standing is even higher. The statue forms one part of Kek Lok Si. Below, but no less imposing, is a seven story wonder called the Pagoda of Ten Thousand Buddhas. It's almost unreal in appearance. The base is Chinese and octagonal, the middle tiers Thai and the golden crown Burmese. It stands exquisitely over temples and ornate gardens in a candy-land extravaganza of colour and shapes. The pagoda and its surrounds look like an epic piece of confectionery or a backdrop for Alice in Wonderland.

Kek Lok Si translates literally as the Temple Of Supreme Bliss. Its founder and first abbot was the Venerable Beow Lean. Born in 1844 his initial calling was in commerce before he switched his devotions from business to Buddhism. He spent the rest of his life searching for enlightenment and dedication to Buddha's teachings. However, the abbot never lost his ability to make a few quid and he passed his financial acumen down through the ages. His shrewd descendants have been employing these skills ever since. Today Kek Lok Si is a growth industry. What Beow Lean started in the late 19th is now a sprawling complex, much of it built post 2000 with a huge bundle of cash.

The Kuan Yin statue was only opened in 2002, a reconstructed replacement for a smaller version which was fire damaged. The completion of the Guan Tong Great Hall and the Aghast Hall are all recent. There's also a new incline lift, an air conditioned box on rails which will take you serenely uphill to the feet of the Goddess herself.

All around is renewal and expenditure. New tiles for the dazzling roofs, paint for the temples. The costs must have been huge but the pace shows no sign of slowing.

Kek Lok Si has always known which side its bread is buttered. Money talks now and it wasn't short of a few words back in the early days. The temple houses "The Big Five", life size sculptures of its original key benefactors. Their wealthy contributions were rewarded with immortality.

The complex is a cornerstone of the Chinese community and they are absolutely unstinting in their generosity. But here's the rub. For a place that is so handsomely bestowed there are signs that it's losing the plot in an endless search for even more cash.

The walk to the temple from the foot of the hill winds through a seemingly endless trail of enclosed walkways crammed full of hawker stalls. It is a rat run of tat. The temple elders may or may not have any say in this crass commercialism but endless offerings of Starbucks T-shirts, Singha beer hats and plastic Eiffel Towers (no, I can't explain that one) don't exactly get you in the mind for the spiritual awe that Kek Lok Si promises. Perhaps it is just my outsider mindset imposing my values on theirs, for none of this seems to bother the locals one tiny jot. My observations may just be the unwelcome voyeurisms of a cultural alien seen through the prism of a lifetime in western society.

OK, that's the political correctness out of the way, on we go.

At the end of the hawker run is a grotty pond full of turtles. They are a warm up act for your wallet. People throw money into the pool or try to land coins on the tiny shells of the poor Testudines (now I'm showing off).

After the turtles the quest for your cash moves into top gear. At the centre of the complex, next to the incline lift, is a gift shop. Not totally unexpected but the size of the place really is. It's a whopper. You can buy all manner of cheap, gaudy, stuff. Row after row of it packed in tight. There's nothing the bargain-hunting pilgrim can't find here. When you leave the monster store you step into the incline lift. A few seconds later you're unloaded.... into another huge gift shop, an immediate second chance to be relieved of your dough. And it's flogging the exact same stuff.

In case punters, sorry, I mean worshippers, are a little anxious about the hefty money-making, posters hang on walls proclaiming profits go to the temple. It hardly looks like it needs it. Perhaps a shout for the poor, lame, lonely or just plain deserving might be more appropriate given the grandness of Kek Lok Si. Whichever direction the funds flow it feels like commercial overkill. But it gets worse.

Inside some of the temples people get to practice their faith under the watchful eye of more stallholders. Who the hell this side of creation could have thought to offer a battery powered cat with moving paws in the middle of a shrine. I fully understand that cats here are supposed to be lucky but selling flailing felines within the temple itself seems disrespectful at best and horrible greed at worst.

And the love affair with cash doesn't stop there. The magnificent interior of the prayer hall is thankfully devoid of free enterprise. Hundreds of people are being guided through the holy rituals of devotion. However, when they finish the departing faithful are immediately confronted outside with guidance of a different type. Posters are prominently displayed which guide them through the process of temple donation.

Enough already!

But there is a final opportunity to splash the cash. A little further down the complex, sitting piously at a stall is a monk. I stood and watched people come and go. His role seemed to be to bless some of the countless religious artefacts bought by the believers. For each blessing a donation was given/extracted (delete where appropriate). Stacked neatly at his side are roof tiles which you can sponsor. Your name can be inscribed on the tile and the good monk will give it his benediction. Blessed are the tilers. Just hand over your money and it's all yours.

It is endless and it is awful. This is not a place short of a shilling or two but the pursuit of growth and renewal seems to have overwhelmed good taste, decency and piety.

At Chinese New Year Kek Lok Si is lit by 10,000 lights. I'm told it is staggering to behold. But contain your excitement, because here's the really special bit. For an appropriate donation you can literally have your name in bright lights. You can sponsor a light bulb. Switch off? You bet.

#

13

SAIGON ON HEAT

Week 7; Ho Chi Minh City, Vietnam; 10,500 kms travelled;
Losses to date - 1 shirt, 1 cap, 1 pair of sunglasses, 1 will to live
(soon rediscovered)

Saigon is a city on heat. District One its smouldering core. Full bore, full on and in your face. It's high octane, high energy and in the backpacker area often simply high.

Not just a city that never sleeps, this place doesn't even take a nap. Each day a hustle, every street corner a scam. Crossing the road an exercise in blind faith. Lots of smiles, millions of motorbikes. Drink, drugs, sex, all constantly offered. Personal space non-existent. Sellers, buyers, traders will all touch and grab. They go through a litany of services searching for your desire.

"You want massage?" No. "You want girl?" No. "You want young girl?" NO. "You want marijuana?" No. "You want sell your shoes"? WHAT! That floored me. Bizarrely it happened three times, I had two offers on my thongs and one on my trainers. I am clearly something of a fashion icon in Ho Chi Minh City, as the place is called these days.

There is a tidal wave of people living in the fast lane or in District One's case, the back lanes. A mass of compact alleyways, or hem, crisscross the backpacker area between Pham Ngau Lao and Bui Vien. No more than three paces wide they overflow with everyday living.

Whole families perched on tiny plastic stools eating, while motorbikes weave past. "More fumes on your noodles?" Kids playing, women chatting, men plotting. People fixing cycles, washing plates, making fans, mending bits of plumbing. Through them prowl the hawkers with vertical piles of rip-off books and dvds, boards full of fake designer sunglasses.

In these warrens people live life in the open. Homes don't get shut until late night. Privacy is only a concern for reserved foreigners. The dwellings are mere slithers, rooms are often tiny.

As you pass you have a peep show on their lives. Elderly people lying on small beds that fill the tiny rooms. People cleaning, cooking, resting from the oppressive heat and humidity.

The alleys are home to scores of little cafes, backpacker hostels and hotels. At any time of day and night stepping out from your oasis of calm into the hem is a violent assault on your senses. Eyes, ears and nose instantly thrashed. The city has a vibrancy that is infectious. It's hard not to be swept up in its swirling energy.

Night-time in Bui Vien is party central. Hundreds of little chairs lined up on either side of the road overflowing with backpackers. As the night progresses more tiny chairs appear from thin air to form new front rows. At times the two sides almost join, sending the constant blare of motorbike horns into new levels of frenzy. Booze is cheap, food a few cents above free and the commodity of fun appears limitless.

But District One is Saigon's schizophrenia. Elsewhere, away from the backpackers' haunt, things are a little more sedate. The area around the Opera House is very sophisticated. Uncle Ho's statue is in a sumptuous setting that could have been transported straight from Paris. It's a little ironic that the man whose life was dedicated to kicking out the foreign imperialists should find his memorial surrounded by grand

French colonial architecture. Elegant buildings, beautiful gardens and international designer shops, capitalism's marquee signature, are his constant companions.

Perhaps the old revolutionary would have liked the joke, especially as he sits in front of the grandest of them all, the old Hotel De Ville, now blandly rebranded as the People's Committee Hall.

Even here, along with everywhere else in Saigon, there's no escaping the traffic. Actually, the motorbikes. Two and a half to three million in Saigon, 30 million more in the rest of Vietnam, according to government figures.

But you won't get out of breath counting private cars. Three huge taxes and seven separate fees price them off the road. A car costing $23,500 in the US would set you back a fraction under $70,000 in Vietnam, that's 30 times the average annual salary. To misquote George Orwell, in Vietnam, 'Two wheels good, four wheels bad.' And so the motorbike is king and the riders know no boundaries.

You quickly learn three rules as a pedestrian. Firstly, don't fall into the trap of believing the pedestrian walkway is for pedestrians. This old school kind of thinking can get you mown down in an instant. Pavements are fair game for scooters to move quickly past other stationary two wheelers. Walkers are mere inconvenient distractions.

Secondly, one-way streets do what they say on the label, they are one-way.... but in each direction. Believing the signs here can leave you complacently looking in one direction for the assumed flow of traffic. A potentially fatal mistake. Instructional signs are for foreigners who don't know any better. The combination of a pavement and a one-way street create the perfect killing zone for tourists cocooned in a lifetime of obeying rules and regulations.

The third element, and probably the hairiest, is the traffic lights. When lights turn red and a few amber gamblers have raced through, don't be tempted to cross. A good rule of thumb is to count slowly to three and then wait. At least one more group will then hurtle through the red light. Once they've gone count to three, again do it slowly. The death-wish brigade will make a final dash through the junction. After that you're good to go.

Having mastered these three basics if you really want to dance with death go to Ben Thanh market. It's a tourist mecca and is situated next to a huge roundabout. Believing you can cross from the market to any one of half a dozen roads is like putting on your underpants outside your trousers and believing it makes you Superman. It is an exercise in total self-delusion.

The usual Saigon rule of 'walk at a steady pace in a straight line' isn't much use either. There is often no space to move into and in the heaving throng of bikes you won't get spotted. Foolhardy tourists who've tried to brazen it out have often found themselves taking up semi-permanent residence in the middle of the road, stuck in an unstoppable wave of traffic, unable to move safely in any direction. The visitors' petrified stance can last so long the city council classifies them as residents and sends them rates bills.

Scooters and motorbikes are everywhere and often 20 abreast in a kind of moving mass symphony that ebbs and flows as one. I have seen nothing like it.

Ho Chi Minh died in 1969, six years before unification. But the North Vietnamese troops carried on singing a song:

Bác vẫn cùng chúng cháu hành quân.

It translates as, "You are still marching with us, Uncle Ho." These days I suspect he'd be more likely to be with them on a motorbike. It would be a heck of a lot safer than being on foot.

#

14

MRS HO - WAR WARRIOR WIDOW

Week 8; Hue, Vietnam; 11,200 kms travelled;
new prescription sunglasses;
1 pair of wonder socks missing, gone for ever?

He was six years old, just a little boy. But fate had not been kind to him. He was having to grow up very quickly, learn fast, make smart decisions. There was no choice, his young life depended on it.

When the attack started he knew exactly what to do, where to go. He'd been through this before.

As the bombs fell he and the other children scattered from their games, terrified and literally running for their lives. In a rush they reached the tunnel entrances, scampering down the holes like rabbits. But the little boy had been left behind, his young legs just not fast enough. A bomb ripped into the ground, the explosion shattering everything in its path.

His mother heard the awful sound and felt the earth tremor as she huddled in fear below. She silently hoped for her child's safety, like she'd done so often before, he'd always made it back to her. But this time was different. He didn't return. Her little boy was gone for ever.

More than 40 years on, now in her 80s, she tells me the story. Her face ravaged by the cruelty of time, her tiny body stick thin and frail. But the awful memory of the day her son was killed was as vivid as ever.

Mrs Cat Ho sat in the shade near the entrance to Vinh Moc Tunnels. The two kilometre complex was dug by villagers just north of the old DMZ (demilitarised zone) on the central coast of Vietnam. It was their only way to escape the aerial and naval bombardment by American forces in the war. These days the tunnels are open to tourists. I was the only one there on a blisteringly hot day.

As I'd passed by she'd raised her bony arm, pointed back at the tunnels and spoke. I was clueless. Twice more she pointed and tried to tell me something.

"She says she helped build the tunnel." My guide, Mr Thang, had come back to join me. "She helped build it and she lived there."

Here was living history. For the next hour we sat at her feet as she told us her extraordinary story.

Mrs Ho had the good fortune to be born in a beautiful setting metres from a sparkling beach. Her awful misfortune was that it was close to the border between north and south Vietnam. With the start of the American War (it's not called the Vietnam War here) US forces set about clearing everything near the DMZ. Tons of bombs were dropped. With nowhere to go the villagers began digging. An underground complex of tunnels and rooms began to take shape. One of the volunteers was Mrs Ho.

For three years she carried sacks of soil on her slight back from the dig site to the sea, mostly in the dead of night. There she would dump it for the water to take so no trace could be seen by US reconnaissance planes. It was gruelling work.

Initially they were 10 metres deep but when the Americans developed bombs that could penetrate underground the villagers doubled the depth.

These days the tunnels are well ventilated, lit and dry. They give a glimpse of the hardship villagers endured in the war but it's impossible to really grasp how it felt.

"It was very wet there. We used to have to stand with water above our ankles for a very long time. The walls were always damp. Many, many people were sick," Mrs Ho told me.

Seventeen babies were born in the tunnels, children had school lessons underground. Cooking and all the other daily routines of life were carried on there.

And throughout there was the bombing.

"Boom, boom, boom," said Mrs Ho and she clutched herself tight, drew in her cheeks and shook her head.

"It was very frightening but we were safe."

Several hundred people at a time could hide underground. None were ever killed in the tunnels. When she wasn't digging Mrs Ho was helping the North Vietnamese war effort. "I took food and supplies to the soldiers. I would carry everything on my back and go right to the front lines. I would be so close I could sometimes see the Americans." She became temporarily lost in the thought and stopped for a few moments before returning to the task in hand of rolling her own cigarette and reliving her memories.

Mrs Ho was awarded a medal after the war. Remarkably it was her second medal and her second war.

In 1954 Ho Chi Minh led North Vietnamese troops against the French. There was fierce fighting around the Vinh Moc area. Mrs Ho helped the soldiers, resupplying them with ammunition and rice. She would crawl through fields while the fighting raged around her, intent on doing her bit. She mimics soldiers shooting and points to a small rise where French troops had once come within metres of her as she hauled guns to the troops.

Mrs Ho was enjoying telling her story, a smile rarely left her face. I mentioned this to her. "Ever since I was a girl I have always smiled. It's important. It helped in the war."

Vietnam is a forward thinking place. Nearly everybody I spoke to looks to the future not the past. The war is long over, Americans are welcome. Or at least that was the picture I'd been getting loud and clear from the young to the middle aged.

I asked Mrs Ho if she'd met any since the war. "No. They don't come here. I think they are afraid."

How did she feel about them? "I don't like them."

And if one came and tried to talk to her how would that be? She paused and then after a little internal debate and a hesitant reluctance the war veteran gave way to the polite old lady. "That would be alright."

Vinh Moc isn't easy travelling. It's more than 100 kilometres north of the ancient capital of Hue. Various tours to the area were touted but my general reluctance to have a 'group experience' had kept me from signing up. The subject had come up with a waitress in my guesthouse and she'd made a couple of calls for me. That's how I'd come across Mr Thang and his motorbike tour, tailor made, personalised and intimate. It also highlighted the advantage of using a local guide.

I love to do my own thing but I would never have met the amazing Mrs Ho without Mr Thang. He'd also taken me to battlefield sites, monuments and war memorials and he did it all at a pace I dictated.

Unfortunately my dawdling meant we were fighting the light getting home. Mr Thang was pushing it a little and was a fraction over the speed limit when we came across the cops. It was tea time once more in Southeast Asia and the uniform boys were doing their usual corrupt best to fill their stomachs. With no tourists around they happily picked on local after local.

Were they speeding? It was far from clear but nobody was arguing. Six or seven of them sat head bowed as money was demanded. Mr Thang was given a surly lecture and then money requested. By now I'd had enough experience of tea time to make a contribution and I don't mean financial.

I got Mr Thang to translate my thoughts to the cops along the lines of "Taking money off me or my driver could cause you lots of headaches." Before you get all impressed by my ballsiness best you know that my physical presence doesn't even intimidate little old ladies in dark alleyways. My face doesn't help much either. My generally happy demeanour creaks and collapses under the strain of the merest attempt at an intimidatory face. My trick is a kind of grown up version of 'my brother is bigger than your brother and he'll smash your face in'. Not terribly sophisticated, I'll admit. Funnily enough it never worked as a kid but as an adult it has a decent track record.

The ace up my sleeve was all those years working for the BBC. Having covered news around the world I'm quite used to getting screwed around in strange places. Sometimes there's not much you can do but journalists spell trouble. Often the hint that you have a readily available line to somebody in authority is enough to make low level officials back down. Mr Thang explained that I worked for BBC News for 18 years. The cops took that as an ongoing thing - their fault not mine. There was a brief discussion and I could almost hear their brains unhappily contemplating phone calls from above. It worked and Mr Thang and I walked off with our wallets intact. I wished I could have done the same for the locals queuing up to be fleeced of their money. Corruption stinks and it's never more nauseating than when it's aimed at the poor and the weak.

Mr Thang was incredibly grateful and my reward was an insistence that I go to his home and join him and his family for dinner.

When we arrived in Hue Mrs Thang did a double-take as I walked into her home but she soon overcame her surprise. The couple lived in one room with their two young children. The four shared one bed. Dinner was served on a mat on the floor and at each new offering I was given the lion's share. It's difficult not to sound patronising but little touches me as much as the generosity of strangers. This is particularly so for those who often have next to nothing but who'll always share whatever they do have. It's a travel cliché but it often happens to ring true.

#

15

TWO WEDDINGS AND A BABY

Week 9; Hue, Vietnam; 11,500 kms travelled; to date - 11 flights;
6 motorbikes; 2 boats; 1 bicycle; 23 different beds

Nine weeks into my travels and I was getting the hang of 'no planning'. Every day was a surprise and it felt very liberating. Jumping on a scooter or motorbike and just driving was becoming a favourite way of spending some hours. Sometimes I had a destination in mind, often it was just a case of following my nose.

The unexpected and the off-beat became my bedfellows. One day in Vietnam I returned from a ride with two marriage proposals and a baby in my backpack. It's true, well almost. The proposals had been made and the baby had actually been in my backpack, it just wasn't there when I got back to the hotel. For any outraged readers, child welfare workers or police officers reading this I best explain that I hadn't dropped it. But to be on the safe side if you do fit one of these categories it's probably best if you skip the next couple of dozen paragraphs. It will ease your troubled minds and save the ink on the Interpol arrest warrant. For the rest of you, here's the story.

I'd got up in the morning and fished out my trusty Balinese coin. Today's choice was drive up into the mountains or head in the opposite direction towards the South China Sea. The toss was made and I left the city of Hue and headed in the general direction of the coast. It was a few miles away and I had a vague idea of the direction. For weeks I had been using an amazing iPad app called MAPS.ME. Even without a wifi connection the app hooked up to a satellite and via GPS I could see on street maps exactly where I was. It's all very Big Brother of course. Conspiracy theorists would say that if I know where I was, 'they' know where I was too. Why the hell they'd want to know is another matter entirely. I've got nothing to hide, well, not much anyway and I don't suppose governments big or small really care that much about the time I....

Whenever I was lost, which was frequently and happily, I switched on the app. It pinpointed my exact location and showed me street names, locations, petrol stations and supermarkets, although not food stalls which was much more my norm for eating.

As I neared the coast the land turned into a sliver between two stretches of water. To the west was an estuary and to the east the sea, which I caught with a few odd glimpses. Much of the ocean side had houses and every couple of hundred metres narrow alleyways cut through them to the beach.

It carried on like this for a couple of kilometres. Eventually I took pot luck and headed up one. Two hundred metres later, just outside the last house, an old man was sitting in the middle of the alleyway. Being used to motorbikes here, there and everywhere he didn't move an inch as I weaved around him. Twenty metres later the path stopped at the foot of a sand hill. Beyond I could hear the break of the waves. I got off my bike and as I was removing my helmet the old man began waving towards me. He pointed to the sun, then to my motorbike and finally to some shade just by him. The penny finally dropped. He was saying, "Hey you, foreign fool, don't park your bike in the sun or you'll have a roasted arse when you get back on." This being rural Vietnam he was, of course, saying it in a much kinder way.

I moved the bike to the shade and as I neared him I noticed he was making a model fishing boat out of wood. I smiled, pointed admiringly at his workmanship, thanked him for his wisdom several more times then headed to the beach. The long coastline was powdery white and the sea deep blue with some semi-rugged walls of white water breaking onto the shoreline. No tourists, not even any locals, but dozens of fishing boats leaning idly on the sand presumably waiting for the next appropriate time and tide before heading back out for a catch.

After 20 minutes or so I made my way back through the sand hills to my bike. The old man was still sitting working on his model boat but now on the ground before him was a small teapot and two glasses. He gestured me to sit with him and as I did he poured me a glass of green tea. For ten minutes we sat, examined his work and I tried a couple of Vietnamese words which kind of boiled down to, "you're a really nice old man and I appreciate your tea. Isn't life great." I think he worked it out even though all I could actually say in Vietnamese was "good", "very good" and "thank you".

After a little while two neighbours came walking up the alleyway. They were taken aback to see a foreigner sitting with their old friend but they were all smiles and handshakes as they joined us. Every few minutes this was repeated until word spread and within quarter of an hour there was a crowd of men, women and children. Some brought along their tiny plastic chairs, others just brought more people. The noise level was high as the excitement rose from the children.

Finally, a woman with a tiny smattering of English arrived and this led to many questions. Somebody in the crowd would ask her something in Vietnamese and she would do her best to translate. One of the men pointed at my ringless finger. The lady smiled and a little shyly managed to find enough English to ask if I was married. I slowly shook my head. But as I repeatedly found in Southeast Asia being middle aged and unmarried was a tough thing to comprehend for many people. It made little sense to them. I mimicked the removal of a wedding ring. Bafflement. The woman's English didn't stretch far enough to grasp the marriage had finished. So clutching at straws I upgraded the gesture to something more dynamic. Out loud I said the word 'marriage' and slowly drew my hand across my throat. It meant marriage dead but was lost in translation and turned into wife beheaded or something equally draconian.

The initial reaction was shock followed by sympathy, particularly from the young women. But one of the men was ahead of the rest and he sensed a mutually beneficial opportunity. He spoke to his wife who quickly disappeared down the alleyway. Two minutes later she was back with her daughter, who I suspect was no more than 25. Both husband and wife smiled and made hand gestures that suggested "here's your next wife". Rather than being shocked at the gross, old foreigner she smiled coquettishly. I defensively put up my hands and smiled politely so as not to offend. The crowd, by now at least 20 strong, were all smiling and pointing at the girl.

But while I desperately fought against their enthusiasm another man got to his feet, shouted down the alleyway and momentarily another girl appeared. Her father repeated the gestures of the previous man and the girl did a kind of half-hearted twirl. The crowd's collective humour raised another few decibels and the women began laughing loudly.

I was desperately hoping no more prospective brides would be proffered. I got my wish. What was actually produced next was the first girl's baby. It was handed to the old man and he thrust it into my arms. Never having had children myself I can tell you my deficient parenting skills brought shrieks from the entire crowd. The old man finally took back the baby and gestured to put it in my backpack. More hilarity and during the next five minutes the seemingly happy baby dangled in and out of my bag.

And then I worked it out. The two girls were clearly unmarried mothers. Their fathers were on the lookout to find them a husband and some financial support. I fitted the bill, regardless of my age.

To be fair everything was done with humour and smiles but I was happy to get away still single and childless. When I finally took my leave I made a note to buy a smaller daypack. I'd ask around in local shops if they sold bags which were too small to hold a baby.

#

16

LOVE YOU, LOVE YOU MORE

Week 10; Zagreb, Croatia; 22,100 kms travelled;
4 wonder socks; 1 jet lag; 1 bad case of hypocrisy

After two and a half months in the region it was time for a change. My Vietnam visa was expiring so I had to leave the country. To be honest I wasn't unhappy to be getting out. Southeast Asia can get under your skin in good ways and bad. The cities are bustling and bursting, high on energy and noise, low on privacy and space. There's terrible traffic pollution, rubbish and garbage indiscriminately defile the landscape. Much of the area is a dumping ground for the world's oversupply of plastic bottles, they are tossed everywhere. Rural transport can be ancient and uncomfortable and 'road' is often a nominal description for interlinking potholes and ruts. Hygiene and cleanliness can be seriously lacking, cold showers can be the norm. Some people will wax lyrical about how refreshing cold water is on a scorching hot day, I am not one of them.

In short, it is an assault on your senses and sensitivities. It was time for a little more gentle refinement. The European summer was well and truly underway. Italy, Spain and France would already be busy but I was heading to another part. I'd gone on to my Kayak flight booking app and just basically searched for cheap flights to anywhere in Europe. The answer was Zagreb in Croatia. I didn't exactly have a plan, that would be breaking the rules, but I have to confess I had a notion or two. Both would involve a journey down the eastern coast of the Adriatic Sea.

I had covered the war in Bosnia in the 1990s and was desperately keen to see how it was faring now. I also wanted to reconnect with my own self from a time long gone. As an 11-year old boy my parents had somehow scraped enough money together to send me on a school cruise. Paying passengers were on one part of the SS Uganda (later pressed into service as a hospital ship in the Falklands war) while hundreds of school kids were in another. For a young boy from north Wales it was beyond exotic. Two of the ports of call were the Greek island of Corfu and the medieval walled city of Dubrovnik in Yugoslavia. After the Croatian and Bosnian wars of the early 90s Yugoslavia no longer existed. However, despite the best efforts of attacking Serbs and Montenegrins the walled city was still there. It would be fabulous to go back. Plus some Aussie friends were due in Dubrovnik the following month. No matter how much you travel and how many amazing people you meet it is great to catch up with friends.

So I bought a one-way plane ticket (alert readers should already be twitching with wisdom) and was due to fly from Ho Chi Minh City to Zagreb.

Unfortunately, two and a half months of travel had made me a little blasé. I had become used to simply dealing with situations as and when they arose. Mistake.

I checked in for my flight at the unearthly hour of 1am. I was given my boarding pass and had walked off towards security when a breathless young lady came running behind me shouting my name. Instantly I knew the problem. I hadn't shown them proof of onwards travel from Croatia and they hadn't asked. They'd obviously just realised the error of their ways. Worse still, I had forgotten to make my false booking to show in case of trouble.

The young lady caught up with me and my hunch was right. "We need to see an onwards ticket please. We forgot to check at the counter."

With no time to think I again played the old BBC card. Simply name-dropping the corporation used to solve many problems large and small. Now I used it again, sorry Auntie.

"I spent 18 years as a BBC TV journalist. I never knew from one day to the next where I would be going. I'm constantly moving from country to country", I said.

I was hoping she hadn't picked up my cunning use of the past tense, would assume I was still an employee and so I could escape without actually telling a lie.

"I can't be expected to have onward travel documents", I added. I wasn't aggressive but I said it in a forceful and confident manner which, truth be told, I wasn't feeling. Taken aback by my assertiveness or thrown off guard by the mention of the BBC she apologised and walked off.

Lesson learned. And the lesson was when you learn a lesson don't forget it. Idiot.

Arriving in Zagreb was quite spellbinding. The airport was immaculately clean and tidy and customs smooth and efficient. Queues were orderly without pushing and shoving or shouting. The signs were clear and the waiting city transfer bus clean.

For the first ten minutes of the drive I was in a daze. Traffic seemed light and drivers obeyed the rules. The roads were excellent, the air was fresh and again I was struck by how clean, neat and tidy everything was. I was delighted to be there.

Living in this kind of environment can make you seriously nonchalant about life. It is so easy to take everything for granted. Health, wealth, cleanliness, safety and infrastructure. I breathed in the orderliness of Europe and loved its welcoming scent.

But travel turns you into a hypocrite. Thirty minutes later I was starting to think it all seemed a little antiseptic, highly organised and prescriptive. The people all behaved in the right way, were orderly and ordered.

Travel tart that I'd become I began to miss the chaos, the freedom and lack of regulation and the sheer unbridled energy of Ho Chi Minh

City. Had I made a mistake coming here?

An hour later yet another act of kindness by a stranger had flipped my mind once more. I had missed my stop on a tram and was clearly looking perplexed. Seeing my confusion an old lady asked where I was going. When I told her she tried to explain that I needed to get off and follow a few simple instructions. Obviously it was too much for me and I must have still looked baffled. So she patiently waited until the next stop, escorted me off the tram, walked me five hundred metres through the light rain and waited until the appropriate tram came along. She sent me on my way but not before boarding the tram and having a word to the driver so he could tell me when I needed to get off. Amazing kindness.

The rest of the journey went without a hitch. I found the small apartment which I'd only booked while sitting in Qatar airport waiting for my onwards flight. With the sun still shining I headed out to the medieval centre of the city. Old Zagreb looked splendid and Southeast Asia once more disappeared from my thoughts. I was sending out the love and Europe was loving me back. Hypocrite!

#

Two facts about Zagreb.

A) 109% of the population smoke

B) The city has 76 million coffee shops - that works out at 97 for each citizen.

Oh, you spotted the exaggerations. Try this then. Replace the word 'facts' with 'impressions' and now you've got a fairly good idea of how it actually feels.

They are the two great passions in the city. When you combine coffee drinking with smoking it adds up to a state of nirvana for the average Zagrebian. Yep, that's also made up but who the hell knows or let alone cares what a citizen of Zagreb is called.

The attractive old part of the city morphs into one huge outdoor coffee lounge. Rows of tables and chairs stretch as far as the eye can see. They're all seemingly there to serve the connoisseurs of coffee.

You'd think this would lead to a wildly manic city full of caffeine fuelled Zagrebists. Strangely, it doesn't. The difference between here and, say the USA, is that coffee shops are really social shops. They are for meeting and greeting, flirting and fighting (only verbally). They are about human contact more than the drink itself. It's where life, business and pretty much everything else happen and it makes for a very communal and relaxed atmosphere.

Look closely and what you'll notice is a whole heap of talking going on and actually not an excess of coffee drinking. A single cup can last an eternity as they animatedly talk the day away. Croatia was ranked 18th in coffee consumption in the latest figures I could find. The biggest consumers? I'd have made an educated guess at the USA. Wrong (no surprise given some of my education), it's Finland. I can't explain it but I'd have a stab in the dark that come winter time there's nothing to do in Finland except drink coffee and practice breeding. Wrong again, at least on the second count, the Finns' birth rate is falling.

A tip for you. If you're planning on going to Zagreb avoid repeating my mistake. I sat down, ordered my coffee and asked for the food menu. There wasn't one. They look like cafes and they sound like cafes but they aren't, not in the sense of a British or Australian cafe. They don't serve food.

What you will find, however, are cigarettes. Billions of them. Zagreberites seem to be permanently lit up. Choose the wrong table and you will disappear in an old fashioned London smog never to be seen again. This despite attempts by the government to restrict smoking.

In offices and public buildings a recently announced ban is generally effective. The only puffers unaffected are those with frayed nerves - the residents of psychiatric wards have official exemptions.

The outlawing of smoking in enclosed bars is a different matter altogether. The ban is in force but it sure as hell isn't enforced, nobody gives a stuff about the rules in bars. There are lots and lots of watering holes in the city, some barely big enough for more than a couple of people. In almost every one you'll see a Zapruder or two with a cancer stick in their mouth.

Small establishments which meet strictly laid down conditions on ventilation, etc, can apply for dispensation to allow smoking. One year after the ban was introduced just 16 bars in the whole country had applied for exemption and then carried out the work. Why bother? Smoking in bars is a national sport and the average petty bureaucrat who should be implementing the rules is almost certainly in the bar flouting them. Good luck to the city worthy who tries to take action. The reality is that Croatians are born to smoke, I suspect babies who are teething are given Marlboro Lights instead of a pacifier and they never get weaned off them.

The same applies to coffee. Mothers who've been downing espressos all their lives no longer produce milk but a kind of light latte. By the age of two the little ones progress to neat cappuccino and on it goes. The good news is that they are probably happy little bunnies as the early introduction to coffee shop culture teaches socialisation.

This may go some small way to explaining Croatia's comparatively low divorce rate. All the more strange then that the capital should be home to the Museum Of Broken Relationships. No, this really isn't a joke, it actually exists. In 2011 it won a prize for being the most innovative museum in Europe.

I came across it in the old town and thought long and hard about entering. Given my own broken relationship from a couple of years earlier I wasn't sure if this was good for my psyche. But I'd already had 14 coffees and passively smoked 40 fags so I reckoned my health, mental and physical, would be better served in the museum than anywhere else in the city. So in I went.

What you find are the personal stories of the broken-hearted along with a donated item which in some way symbolised the relationship or its demise. There are bikes, wedding dresses, teddy bears, an iron, handcuffs (everybody in the museum stopped and read that story). There is pain, sadness, a little hope, rather a lot of anger and bucket loads of bitterness.

The range of human emotions should have made it compelling but for me it didn't quite work and I'm not entirely sure why. It could have been the setting, the storytelling or the uneasy sense of voyeurism. Having a ringside seat at a stranger's broken heart left me with an uneasy sense of intrusion. For the people who told their stories I presumed it was generally a cathartic experience. The museum was always on the lookout for new stories and associated items. That got me wondering for a while but I decided the world would not be a better place for knowing my personal ups and downs. And what would I donate? I couldn't part with Gonga, you remember him, the furry friend from the introduction.

By the time I left I felt oddly flat. I wandered along lost in contemplative thought. However, being Zagreb it may just have been a cloud of smoke I'd stumbled into.

(Footnote: in case it comes up in a trivia quiz, the citizens of Zagreb are called Zagrebcan or Zagrebchan. Don't say this book isn't educational.

#

17

THE WORST WRONG TURN IN HISTORY

Week 11; Sarajevo, Bosnia; 22,950 kms travelled;
3rd pair of thongs; T-shirts now beyond washing;

Sarajevo, June 28th. There was only me, a lone witness for the world. I stood silently at the spot where he stood and waited for the moment to arrive. I tried to put my mind in his but it was utterly beyond me.

People passed by oblivious as the hands of time and history reached 11.15am. From this very spot, at this precise minute, on this exact day in 1914, Gavrilo Princip fired a shot that convulsed the world. It was arguably the biggest individual act of consequence in the history of mankind. And it still goes echoing on.

Princip's assassination of Archduke Franz Ferdinand of Austria unleashed a cataclysmic chain of events. Within two months the fragile world had tipped into the abyss and ushered in the carnage of the First World War. There followed a direct line of cause and effect to the Second World War.

Today in Sarajevo there is a stone inscription and a small museum at the point from which the nineteen year old Serb nationalist fired his lethal shot. Princip acted alone only because six other plotters had fled after botching an assassination attempt earlier in the day. A grenade they'd thrown had hit the Archduke's car, bounced underneath a following vehicle and exploded. More than a dozen people were injured but the Archduke was unscathed.

The angry aristocrat carried on to a planned reception in Sarajevo town hall. Despite fears for his safety he later insisted on visiting his injured men in hospital before hightailing it out of the city. Unfortunately nobody remembered to tell the driver, Leopold Lojke, of the new plan.

He set off along Appel Quay and opposite the Latin Bridge he began turning into Franz Josef Street. At this point there was a shout from a following vehicle telling him he'd taken a wrong turning.

He immediately stopped the car and began clunking through the gearbox so he could reverse back to the correct road. Unfortunately for him, the Archduke and tens of millions of people, it would prove to be the biggest motoring cock up of all time.

He had stopped literally alongside a stunned, allegedly sandwich munching Princip. Not believing his luck the young Serb dropped his butty, took out his gun and fired. The Archduke and his wife Sophie were both killed.

I say 'allegedly sandwich munching' as this has become the widely accepted version of events. It features in books, documentaries, in DVDs used by school projects and is all over the net. However, some recent detailed analysis of the assassination and of court, police and witness records shows nobody ever mentioned a sandwich. It was only at the start of this century that it cropped up in a historical fantasy by a Brazilian TV host. That idea was in turn featured in a programme aired by the BBC and from there the intriguing inaccuracy has become widely accepted. From fiction to accepted fact in a decade.

All these years after the assassination I stood in Princip's footsteps. I asked a few passers-by if they were aware of the anniversary. For young and old, locals and tourists, there was collective amnesia. It appears to be the same each year other than for the 100th anniversary when major commemorations were held to mark the occasion. We humans are suckers for round number events.

Sarajevo captured the world's attention then in the early years of the 20th century and once again near its end. War came to the city in 1992 and was the focal point of the Bosnian conflict. It was brutally besieged for almost four years, three times longer than the siege of Stalingrad.

Eleven thousand people lost their lives. At its lethal peak more than 3500 shells rained down on Sarajevo in a single day. The International War Crimes Tribunal would later hear the city was reduced to a state of 'medieval deprivation'. It was not alone. At least ninety thousand more people died in the rest of the country.

I spent a total of six months in Bosnia during the war working for BBC News; this was my first visit since hostilities ended. The last time I was in the city it was a wasteland, an awful canvas of destruction. The essentials of modern life, food, water and electricity absent, the twin evils of fear and barbarity everywhere.

Now most of the city was happily unrecognisable. Half a dozen shiny shopping centres had been built. There were new office blocks, mainly for banks, and Porsche had even opened up a showroom. In the old town life was also back to normal. Weathered men sat and talked in coffee shops, young couples ate cevapi. The atmosphere on an easy summer morning was relaxed contentment. People went about their daily routines, working, shopping and living. Such everyday normality would have been unthinkable in the early 90s.

Despite the change reminders of the past were plentiful. Many buildings remain pockmarked by bullets, a few stand abandoned, devastated by shelling. And then there are the flowers.

Sarajevo Roses, as they are called, are the impact marks from exploding mortars. Where people were known to have been killed, the lightly scattered scars in the ground are filled with red resin. This often gives them a floral look and hence the name Sarajevo Roses. Through city renewal they are slowly disappearing but in the Old Town many of these raw, tragic stains of death remain. To suddenly look down and see them in the most normal of modern day surroundings is an instant jolt back to the dreadful suffering of a besieged and neglected people.

Outside the city the picture is at best patchy. Towns like Vitez, predominantly Croat except the old centre, have enjoyed remarkable investment and growth. Most of the money has come from over the border in nearby Croatia. Other places such as Mostar have fared far worse. The city is still ethnically divided, the west mainly Croat, the east Bosniak (Muslim). Its split community seems stuck in time. Since the end of the war there have been separate universities, healthcare and even phone systems for the two groups. The place has a raw undercurrent of anxiety.

A couple of people mentioned the football matches to me. These, they said, were the worst of times. Nobody mentioned the best of times. I was told Mostar seethed with unrestrained hatred when teams from the different ethnic groups played each other. The days before and after the games are a fearful time and violence and even death has revisited the city.

Over in Republica Serbska, the Bosnian Serb controlled part of Bosnia, the town of Pale feels sullen and rooted in an angry past. It was the notorious centre of Radovan Karadzic and his military leader General Ratko Mladic. From here the Bosnian Serbs dictated some of the worst crimes of the war, although no side was entirely blameless.

Pale still feels like a paramilitary town, many of the men and teenage boys dress in army fatigues. There are a couple of military memorials. Foremost of these is an aggressive, grenade tossing 'patriot' and it speaks volumes of the mindset up in the hills.

The country's ethnic fissures are still clearly everywhere. Healing doesn't feel like it's running far ahead of hatred. Bosnia's three main groups of Croats, Bosniaks, and Serbs are a million miles away from a full and happy integrated co-existence. The Dayton Peace Plan ended the war but it failed to build a viable state. Instead, Bosnia is now a hapless victim of a hotchpotch of shared power and ethnic quotas. The grand plan to prevent domination by one group has created a complex system of over-government. It is an almighty mess.

I met Mirza and his family. He told me the country's politicians are full of self-interest, but short on the national stuff. Ethnicity drives their thinking, political corruption is also rife, he said. Mirza would leave if he could, his views are not uncommon.

He cited the lengthy dispute over new identity card registration. Ethnic politicking had gridlocked the issue in parliament for months. The sides disagreed about what information would be contained on the cards. The fear, for some, was that a specific reference to the user's home area would be a pretty clear indicator of ethnic origin. It's one of the many prices of ethnic cleansing, Bosnia is far less integrated post-war than it was pre-conflict.

The ID card row had festered in parliament and as a consequence 1500 new born babies were without official registration. In Bosnia that also meant no medical card could be authorised and without one there would be no access to doctors or passports.

Deadlocked, and with no sign of a breakthrough, furious mothers besieged the parliament trapping hundreds of people inside for 14 hours.

Mirza also told me of schools with separate entrances for children from different ethnic groups. Once inside the pupils followed different curricula. That's bad but what awaits them after school is maybe worse. When teenagers complete their education their prospects are bleak. More than 40% of the Bosnian population are unemployed. In some areas the figure at youth level is a staggering 75%. It's worth repeating. SEVENTY FIVE per cent of youngsters have no job and really no obvious prospect of one in the near future. This alone does not bode well for the country's future. Coupled with plenty of other factors the country's future as a peaceful and prosperous place is far from certain.

I asked a number of people if they believed Bosnia could ever lapse back into war. It was a terrible question to ask, worse still to answer. But Mirza and many more say the awful possibility is a real one. There are others who disagree but the doubt and the underlying fear is there.

I talked with Anna, she was young and optimistic. She believes the fighting is over for good. She's desperate for Bosnia to join the EU and other international organisations in the hope that this will help bind the country into stability.

Anna worked as a guide at Gallery 11/07/95, a museum dedicated to genocide. On a daily basis she talked visitors through the horrifying details of Srebrenica, the town where more than 8,000 people were systematically executed in the war. She, more than anybody, had to have hope that there would be no going back to the insane evil of that time.

As I stood in Princip's footsteps I could only hope that in this new century Anna's youthful optimism triumphs over his idealistic nationalism.

#

18

WORLD'S SMALLEST GOLF CLUB?

"Are there any golf courses in Bosnia?" I'd asked a few people and had been met with shrugs and blank stares. Now it was Hamza the waiter's turn.

He was adamant. "No, no. We have none."

He finished with a laugh that strongly implied it was a stupid question. In truth it probably was and I can't exactly tell you why I asked it. I play the game myself, or at least have a parody of a golf swing, but on my travels nothing had been further from my mind. Backpackers are a little sparse on the world golfing scene. But having been through too many conversations about the bleak side of Bosnia's predicament I was probably in search of something that would feel normal, not burdened by ethnicity and its spreading tentacles of division. Golf may appear decidedly dull for non-enthusiasts but there is something about it which makes it quite a reliable indicator of a stable and solid society. I desperately wanted it to be weaving its way into the fabric of Bosnia.

Having asked around and come up with nothing I turned to the web in a half-hearted final attempt to see if the game existed in the country.

I went to the World Golf Foundation site, opened up its country file and headed down to 'B'. Surprise, surprise, there were actually two courses listed in the country. Both had only nine holes (for the uninitiated 18 is the norm) but here was proof golf in Bosnia existed.

One course was at Posusje, near the Croatian border, the other, the VF Golf Club, Sarajevo, was in the suburbs of the capital.

According to the website the country had just 123 registered players, 30 of them women. Those numbers qualified Bosnia as an outpost of world golf and that alone meant it was worth a bus ride to take a peek.

With so few members I'd mentally pictured a shack for a clubhouse and maybe not even that. What I actually found was literally jaw dropping. The building had been designed by one of Bosnia's top architects and no expense had been spared in its construction. The clubhouse was made of natural stone and wood and its inside was designer plush. That night there was even a band warming up to entertain the members.

I asked the barman if the club had a golf professional, a long shot given the paucity of its members. Next shock, yes it did, and he was outside giving a lesson. I went to look for him and couldn't believe what I found, a top quality, all-weather, covered driving range and it was floodlit. Members turn up whenever they want, flick a switch and hit until their patience or golf glove wears out.

There were also a couple of greens for chipping and putting practice as well as sand bunkers. All were in tip top condition. These are some of the very best facilities I've ever seen at a nine hole course. But here I hit a snag.

"We don't have nine holes," the pro Dejan Saran told me when I met him.

"Really. The website says you do."

"It's wrong. We only have six."

"Six holes. That's all?" I asked.

"Yes."

"I hope you don't mind me asking this but doesn't that get a little.... boring?"

"No. We're happy. Until a couple of years ago we only had four holes."

We were now in unchartered waters, I'd never heard of a club with six holes let alone one with only four.

As I wrestled with the concept we were joined by Vedran Kosic. He explained the club's unusual background. The course was the brainchild of his father-in-law, Jasmin Selmanagic, a golf fanatic who had nowhere in his home country to indulge his passion. His only option was to travel abroad for a game.

Fortunately Jasmin is a wealthy man so in 2001 he did the only practical thing possible and built one himself. He also played a major part in the design. He'd love to extend the current number of holes but the adjoining land is owned by the government, they don't want to sell and even if they did it would be hugely expensive.

The next eye-opener was the discovery that the tiny club had a Pro Shop. Admittedly it was hardly over-stocked and had just two sets of clubs for sale, one for men the other for ladies. For custom fitting members needed to jump in their cars, drive north a few hundred kilometres, show their passports at the border and find a golf shop in Croatia.

Finally, the biggest surprise of all, the course itself. I admit that I thought a six holer would be a little, well, you know, Mickey Mouse. Turns out it actually had quite a roar.

The views on the first tee were magnificent, however, golfers would have their minds on the opening shot, it's seriously intimidating. The hole is a precision par three with angled green, water right, a steep bank left and bunkers short and long. And so it continues. There are blind shots, drives with long carries over water, lots of sand, endless slopes.

Unsurprisingly the average handicap is quite high. I asked Vedran where my 12 handicap would rank me in the country. Definitely top 20, he told me. Top ten is not out of the question. I blushed at my own Bosnian brilliance and instantly decided to move there.

My star rating looked even better when Vedran informed me the website is out of date. He believed Bosnia now had well over 200 •

players, still hardly enough to cause a queue on the first tee.

Visitors are rare, each week they can be counted on the fingers of one hand. Members have peace and quiet to enjoy their competitions. All are played over 18 holes, which means three laps of the course. Do they ever get bored? Apparently not. If anything they relish the mental challenge of competing against a hole which may have bruised them once or even twice already in the round.

The missing holes are an oddity but this is a proper golf club in every other sense. Beautifully equipped, in top quality condition and with good greens. This place punches well above its weight. It might just be the best small golf club in the world.

#

19

SEX TAPES, BOOZE AND HAIRCUTS

Week 13; Dubrovnik, Croatia; 23,200 kms travelled;
12 million steps climbed; 1 pair of undies lost??
1 pair sagging with elasticity issues

He had the look of an ageing and slightly punch-drunk heavyweight boxer, a beast of a man. I was dwarfed as he circled around me. In his giant hands he wielded a cut throat razor inches from my face.

I glimpsed two, maybe three, front teeth. A drop of sweat hung precariously to the end of his nose. The heat was no friend to his size. The bruiser paused, stood back a little, and then took a drink from an ice cold beer. His thirst quenched he picked up his razor and returned to the task in hand. My haircut was back on track.

Hrvoje Cikato has been cutting hair, he'd never say styling, for more than 50 years. His shop is a monument to the bizarre. It houses an eccentric collection of clocks, caged birds and old hairdressing paraphernalia. Religious artefacts sit next to racy calendars from the 1980s, girlies next to God, you could say. All manner of weird and wonderful pictures hang from every last inch of the wall.

It is a small room in the ancient walled city of Dubrovnik. The

Croatian city is UNESCO world heritage listed. The UN would be well advised to consider a separate listing for Hrvoje and his shop.

Hairdressing is in the blood, his father Angelo was a barber for 50 years. They've used the shop since the 1940s save for the time the Serbs and Montenegrins laid siege to the citadel in the early 1990s. Around 100 people were killed and two thirds of the Old Town buildings were damaged. Among them was the salon. It took a direct hit. Father and son had completed an expensive refit of the shop only a few weeks earlier. They moved to temporary premises just down the alleyway and couldn't return for a decade.

The shop is rarely empty. Most callers are friends who come to chat, they also bring Hrvoje some bottles of beer. I hoped I'd timed my cut so that the beer would be a help rather than an intoxicating hindrance. His friends assured me he never has more than two or three bottles a day. There are a few empties around the salon including a bottle of cognac and a Jack Daniel's but who's counting.

Hrvoje's premises is a draw for tourists who venture down the alleyways off the Stradum, the Old Town's 13th century limestone cobbled thoroughfare. In summertime the city heaves with visitors. Four cruise ships disgorged 11,000 in a single day while I was there. At these times a walk along Dubrovnik's walls can take hours.

That said, arrival by ship is a fabulous way to enter Dubrovnik. Better still if the journey has been along the breathtaking Croatian coastline. I'd come down by boat from the ancient island of Hvar just off Split. It hadn't been a cruise liner exactly but I'd had a million dollar experience. Surprisingly the million dollars had only cost me 16 Euros, an absolute bargain. It felt like Christmas had come early. I actually thought it had as the ferry's audio system inexplicably began playing Mariah Carey's version of 'All I Want For Christmas Is You'. There's a time and a place for the song but the middle of July in the height of a European summer is not it.

The ferry journey took about eight hours. It was a smooth glide between beautiful islands and permanently hugged the steep, rugged coastline. I'd recommend it as one of the best bargains the continent has to offer.

The ferry actually only costs a tad more than a haircut at Hrvoje's shop. Many tourists stumble upon his salon, peer inside and when they spot the exotica their cameras begin to whir. He never complains, knowing some will venture in for a cut. Thank you letters from around the world adorn his walls.

Pride of place is a photo of film star Richard Gere who dropped in one day for a trim. The gentle and personable giant even has a photograph of a member of the Obama clan getting a cut. He's very proud of this one, even if my enquiries can't quite work out the exact relationship with the man in the picture and the man in the White House. But the beer will probably aid his memory later in the day.

One star whose hair he won't be cutting is Severina, Croatia's version of Kylie Minogue. While I was in town she gave a free concert in the Stradum to celebrate the country's membership of the European Union. The Old Town was packed tight that night. I knew nothing of the diva but a quick search of the net revealed her star status.

Like any pop princess she has a history of controversy. Her main stab at notoriety was an affair with a married businessman despite earlier public protestations that she was a good Catholic girl opposed to premarital sex. The leaking of a sex tape from the tryst added to the outrage. But, as the saying goes, there's no such thing as bad publicity.

This was back in 2004. Sex tapes are a little old hat for current pop stars so the Dubrovnik performance featured her kissing women on stage. Much more en vogue.

The next night was a gentler affair, the Dubrovnik Symphony Orchestra, opera singers, classical guitarists, dancers and choristers did their bit for the EU. I'm not aware of any of the performers having a leaked sex tape.... in some cases this is definitely a very good thing.

The setting was the Rector's Palace, an inspiring mix of ancient architecture. It was a wonderful night except I missed my last bus home. I was left with a three kilometre walk and two staircases with a total of 400 plus steps.

Which reminds me, if you're planning on going to Dubrovnik do yourself a favour, visit outside the busy peak summertime and enrol yourself at your local gym's step class a few months in advance. Dubrovnik has a world monopoly on steps and they will take their toll. They are everywhere and they don't just come in ones or two.

The good news is that Hrvoje's shop is in the flat part of the Old Town. Call in and he might share a beer with you while he cuts your hair. It will steady his hands and your nerves.

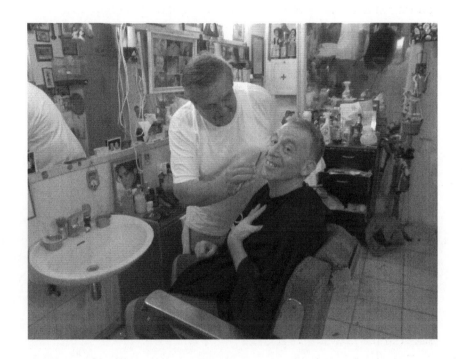

#

20

THE BEST VIEW IN THE WORLD?

Week 14; Kotor Bay, Montenegro; 23,300 kms travelled;
2 lost keys for backpack lock; 1 landlady with hacksaw

In my original plan I'd allowed myself three months of travel. It was an arbitrary deadline but one I'd originally spent a fair while trying to organize. That point had now been passed. Yet here I was full of happiness, excitement and enthusiasm for more. I sat quietly on the bus from Dubrovnik and looked at scenery too beautiful to describe. I was on the edge of Kotor Bay. I'd never heard of it until a Norwegian guy I befriended in Dubrovnik raved about it. "It is more than a must," he had told me and he was right.

I sat taking it all in and thinking to myself that this spellbinding vision of beauty would have been missed if I'd stuck to the plan. From here on in everything would be a bonus and I was determined to seize the great good fortune that had made me decide to travel without restraint.

Kotor is dwarfed by soaring hills, they provide vantage points over the old town and the bay. Scaling them, my friend had told me, was also 'a must'. Armed with his advice I set out the next day through the ancient buildings of the town and soon began the long ascent.

Three hundred and fifty gruelling steps up the sheer Hill of St John a teenage boy sat waiting. Next to him was an old, battered, cooler box. It was the perfect place and he had the perfect pitch.

"Cold drink?" he nonchalantly asked. It was early afternoon and blisteringly hot. However, I was focused, a man on a mission and I declined his offer.

But the kid was no fool and he allowed me to draw level before following up with his killer line, "You have a thousand more steps to go". I physically wilted, stopped and bought a drink.

Trekking along the zigzag walls up to the fort is no easy hike and the last section of the 1350 steps is classed as a 'high risk zone'. That seemed to be to be overstating it, however, risk or no risk the rewards for perseverance are priceless. The medieval buildings are interesting but to be honest they're a sideshow. What I'd gone for was the view of Montenegro's Kotor Bay.

Wide eyed and awestruck I felt as if I was perched with the gods supping up the full glory of the world. It was an unblemished vision of beauty.

The bay is sometimes called the fjord of the south. It cuts in from the Adriatic Sea in a wide arc before funnelling into a narrow channel of water. After this slender entrance the water turns at a right angle and the Bay opens to the south east to reveal its glory. Luscious blue water is towered over by almost vertical mountains. Immense, sheer, dry rock wall on one side, dark green and forested slopes on the other. It is magnificent and humbling. The most stunning view of my journey to date.

At the end of the bay and almost vertically down from my vantage point lay the ancient town of Kotor. It has a fragile foothold on the mountain at the edge of the water.

The Old Town teems with history and is an enclosed triangle. The walls which protect it were gradually built up from the ninth century onwards. Within is a maze of medieval piazzas and a crisscross of alleyways. They are home to scores of little shops and dozens of restaurants and coffee shops. Like Dubrovnik the Old Town is still inhabited by people living in antiquated homes.

I took a couple of bus trips along both sides of the bay. Vehicles cling on by inches to the edge of the road. Along the eastern side is the historic village of Prabast, a UNESCO Heritage site and the entrance to the bay. It is the place to catch a short boat ride to the small island of Our Lady Of The Rocks.

Legend tells of it being formed by sailors throwing rocks in the bay after a successful voyage. Over time, the islet emerged. The custom is kept alive each July when villagers take their boats out and throw rocks into the water.

Montenegro is a new country. Formerly part of Yugoslavia it didn't acquire statehood until 2006 and is yet to get established on the tourism trail. The country is in the shadow of its better known neighbour Croatia, currently one of the world's en vogue travel destinations. Its sun drenched islands and rugged coastline are a magnet for charter sail boats and landlubbers alike. Most visitors stop at the beautiful city of Dubrovnik and never venture the extra few kilometres to Montenegro. But they're missing out. I nearly missed out too.

While in Dubrovnik I began thinking of my next options. There were two obvious candidates, Italy away to the west and the Greek Islands to the south, both had five star appeal. I was on the verge of a coin toss when I bumped into a young Norwegian traveller in my guesthouse. He'd just come from Greece via Albania and Montenegro. He had three main thoughts to contribute. The route had gorgeous scenery; Albania in particular was free of tourists; transport was unreliable, uncomfortable, a hassle but absolutely doable. I tossed the coin, away that is. My decision was easy, I'd keep heading south.

After Croatia the Adriatic coast continues south in spectacular style. The journey of an hour or two took me through dozens of little bays, the stony beaches were packed with Montenegrins enjoying the coast. There are plenty of foreigners too, usually from Russia and Ukraine, not a happy combination these days, so the towns here have a different feel to Croatian tourist spots.

After Kotor Bay Budva is the principal attraction. It's very appealing, particularly with its Stari Grad or Old Town, an historic setting overlooking the bay. However, it does get very crowded and it's clearly in a rapid phase of development. As the buildings go up its appeal will go down, at least for me.

Montenegro's interior is a five star draw. It's a hiker's paradise of magnificent mountains and superb views to match. The country is small and has a population of just 630,000 but its infrastructure is surprisingly good and it feels like a country on the up.

Do yourself a favour, go there soon. And if you take a walk up Kotor's stunning Hill of St John, stop and buy a cold drink. Better still, buy two. One for you and one for the gods.

#

21

ON THE BUSES ALBANIA STYLE

Week 15; Shkodra, Albania; 23,400 kms travelled;
wonder socks all good; underpants not good at all

The 1.30pm bus to Albania left right on time…. at 1.15pm.
Confused? It gets worse.

A week later I was stranded when the daily bus from Vlore to
Sarande never left at all. The same day I stumbled across a second bus
which nobody knew existed, left from a bus stop that wasn't really there
and was only a minute or two behind schedule, not that there was one.

Welcome to life on the buses Albania style.

For forty one years the Stalinist dictator Enver Hoxha had total
control of his country and absolutely no control of his senses. He
turned Albania into a nightmare state, isolated, fearful and paranoid. It's
currently the third poorest country in Europe. It was routinely at the
bottom of the pile until the break up of the Soviet Union created
pauper states. Moldova now has the 'honour'.

Albania's buses epitomise the country's mess. There are no
published timetables, no bus stations, many of the buses or minibuses,
known as furgons, are ancient and the roads are regularly rough as all
hell.

On the plus side they are dirt cheap, kind of work when you understand the 'system' and travel through some mesmerising scenery, admittedly sometimes at a pace slightly slower than an asthmatic donkey with a limp.

I'd used buses in Bosnia and Montenegro and both worked fine. But the Albanian bus taking me into the country began the slide into chaos. At the Montenegro terminal there was a printed timetable and even a TV screen, both confirmed the bus was scheduled for 1.30.

However, my ticket stated 1.15. I checked with an inspector. He looked and he shrugged. It pays to get used to this particular look, in this part of the world it's fairly common and perfected only after extensive training.

The bus did actually pull out at about 1.15. We reversed ten metres until a passenger screamed that the luggage door was wide open.

After a quick check from the driver all was sorted and we started again. Just two revolutions of the wheels later there was a yelp. Somebody was on the wrong bus. Poor form really as there were only two to choose from.

Third time lucky? Sadly not. Before the driver could start moving again another passenger asked to get off to go to the toilet. We inched back to where we started.

As Mr Bladder returned four flushed Scandinavian backpackers scrambled on board cursing and mumbling something about a 1.30 scheduled departure time. We gave sympathetic shrugs. Finally at 1.27 we pulled out, 12 minutes late or three minutes early. I really hadn't got a clue which.

The bus was ancient, steam powered, I think. Its windscreen was a spiderweb of cracks. As it chugged through the hillsides the ravines to either side increased in severity. Two weeks earlier 18 tourists were killed nearby when their bus careered off the road and crashed 40 metres down a hill. The government immediately made a solemn pledge that road safety would be a national priority. Somebody clearly forgot to inform our driver.

Twenty minutes into the journey his mobile rang.

"Please don't," I said quietly to myself.

"Let it ring, ignore it. Pleeeease."

My prayers went unanswered, the phone didn't. He picked up and drove with one hand on the wheel. For gear changes he had the phone in his left hand, the gear stick in the right and he balanced his left elbow on the wheel to steer. This was Albania's version of hands free.

On severe bends his safety training finally kicked in. He jammed the mobile between his hunched up shoulder and his ear freeing the left hand to guide us.

Albania's buses and furgons park on various streets in the towns and cities. The locals mostly know where they are, tourists don't. They have approximate departure times but only leave when full or overflowing. This can be an hour or two behind 'schedule'.

My most spectacular furgon trip was through the Llogara Pass. The old minibus wheezed and spluttered up over 1000 spectacular metres. From the top the Albanian Riviera looked poetic, all dreamy blue sea at the foot of a vertical mountain.

However, the poetry died with the descent. The narrow road twists and clings to the mountain and constantly doubles back on itself. Safety barriers are almost entirely absent. The previous year 13 people were killed and two dozen were injured when their bus crashed down a cliff further along this road. The region has more than its fair share of these accidents and it's not difficult to see why.

Our driver fought like a bull rider as the battered old furgon bucked and kicked underneath him. The brakes went into overdrive. There was squealing and what sounded like air brakes but it may actually have been bowel movements from the increasingly nervous passengers. An atheist like myself can be a little short on help at times like this so I began silently praying to the gods of every mainstream religion.

A few turns took us close to the precipice and I broadened my prayers to include every nutcase, lunatic fringe religion on the planet. Any kind of help would be welcome now.

We finally made it safely down and stopped for a break and a clean-up. I took the opportunity to consider if my prayers were a factor in our safe arrival. If so, which religion or cult had done the trick? Although grateful to be alive I was kind of hoping my prayers hadn't been answered by the bizarre 'Prince Philip Movement'. Its members seriously believe the queen's husband to be a divine being, a view seemingly shared only with Prime Minister Tony Abbott of Australia.

I quickly dismissed the idea. I suspect there's more chance of an Albanian bus leaving on time than of Phil the Greek being a god.

#

22

HITCHHIKING IN GANGSTER LAND

Week 16; 23,450 kms travelled;
depleted undies means regular re-use;
hand-wash contemplated; 7 countries visited

"I think we're being kidnapped."

"What?"

"They've locked the doors and closed our windows and it was odd that they just picked us up off the street."

This was not an ideal start to the morning.

My companion for the day was Gloria, a well-travelled, thirty something, spunky American. This morning, however, she was a little spooked.

It was probably my fault. I'd filled her in on Albania's reputation for rampant crime and gangsterism. I said it was a crazy stereotype and invited her to join me in a scheme to prove this is a safe destination.

The plan was to get a ride to the Prokletije mountain range, take a ferry along Lake Koman and then hitchhike back to Shkodra. We'd be thumbing our way back from a fairly remote area. If all went well it would take about four or five hours. If it didn't go to plan.... who knew, especially if the stereotype turned out to be based on truth.

I tried to convince Gloria we weren't being snatched but it wasn't an easy idea to sell. The driver and his sidekick had no English and were lifted straight out of 'The Sopranos'.

A few moments after picking us up off the street they made a mobile call to some mystery man. The conversation was all hushed tones and was accompanied by a few stolen looks into the mirror at the two foreigners in the rear.

Gloria's fertile mind was also being fed some disturbing imagery. Ten minutes into our journey the driver stopped and got out. He'd parked immediately next to a street butcher. The carcass of a pig was hanging and swaying from a stand. It filled the view from Gloria's window. A grotesque smile on the dead porker's face added to the uneasy atmosphere.

The driver soon returned and our would-be kidnappers drove us into the mountains. It was utterly remote and the deserted road soon turned into loose shale and stones. Heavy, forbidding clouds hung over the wilderness and I quietly began to wonder whether my companion might have a point as the mute Albanians drove on, doors still locked.

Ninety minutes later we entered a roughly cut tunnel. Water dripped from the roof and jagged rock made the passage a tight fit. When we emerged on the other side we were thankfully at the lake. A few battered vehicles were around and a handful of tourists. There was a ticket office and a cafe. Both looked a little bleak, neither looked even close to inviting. But they were proof that the kidnap was just in Gloria's imagination, Albanian stereotyping had infected her thoughts.

However, for the next 25 minutes we were given the run around by a master in the art of lies and deception. The number of ferries, time and cost were all variable depending on which of us asked the question.

But finally the details were agreed all 16 tourists who'd made it there would be leaving on the one and only operational ferry on the lake. We were loaded on board and began our journey.

Almost immediately followed a second ferry which we'd absolutely been promised didn't exist. Why and for what purpose I have no idea.

Lake Koman was created in the 1980s when the Drini Valley was dammed. It stretches for 30 kilometres from Fierze in the northeast to

Vau I Dejes, in the south. Those are the bare inessentials. What you really need to know is that the setting is the rarest of European jewels. Staggeringly beautiful, mostly pristine and, save for we hardy few, devoid of tourists and river traffic. It was beauty on an epic scale.

The area was essentially untouched. Every so often a sparse track led up through the trees to an isolated home, otherwise this was wilderness.

At first the landscape was pretty. Soon it was almost literally overpowering. Hills gave way to sheer, limestone cliffs. They towered over our small vessel and crowded in on us. At times it looked like we were heading into solid, impenetrable walls of rock. The gorges were tight and magnificent.

It was a magical two and a half hour ride to Fierze. Normally the ferry won't return until the next morning but today only a hardy Dutch family planned to overnight. A one hour lunch stop was announced. As we ate in a nearby cafe I kept an eye on the road Gloria and I would be thumbing along. It was clearly not a major arterial route. In 45 minutes of keen observation I observed nothing, or pretty close to that. Two vehicles were all that ventured down there and one of those quickly disappeared up a short drive to a farmhouse. I made a quick calculation and decided that the odds of getting back to Shkodra this side of Armageddon were not great. On the plus side this remote backwater will almost certainly miss out on the end of the world. News of the world's end will probably never make it to this isolated outpost.

I was thinking of tossing my coin to decide whether to hitchhike or catch the boat. Fortunately common sense and Gloria got the better of me and we hastily ditched the hitch idea and raced back to the ferry, Gloria trailed in my wake as my self(ish) preservation kicked in.

The wonderful appeal of the morning journey wasn't quite recaptured on the return journey. Backsides became a little sore and the sun radiated intense heat. I'd managed to miss out on any shade and started to bake and shrivel. By the time we arrived back at our starting point everybody was weary.

Unfortunately all was not well. The taxis we were promised would be waiting for us were nowhere to be seen. Our protestations and pleadings were not soothed by regular promises of their imminent arrival and it was 45 minutes before our 'taxi' appeared. Actually it had been there all the time and had been cunningly masquerading as some bloke's old ute. Five of us were put in the snug cabin and three locals were perched on the back. The journey was endless. We stopped for every conceivable reason, including foraging bits of scrap metal lying alongside the road.

Hitchhiking would have been easier and probably faster. I'm sorry to have missed out, if only for the reason that I'd already come up with the headline for this chapter, Hitchhiking In Gangster Land.

However, fate came to my aid a week later. I had travelled on to the Albanian capital Tirana and after a few days moved to Berat. It's known as the town of a thousand windows, full of preserved, classical, Ottoman architecture.

As I sat drinking coffee one afternoon on my guesthouse terrace I spotted Gloria. This was not as strange in Albania as it would be in many other countries. There are so few tourists that you will regularly bump into familiar faces. It happened to me days later when I again bumped into the lovely Dutch family from Lake Koman.

On this particular day Gloria was on a trip from Tirana. Time was running out and she didn't have long before her bus was due to return. As previously mentioned the schedules and punctuality of Albanian buses is more concept than reality. However, this was the last bus of the day so there was a chance the driver would leave 'on time', keen to get home for his dinner. Sod's Law has been mathematically proven to beat all others so Gloria was a woman on a mission and keen to meet her deadline.

She was on her way to Berat's star attraction, Kala, a huge castle complex perched on the top of a very steep hill. I decided to join her and we barely had enough time for a decent look around. We were now behind the clock and the walk back down the hill was treacherous. The surface was made of cobblestones and over centuries they'd become worn and slippery. Both of us were wearing thongs (flip flops if you are in the northern hemisphere). Making it down for Gloria's last bus home would be very tight.

Then I heard the sound of salvation. Behind us an old Mercedes was inching slowly down the hill. Instinctively I stuck out my thumb and the car came to a halt. The fact that I stood in the middle of the road may have helped. I went to the driver's door and spoke a language he didn't understand before reverting to gesticulation. The slightly startled elderly driver finally grasped my meaning and motioned us to get in.

As the door shut and the old man pressed lightly on the accelerator a big beam lit up my face. Finally, I was hitchhiking in gangster land. Now, if we could just escape without being kidnapped by our pensioner saviour I would have my tale.

Four hundred brief metres later we reached the bottom of the hill, the car stopped and our ride was over. To be perfectly honest this wasn't quite what I had in mind when I wrote the headline. But it was enough. Hand on heart I can now tell you that 100% of my hitchhikes in Albania were crime free and perfectly safe.

It all goes to prove you shouldn't believe stereotypes... or statistics!

#

23

TIRANA - PAINTING OVER THE CRACKS

Week 17; Tirana, Albania; 23,550 kms travelled;
kidnappings - nil; wonder socks - 3;
undies in need of a wash - all; weight 72.5 kgs;

Four and a half months of travel and I thought I'd seen the lot when it came to accommodation. From rooms in exquisite settings to others where $10 a night was about $5 over the odds. But, hey, it's all part of this NONY backpacking idea. Rough with the smooth and all that.

However, my arrival at the apartment in the Albanian coastal town of Vlore topped the lot. My host generously picked me up and drove me to the digs. He spoke scratchy English and as we drew up to the large metal gates in front of his property he managed to proudly say "Welcome to my home."

My Albanian language skills weren't up to a reply, in this instance my English would also have been a little lacking. I sat a little dumbfounded while I should have been asking a couple of probing questions such as, "Where are the walls, the roof, the rooms, the....". You get the drift.

All I could see from my car seat was an empty vessel, a shell of a building. Fortunately as he drove us into his driveway I saw one level of apartments had been completed. Al fresco sleeping had thankfully just been averted. The owner explained that his family had run out of money so the rest of the building work had stopped. I sympathised.

A little later I noticed the building next door. A hotel was under construction. Except, I was informed, everything there had ground to a halt five years earlier. Apparently the owner had run out of money without even one level having been completed. There was a theme developing here.

Vlore is unfortunately a bit of a concrete jungle. There are lots and lots of new apartment blocks. Many finished but short on residents, dozens more incomplete. The same goes for private houses. Shell after shell after shell. It's like Schubert had given up music, was working on a thousand different building projects then....poof. Dead. Gone. Leaving behind an Unfinished Sea City (I'll admit that's a lousy attempt at humour and you'll need to work a little to get it. And if you do the work you'll know it wasn't worth your effort anyway. But thanks for trying).

The reason for Vlore's mess? After decades of dictatorship the country had slowly opened up and the people began to get a taste for the riches of capitalism. 'Investment opportunities' sprang up offering astronomical returns, anything from 19% a year to 100% PER MONTH. You and I know these 'opportunities' as pyramid schemes, most of us wouldn't touch them with a barge pole but this was all new to gullible Albanians who dreamt of an easier life after years of deprivation. Unfortunately their inevitable collapse cost people their life savings and led to widespread civil unrest.

Ten years later the country had recovered pretty well. Banks were privatised, the economy grew rapidly and money from the Albanian émigrés poured in.

In Vlore the newly confident people took a second stab at capitalism and began to borrow money to invest in the tourist boom they saw coming their way. Hotels and apartment blocks began springing up. Others set out to build their dream homes as bad times turned to good. Unfortunately the newly resurgent thirst for moneymaking coincided with the Global Financial Crisis. The shrinking world economy meant money quickly dried up and the hoped for invasion of travellers didn't happen. Building work all over the city ground to a halt.

I wandered around the hills overlooking Vlore. There were some fabulous homes with stunning views over the southern Adriatic Sea. But for every house that was built there was another in a state of half-built abandonment. Some people were able to live on the ground floor where they now waited patiently for the county's third big push at capitalism. Until that time comes you can see more shells in the hills than on the beach.

Tirana, the capital, has a different building issue. It has a thoroughly deserved worldwide reputation for being utterly drab and grey. The city is undeniably full of ugly, decaying, communist era apartment blocks.

Or at least it was until 2000 when along came the new mayor Edi Rama, a former artist. He launched an imaginative programme to subsidise paint so buildings could be given a cheap facelift. There were no limits on design but monotony was definitely off the agenda.

"We have enough grey to last us a lifetime," he said of the city.

The first building to get the paint treatment was done out in a vivid orange. Stunned Albanian motorists stopped their cars to stare in awe at a sudden transfusion of life into their dull environment. The money for the paint actually came from an EU subsidy and one of its technocrats was not best pleased on hearing the cash was being spent on such a gaudy colour. According to the mayor the official informed him orange is not a designated EU colour. Big Edi apparently told him in his politest Albanian to bugger off and orange kicked off Tirana's urban revolution

More and more buildings were painted, riots of vibrant colours in amazing designs sprang up around the city. The result can be a little frenzied as the improvements were unrestrained. Critics point out that the decay is still there and that it has simply been painted over. But overall it was a brushstroke of genius. The painting project led to a mood change in the people and vastly increased civic pride. Crime dropped, littering was reduced and people were reportedly happier.

"It gave people hope and light. It brought a different spirit to our lives," said the mayor in a lecture.

Edi now has a bigger stage having been elected Albania's prime minister. Unfortunately, on taking office he soon discovered a huge hole in the country's finances. The outgoing government was corrupt and closely tied in with the Mafia. According to documents published by WikiLeaks, the US saw the previous government as 'Law breakers turned law makers.' The artist formerly known as the Mayor of Tirana won't be able to just paint over the cracks this time.

Apart from the riots of colour amid some serious drabness Tirana has one other obvious quirk. Dotted around city centre gardens and streets are men and women with weighing scales. At first I couldn't believe they were for people to check their weight but sure enough that was their purpose. Trade was hardly buzzing but the odd citizen would walk up, hand over some change and step on the scales.

I could only presume that as the country is so dirt poor these would have been luxury items in people's homes. And the L word is not something that goes hand in hand with daily life in Albania.

I watched for a while to check I hadn't got it wrong and then I decided to give it a go. I wandered over to a little old lady, gestured that I was a candidate for Albania's 'Biggest Loser' and would like some good news. She guided me on to the scales and the numbers whizzed back and forth around a bent and rusty needle. How accurate they were was highly debatable but when the pointer stayed fixed at 72.5kgs off I got. I was very happy with the result, like all her customers, I suspect. In a grim place like Tirana everybody's had more than their fill of grim stuff. Along with the former mayor everybody needs to lighten up a little.

#

24

LIVING HELL IN HOSTELS

*Week 18; Somewhere in Albania; 23,870 kms travelled;
seriously smelly; first hand-wash; last hand-wash?;
will to live lost again - probably with wonder socks in backpack*

I am a sucker for good accommodation reviews and, it must be said,
I can be quite a sucker for punishment. I had stayed in three hostels up
to this point on the trip for no other reason than curiosity. It had been
three decades since I'd last stayed in a dorm. I wondered whether a
NONY could stay in a hostel and either: a) sleep b) not look like some
weird middle-aged bloke surrounded by disinterested or disgusted
young people.

The hostel in the Albanian city of Shkodra had been a good
experience. It's where I'd met Gloria. It was clean, spacious, quiet and
the across-the-spectrum age group staying there were fun company.

In Montenegro I'd paid a little extra to share a two man room at a
hostel. This was done to improve my odds of not having a snorer
wreck my sleep. My buddy for the night was a 30-something Bosnian
who littered the room with a dozen beer bottles but ate not a single
thing. He couldn't afford food, he said. But hey, beer is beer. For my
two nights with the boozy Bosnian I slept with my valuable possessions
strapped to my body, just in case he changed his mind and decided

food was actually a necessity and money was required to pay for it.

However, I met some fun people there including an incorrigible pair of Norwegian girls. We swapped tales of life on the road, their travel highlight was in India. They'd paid a tuk tuk driver to let them take his vehicle for the afternoon. They got bogged on a beach, picked up a disabled old man, treated him to lunch then dumped him when he decided they were potentially future brides. He let it be known he'd be returning to their quarters with them that night as part of the selection process.

Next on my hostel stay list was Split. The Croatian coastal city served up an altogether different experience. The place was positioned right at the entrance to the old town, a beautiful example of bygone Europe. Its hand-on-history feel of stone walkways and squares of alfresco cafes was enchanting. I sat smiling at every passer-by, happy to be part of the brotherhood of man.

The hostel experience, on the other hand, made me want to buy a sub-machine gun and slaughter every young American in sight. It was a totally hellish experience, pulling out my own eyeballs out would have been light relief.

I knew Split was a party town for the young. However, I'd made an unbreakable pact with myself that while I was in the hostel I would take whatever experience presented on the chin. I was determined not to play the middle-aged guy moaning about late night noise or whatever. I was here as a passive observer, a social analyst of youth culture. A guinea pig for other NONY types who might wonder what a modern hostel experience is like.

The place was several floors up in an old apartment block. My dorm had eight beds but I would only be sharing with three Americans, according to the night porter. He said they'd already gone out and warned me they'd probably be late back. Fair enough, let the experiment begin.

I changed clothes. Actually, I didn't, I was weary and smelly after an eight hour train journey. But best to give you an impression my standards never slipped, whereas in reality they were by now somewhere down around my ankles. I headed out for a late dinner and was back in the dorm around midnight. No sign of the Americans as I fell into a coma.

At 4.45am the door flew open and I was literally yanked from my sleep. "Dudes it's f***in' hot in here," said Loudmouth One to his compatriots.

"Hey dudes, there's a f****in' dude in here," that was Loudmouth Two having just spotted me rousing. No apologies, no other acknowledgement.

To cut a long story short, Loudmouth Three, the quiet one, swore a little, said "dude" a lot then crashed. He instantly began snoring

Unfortunately One and Two spent the next 30 minutes taking it in turn to loudly and endlessly repeat a single drunken, crude, mantra at their sleeping mate, "Dude, if you don't shut the f**k up I'm going to stick my p***s down your throat." They took it in turn to find this threat utterly hilarious.

Each and every single snore would bring a repetition of the monotonous warning. The record never changed, their laughter never died.

If I'd been drunk beyond comprehension I might, just might, for the briefest of moments, have found it slightly funny. Being even mildly sober and anything less than a mindless moron it was insanely crude and annoying.

On the fiftieth rendition of the p***s threat I snapped.

"Will you shut the f**k up and go to sleep." I really wasn't proud at becoming Loudmouth Four and using foul language but it did the trick. Unfortunately I'd broken my self-pledge of being a passive observer of hostel behaviour. I now have no idea whether they would have kept their inane, repetitive banter up much longer. My strong hunch is that they were in for the long haul.

In the morning I woke at 8, showered and left. The trio of trolls were dead to the world. That's a little short on details but anything I tell you about my slamming of doors and playing of loud music wouldn't give you a good impression of me. I'll just leave it to your imagination.

Oh, and for those of you are au fait with the Foo Fighters, you will know that 'Pretender' is a very, very loud song. Cue my childish smirk.

So that had been the total of my hostel experience as I arrived in Southern Albania. I'm being a little coy about exactly where in the interests of the sensitivities of an extremely sensitive soul.

I'd found one of the top rated hostels in the country via Hostelbookers and Hostelworld, both are hugely successful booking websites for hostel accommodation. They are to hostels what TripAdvisor is to hotels. They carry lots of independent reviews from users.

The place I found was highly ranked on both sites. The reviews were glowing, particularly about the owner/manager who came across as a gem of a human being. As always my booking was made late, the downside of travelling without a forward plan. Often accommodation is booked out or prices have risen. But this day I soon had my confirmation back. I was in.

My five hour bus ride brought me close to the hostel building, another high rise apartment. It was about 5pm as I rang the ground floor intercom to gain access. I got nothing back. Disappointing as I'd specified a rough arrival time.

I repeated the ringing for the next 15 frustrating minutes with no luck. Finally a resident came out of the building, I grabbed the door and entered. Neither the small lift nor the buzzer outside gave any clue as to which floor the hostel was on. I tried every one, there were about ten, and could make out nothing even vaguely suggesting a hostel. I eventually found somebody in a corridor and they sent me to the correct floor. I knocked on an unmarked door and a young guy opened it up. I asked for Mikka (not his real name) and was grumpily told he was out. I was talking to a 'guest'.

The hostel was small, probably three rooms with six to eight beds in each and a central kitchen. A couple of young guys were there but attempts at conversation were met with grunted non-communication.

Twenty minutes later Mikka arrived.

"Who are you?" He was hardly overflowing with warmth.

"My name is Arthur Penlington and I have a reservation."

"No, you don't".

"Yes, I do." I showed him the confirmation on my iPad.

"I don't have that reservation. They have made a mistake, you have no booking. You will have to go somewhere else."

Fortunately, I had been looking over his shoulder at the computer screen and there in his emails I saw my name and my reservation. I pointed this out to him and he took a deep sigh of inconvenience.

"You can't stay here. I am fully booked," was his repetitive answer.

After ten minutes of increasingly heated to and fro he announced that I could stay in a friend's apartment. There were no facilities, no wifi but there was a bed. I would be given the access code to the hostel and could use the wifi there. My inclusive breakfast would also be available back in the hostel from 8am.

An unhappy Mikka took me up the road and showed me my digs. There were three beds and no other guests. Fine. I told him I needed to use the Internet back in the hostel and would be there in 20 minutes. He promised he'd hang around until I showed up.

Fifteen minutes later I was at the hostel. Mikka wasn't. The only person around was a guest in his late 60s. He knew nothing of wifi passwords, I wasn't happy. After many fruitless guesses at the password I went out to look around town and eat dinner. I returned to my room and slept very well. When I woke up in the morning I had a feeling that things were on the up.

At quarter past eight I went to the hostel for breakfast. It was shut and bizarrely my access code failed to open it. Breakfast should have been on the go 15 minutes earlier but as I put my ear to the door and listened all was peace and quiet. I knocked gently not wanting to disturb the sleeping hostellers, the young and early mornings do not have a close relationship. There was still no reply.

Fifteen minutes later Mikka arrived, apologised, and let me in. In the middle of the kitchen floor was a teenage girl, fast asleep in a sleeping bag. Her deal was even worse than mine. I sat at the table, her feet inches from my chair.

"I didn't have time to buy bread," said Mikka, "there is no food."

"Nothing? Not even cereal? "I asked in a disbelieving but hushed voice.

"Nothing. Things are difficult for me, very difficult. You don't understand."

Mikka's moaning didn't help my mindset but I bit my lip and whispered back that I'd just have a cup of tea.

"Sorry, no tea. I only have coffee. Black."

That was the straw. In my best heated whisper I let him have it.

"You say things are difficult for you? Yesterday I couldn't get into the building; when I did get in I wandered around lost because there was no sign at your door; I was told I had no reservation; my bed is up the road; you promised to connect me to wifi but you vanished; you are 30 minutes late for breakfast; and now there is neither food nor tea. I'm paying for this and you tell me I don't understand. I understand perfectly. This place is a nightmare, a NIGHTMARE." Mikka's face dropped and his lip trembled, an emphasised word in a whisper is obviously a crushing weapon.

With that I tiptoed over Sleeping Beauty and headed out of the door in an exaggerated but silent fury.

Mikka immediately followed. I anticipated a scene and I got one. But where I expected raised voices what I got was Mikka's interpretation of the death scene from Don Giovanni. He began wailing, his face wracked by emotion.

"You don't understand. You don't understand. I am here on my own, my girlfriend is in Germany and I do all this on my own. I can't do it, I can't do it."

My sympathy was zero. "Mikka, you have done precisely nothing. It has been a NIGHTMARE." No whisper required this time.

I hadn't realised he'd been holding his finest theatrics in reserve but now he unleashed some serious wailing. His hands grabbed his tortured face, his short, chubby body convulsed and he began bawling.

'I can't do it, I can't do it." On he went, warming into his role as a volcanic and histrionic shrieker. By now his hands were grasping at his long, straggly hair and his words were interspersed with gulps. Had it truly been opera this was the point at which the audience would know death is imminent.

Not having any desire to put my lips on his to give him CPR I decided I had to calm him down. Slowly but surely I managed to convince him that the whole experience had been a mere bump on the road of life. It did the trick. The convulsions and the wailing stopped. He put out his arms for a conciliatory hug and I hugged unenthusiastically back. There it should have ended.

"Come back inside and I will make you tea," he said, all conciliatory.

"Mikka, you don't have any tea." My frustration was again undisguised. It was a starting pistol for round two of the hysteria. Off he went, the rolls of fat around his waistline began vibrating like a pneumatic drill.

"I will buy you breakfast at my friend's restaurant," he finally burbled. I happily acquiesced and with that he led me out of the building along the waterfront and into a rather nice cafe overlooking the stony beach. I have to confess the place was one up on the hostel dining room and that this seemed quite a good result.

A nice breakfast was served and as I ate Mikka offered by turns his apologies and his tale of woe. I hadn't wised up that this was all leading somewhere. But it most assuredly was. His online reputation.

In my earlier anger I'd seriously doubted the idea that his hostel was rated highly on accommodation websites. I'd threatened to write a stinking review.

Breakfast was his attempt to undo the damage. It was fascinating to see the influence these websites can have. Number one rankings and glowing reviews translate into bookings which in turn mean more money.

"You said my place was a nightmare. Nobody has ever said that,' whimpered Mikka. "Now I will be ruined on TripAdvisor."

I tried to ease his troubled mind but it was no good. "A nightmare,' he kept repeating, 'You said it was a nightmare".

"Alright, perhaps nightmare was overstating it. But you have to admit the whole experience was....".

I hesitated for fear of more wailing. Eventually I settled for a timidly watered down, "not quite what I'd been expecting.'

Oh dear lord, that hit a raw nerve. Tears began falling down Mikka's face. "I will be ruined," he sobbed. "You said a nightmare, a nightmare."

Stunned diners looked on at what they must have guessed was a lovers' early morning tiff. This really was a nightmare. I knew by now what he was after and I happily conceded it to him.

'Don't worry. I won't write any reviews."

"You promise? You won't say it was a nightmare."

"I promise. No reviews."

The tears dried in an instant. Very shortly after Mikka got up from the table and returned to his hostel to tend to his other 'guests'. They, presumably, wouldn't be getting the beachside breakfast bonus.

So there you have it. Judas sold Jesus down the river for 30 pieces of silver, Mikka bought me off for the price of an omelette and weak tea. I felt bad for future guests who might suffer the same kind of jerking around that I'd had. My awful experience would never be shared on the net and Mikka's number one ranking would be preserved.

I doubted I was the first to have his silence bought. I regularly read accommodation review sites before making bookings, they are often a big factor in my decisions. But, like many things, they are clearly open to manipulation.

I finished my breakfast watching a large digger moving stones around on the beach. Its huge bucket rose and fell just inches away from unperturbed Albanian sunbathers. They moved not one fraction nor acknowledged the mechanical monster's presence. In Albania you take your pleasures where you can and don't complain. I had just learned that lesson myself.

I headed back to my room, packed my bag and went to see Mikka to pay my bill. In a highly conspiratorial manner he called me into a deserted dorm room, looked around and said, "I am so sad. You said it was a nightmare."

Oh hell, let it go.

I made the review pledge once again and then headed outside to catch the ferry to Greece.

Lo and behold there for the third time in a few weeks was an overloaded Gloria. After hugs and greetings she asked me if I had any hostel recommendations. Yes, I certainly did. Avoid that place over there like the plague.... unless you are in need of a free cooked breakfast. In which case I know the magic word and it starts with the letter 'N'.

\#

25

BILLY THE PSYCHOPATH - ALL ROUND GOOD GUY

Week 19; Sidari, Corfu, Greece; 23,980 kms travelled;
shopping time - 4 new shirts, 1 shorts, 1 deck shoes, anti-perspirant;
my smell - fragrant; hitchhikes - 2

Just across the water from Albania lies Greece and more specifically Corfu. Despite its massive financial troubles it basks in first world heaven in comparison to its third world neighbour.

In terms of hoteliers it also has a gem. His name is Billy. Actually it isn't, but 'Billy' keeps things easy for his mainly English guests.

Like Mikka, he sits high up the TripAdvisor rankings. He is also a little theatrical but there the comparisons end. Billy will never be troubled by absent girlfriends in Germany, he is cut from a different cloth. He also has compassion, humour and the merest hint of an underlying edge. Billy is also wonderfully warm, engaging, highly efficient and, to read his online reviews, sainthood is not far away.

After a night in Corfu Town I'd caught a public bus up to the north coast of the island, for privacy's sake I'll keep the exact location to myself. I was in search of peace and quiet to do some serious writing (at this point you might be wondering what happened to it).

The ride up was spectacular. Corfu is a tourist mecca but the visitors mostly congregate around the coast to worship the sun and the sea.

Inland is quiet and breathtakingly beautiful. The road bent and buckled through rugged fir covered mountains and gorges. Corfu is the greenest of all the Greek islands and the most northerly.

I hadn't been there for 40 something years but the place had stayed with me. The island has a beautiful fragrance, the inland air is an unforgettably evocative mix of fir trees and dry rock. Through the bus window it seeped and wafted me back to my early years. The whole memory was incredibly powerful. I closed my eyes and thought about a little boy long since gone and his wide-eyed wonder at this magical place.

The bus eventually dropped me at my destination. I'll confess right here and now it wasn't what I had in mind. The town had lots of bars with tribute bands, menus all in English, everything done to make it the UK with sunshine.

I'd not researched the town and had only chosen it as a destination after arriving at Corfu Town bus station and checking options on the timetable. If there were choices I'd retrieve my trusty coin from Bali and toss away. On this occasion there wasn't much choice at all. The first bus was going north so my decision was easy.

On my travels I generally started moving early to mid-morning. I'd head to a bus or train station or sometimes a ferry terminal, pick a destination and off I'd go. Sometimes, to be honest, I did a little research in advance or had a word of mouth recommendation. But often there was no set plan. Now and then the coin would send me to a dud, other times it struck gold.

I'd learned that unless I'd booked accommodation in advance it was best not to arrive at a destination beyond mid-afternoon. Night-time searches are a pain, the world hides itself when dark descends. Arrive in the light, tramp around and ask around. If that doesn't work fire up the wifi and make a quick decision. It saves a lot of time pratting around and believe me, in the early part of my travels I pratted.

After arriving at my destination I'd found a cafe with free internet, jumped on to TripAdvisor and found Billy's hotel with its high ranking and glowing recommendations. It had the advantage of being out of town. I went on to Agoda, the hotel booking website, to check availability and made a reservation. Unfortunately, I didn't get back an immediate confirmation. It was not a done deal.

I headed optimistically off in the direction of the hotel. In the early afternoon heat five kilometres with a backpack was a hot walk. On arrival I was met immediately by Billy, small, slight, extravagant. I gave him my name and soon had the sense my last minute booking was causing some kind of issue. Unlike Mikka's nightmare this was a drama that was mostly kept hidden away from me and in the end was no drama at all.

Billy asked me for a little patience, soon produced my key and I was in. The hotel was lovely, its rooms modern, comfortable and spacious and all set around a large swimming pool. That night I stayed at the hotel for dinner, all the other guests headed to town. I began to get to know Billy.

Over the course of the next three days we talked, gossiped and laughed. He was fantastic fun. I told Billy I was trying to write a book and that sadly, as lovely as his hotel was, I would have to go and find somewhere, smaller and quieter with no children playing in the pool. I couldn't afford noisy distractions.

Most hoteliers would have seen a source of revenue drying up and washed their hands of me, not Billy. He told me to leave it to him and he would ask around.

By next lunchtime he had a potential solution. I was to ride my newly rented motorbike a dozen kilometres through the countryside. On arriving at a tiny village I was to wait outside a shop for a man on a motorbike, Billy didn't know his name. The directions couldn't quite compete with Greek road signs and multiple unmarked lanes but eventually I arrived. After 20 minutes along came a man on a motorbike. With barely a word he indicated I should follow him. For several kilometres we rode through narrow, twisting, potholed roads of the Corfu countryside. Finally he headed down an unmade track past a couple of homes. The most stunning coastline panorama opened up before me and at almost the same moment a small two storey complex of studios. We turned in and I was greeted by Katerina an archetypal Greek mama. Her English was excellent, her husband, who I'd followed on the bike, was Alekos, his English was a little rustier.

Katerina took me to see a room. In it were two single beds under mosquito nets, a small fridge, two hot plates for cooking and a wardrobe. The selling point was outside, a decent size balcony with a table and chair and from it an uninterrupted view over the mile long bay. Beautiful, rich blue ocean framed on either side by high rocky headlands. Outside the studios was the perfect sound of silence.

I explained that as long as the peace and quiet were as they appeared I might hang around for a while. Katerina took me through her pricing proposal. Thirty Euros a night if I stayed one week and the sliding scale went all the way down to 25 Euros a night if I spent a month there.

Breakfast, if I wanted it, would be five Euros a day, and would be served under a canopy of flowers next to their olive grove. It was all totally enchanting in a thoroughly Greek setting.

The stay was so utterly blissful that I stayed six weeks. And it was all down to Billy's generosity. He'd made some phone calls, mentioned me to some people and they in turn had come up with Katerina's place.

I made a couple of trips back to Billy's place. One night I mentioned to him that I was working on a crime/legal/political thriller (you'll no doubt be delighted to hear it's next off the production line). He asked if I could base a character on him. Unfortunately, I had to tell him that I only had one character left to work on and that this was a serious villain. Billy was way too loved by all his guests to fit the bill.

With one of his great theatrical looks he leant in a little to the table and said, "But Arthur, I have a dark side." Billy began to tell me more of his story. Some of it rather personal. He confided in me that an Englishman had broken his heart a few years ago. Billy had since taken a number of lovers, several of them were married.

Once more he leant in from across the table, appraised me with his eyes and said with a twinkle, "Arthur, I can turn any man."

"Any man Billy?" My voice may have quivered a little as I spoke.

"Any man," he confirmed with a twinkling nod.

My mind went back to the Gili Islands and Harry The Crocodile. Interesting, the people you meet and the things they tell you.

Billy, of course, didn't really have much of a dark side, or at least not one that I saw. He has a bit of history but we all do, don't we? In the end, however, I did try and mould some of Billy's character into my villain. It was utterly hopeless. But in honour of a truly fun, gregarious and generous human being my evil, emotionless, psychopathic villain will be named …. Billy.

#

AROUND THE WORLD IN WONDER SOCKS

26

BOOT CAMP FOR HIPPIES

Week 20; Agios Georgios, Corfu, Greece; 24,060 kms travelled;
2 undies culled, 4 remaining; 2 wonder socks MIA

"Let us all om".

On the command 130 people moved their arms serenely outwards and aloft. Then they began. The room filled with a low rumble.

"Ommmmmmmmmmmmmmm".

My arms were half in, half out and only half-heartedly raised. My sound more erm than om. I was self-conscious and well outside my comfort zone.

Then a brief panic. Should my eyes be closed while oming? In my uncertainty I half-closed them and snuck a crafty peek at my neighbours. The evidence was mixed.

Om, or Aum, is the chant you hear at yoga, in Buddhism or Hinduism. It is supposed to be the sound of the universe or divinity.

On this particular night it marked the beginning of a concert at Buddha Hall in Magoulades, a small village in Corfu. It was the venue for something called Light of Love 2, a week-long 'healing world of mantras, songs and circle dances.' Each morning participants undertook two hours of 'ecstatic chanting'. Apparently it's extremely popular and people come from all over the world.

Sounded to me like boot camp for hippies. Not quite what I envisaged when I arrived in Corfu, one of Europe's top beach holiday destinations. I'd pictured beautiful mountains lined with cypress trees and beaches packed with bronzed gods and goddesses.

This spiritual 'thing' has never really been 'my thing'. I am admittedly a one-dimensional, born, live, die, The End, kind of guy. In other words an atheist and also rather short on spirituality. But on my travels I'd set myself the goal of opening my mind to experiences.

Whenever I'd seen the Light Of Lovers around town I'd been struck by how happy they all seemed. So when I heard about the concert I decided to see what dancing in circles could do for people, other than making them dizzy.

My early prejudices were perfectly met. The flower power generation appeared to have been transported from 1960s California to 21st century Corfu. There was a fair amount of long hair, although mostly now grey. There were also lots of flowery clothes, perhaps a little more tailored these days. But there was no sign of the free love that so shocked the swinging sixties. I think for some of the older members love now costs, the price being a little purple pill. But I had to admit they seemed genuinely happy.

This being the Buddha Hall they were all sitting on the floor. In the middle of the room were Miten, Deva Premal and Manose. They led us through the next couple of hours. Mostly it was gentle songs of love, respect and god, not the Christian version but something more individual and at the same time universal.... I think. I was a little confused.

Two hours later my night came to an end. As I headed home I was struck by feelings of calm and peacefulness. I had been touched by the concert and really enjoyed the experience. Oh hell, my hippy sneer was on the slide.

The following weekend there was confirmation. It was Miten's birthday bash. A morning of songs was to be held in an ancient olive grove. All invited. Two rules, arrive quietly and dressed in red and white. I rocked up a little late as my motorbike had decided it only worked weekday hours and would be taking the weekend off. I was appropriately dressed in pink shirt and faded white, three-quarter length, jungle trousers. Not normally a great look but with the olive grove crowd I blended in perfectly.

What was immediately clear was a tangible feeling of goodwill, a genuine warmth. The sun shone brightly and the olive grove had a very earthy and welcoming air. The music wafted softly through the ancient trees. Gentleness was all around, I was feeling the love. Then came a beautiful and tender rendition of the Beatles song 'Here Comes The Sun'. It was a warm, soft, gentle sound. Contentment wrapped around every fibre of my body.

The music seeped into the souls of the gathering and people began to stand, raise their arms skywards and start to sway. I too found myself standing. It all felt so deeply blissful and soothing.

But that's where it ended for me. I was still self-conscious and my arms stayed firmly down by my side. Deep within me I knew this was still not really my thing.

The best I can say is that my obvious prejudices had been shifted. These people didn't dress like me, didn't think like me but I understood they were searching for something and on the way to finding it they were enjoying the moment. I no longer dismissed them as hippies. Perhaps that morning, there in the olive grove, happies was a better word.

It was good to prise my shuttered mind open slightly to let in just a few rays of the Light Of Love.

#

27

WHAT GERMANS DO WITH TOWELS AT NIGHT

Week 21; Agios Georgios, Corfu, Greece; 24,060 kms travelled;
missing wonder socks found; 4th pair of thongs;
month-long stay in one place - nice;

Greece in the summertime conjures up highly evocative images of beaches, romance, history, culture and festivals. They all come wrapped in a warm sultry cocoon.

Of course there is the other side. Crowds and queues, young Brits abroad, older Brits abroad. And then there are the Germans. If you grew up in the UK there are three main stereotypes about Germans. Firstly, they are aloof and have no sense of humour; secondly they are highly efficient; finally, they get up early on their holidays to put their towels down on sunbeds to claim them for the day.

The first stereotype I'll come back to in a moment but the second I can vouch for. As for the third, well I can't really help as the small studio complex I was staying at didn't have a pool and I didn't go to the beach early in the morning. But I do have another little gem for you. Have you ever wondered what German folk do with their towels at the other end of the day? Let me shed some light on one of the great overlooked mysteries of world stereotyping.

While I was staying at the idyllic Corfu studios the Perseid meteor shower was due. Potentially several hours of shooting stars, one of the greatest free shows on earth, at least if you're in the northern hemisphere in August. The Perseids are visible when the Earth passes through material from the tail of the Comet Swift-Tuttle. Small fragments of ice and dust strike the Earth's atmosphere and burn up. Here on planet earth we see them as spectacular streaks of light across the night sky. The best time to view them is from about half an hour after midnight until the wee small hours.

I had a deliberately late night in the nearby village of Arillas. It was party central for the Light of Lovers, or at least the place where they hung out. This night I'd stayed back late and by the time I reached home it was half past midnight. I went to my room collected the duvet off my bed and climbed the staircase up to the flat roof of the studios.

All around was dark and quiet, perfect for the meteors. I stood and looked at the night sky, keen to know if the shower storm was underway. Nothing obvious yet so I walked to the centre of the unlit roof. Five paces later my foot smacked against something hard. I stumbled forward and as I flailed around my other foot landed on something soft. Whatever it was it yelped in pain with a high female pitch. One more stumble, another cry, this time the thing had changed sex from female to male. I had a few more lurches before regaining my balance. What the hell?

It took a few moments but I realized people were lying on the floor. I gave a few surprised apologies into the dark and back came a voice, a German voice. "It's ok. Are you ok?"

"I'm fine," I told the empty, black void before me.

Slowly my eyes adjusted and the outline of several bodies became barely visible. They had their duvets for warmth and then I realized their towels were on the floor. Had they put them down hours earlier to reserve their spot? Probably not but I was far too respectful to ask.

Moments later I could also make out the telltale sound of glasses and bottles of wine. They weren't just Germans they were well prepared, efficient Germans. It was two ticks in the box for stereotyping. But the voices from the dark proceeded to take a sledgehammer to the third stereotype of aloofness and the perceived lack of humour.

The group turned out to be two mothers, one with a teenage son the other a teenage daughter. Over the next several hours we talked and laughed and they offered me wine and nibbles. I had nothing to offer in return, except for a thousand apologies, but they didn't care a jot.

Over the next few days we became firm friends. Each night they would invite me onto their balcony to share food, drink, company and more than anything else humour. They were great fun, so much so in fact that later in the summer I went to Germany to visit them.

The five of us were the only people staying at the studios. Before Angelika and Karin arrived only two other couples had stayed at the studios, both German. They were interesting, kind people and all four loved to laugh and tell their funny stories. If I was to give an award for my favourite nationality during my year's travels the Germans would be in first place. By and large they were educated, humorous, kind and with excellent English.

Bottom of the list I hear you wondering? It wouldn't be right for me to engage in this. I've warned before about stereotyping and the fact is all countries have their good and bad. In any case if I was to 'out' this country its president would almost certainly annexe part of my body and secretly fund other parts of me to rebel. So I will resist the opportunity to Put In any cheap clues....there again.

Agios Georgios became an essentially German town in summer. Up the coast others such as Sidari were mainly British outposts. It's nowhere near 100% of either and many other towns are a jumble of nationalities but it's clear some kind of nationality factor is often at play. I suspect it mostly comes down to the tour operator. British travel agents book out hotels in specific towns and the same applies for German operators. Presumably, over the years they have tended to ghettoise these places so that holidays are spent mostly in the company of people who talk, think and drink the same.

Restaurants, bars and shops then reinforce the identity by targeting these customers. Some places have English only menus, others have German at the front. Some bars advertise English football, others the German Bundesliga.

Another German friend I'd made invited me over to her complex and when she introduced me to other holidaymakers I took on the role of novelty item. They were very welcoming but it felt like I was the only foreigner in their midst. Further up the coast I suspect the roles would be reversed in British camps.

It all felt a little insular. A pity as we tend to be at our most relaxed on holiday, with minds prised a little open. It's a chance to confront the stereotypes we often create in our heads. I'm not denying that some have a grain of truth about them. So if you're ever in Corfu in August and want to watch the Perseid meteor shower get your towel out early at night, just to be sure.

#

One more tip for Corfu in August is to make sure you have a pre-arranged ticket out or plenty of time on your hands. My spur-of-the-moment travel had worked well to this point, give or take a couple of minor irritants. But the peak month of the European holidays is not ideal travel time. Demand is so high that seats on planes, trains and boats are fully booked or the price of getting on board is astronomical.

For once I had a pre-determined destination. My mate Matt Sydney was turning 40 and I was invited to his bash in London. Rather than head straight there I planned to take up another offer to go via Brussels to visit Leela, a friend I'd met while travelling. I'd also have time to visit Ypres the Flanders battlefields, site of some of the worst horrors of the First World War.

It felt a little like cheating having a brief plan but I was looking forward to it all with great anticipation. So when I'd finally had my fill of Corfu I naively tried to put the scheme into operation by booking a flight. Fat chance.

I ended up late at night standing in a grim little cafe outside Corfu Town docks using scratchy wifi to search ferry schedules. After an eternity I cobbled together a plan which would involve boats, buses, a plane and a night sleeping on chairs. This was the only realistic way off the island for a couple of weeks. The unappealing scenario which faced me was going to cost a princely sum. However, a direct flight out would have cost more than the Greek national debt – I probably couldn't afford it, the country definitely couldn't.

#

28

CHARITY AND THE TWO FOR ONE SPECIAL

Week 23; Wales and London, UK; 26,860 kms travelled;
weather cool, new Greek clothes redundant;
15 flights; 10 motorbikes; 5 boats; 51 beds

The next few weeks were spent travelling through Belgium, northern France and finally on to London for the birthday bash. While there I met up with many old friends and colleagues, some I hadn't seen for years. It was a fun time, London is buzzing these days. Leaving wasn't easy but deciding on my destination was simple.

Wales, the land of my fathers, the blood in my veins, the place that stirs my heart. But also down on its luck, not that it's ever had much. Conquered by the English centuries ago it sits out to the west, sometimes a little moodily, often just ignored by the rest of the UK and unknown to much of the world. Psychologically out on the margins of the Celtic fringe and you can't get much fringier than that.

Not many people, even fewer jobs, an economy that earns pocket money. Its stereotypes revolve around sheep, singing, rugby, sheep, Tom Jones, Dylan Thomas and sheep (you'll need a few more fingers and thumbs if you ever plan to count them all, they're everywhere).

In the most positive and endearing sense of the word it is a simple place. There are few airs and graces or pretension about the Welsh, what you see is what you get. Labour heartland, beautiful scenery.

The unfortunate thing is that apart from crap weather and a rich musical and cultural tradition Wales lacks things; investment, resources, high value businesses, somebody to fix the line-out (you need to be a rugby fan to get that one). There's not much money to go around except for its capital city Cardiff which is actually doing rather nicely, thank you. But 30 minutes or so along the M4 is Bridgend. My sister, Avril, and her husband, Nigel, live just outside the town in Brackla. Their daughters, Leah, Ceri, and their own children are also there. It's friendly and quite tightly-knit and is actually growing.

Pitching up in my sister's place after nearly five months on the road and for our first get-together in three years was great.... once she'd passed her initial shock.

"My God, you look like a tramp," was her greeting. What she didn't know was I'd actually tidied myself up on the train over from London. Hmm, my standards might be slipping here.

Over the course of the week we happily lapsed back into the easy ways of family. Stories, laughter, cups of tea, biscuits, dinners and gossip.

Two or three times I went into Bridgend, a town with a population of about 40,000. It's a straight up and down working class place, typical of much of my homeland. But when you've been away, as I have for the best part of a decade, some things really stand out. There were always street stalls selling everyday items but now a couple were selling lawyers, or at least their services. Big and bold they advertised a single service - suing. For accidents, unfair dismissal, tight fitting underwear, you name it, they'll take law suits out against it. America has exported its omnipotent legal culture to the UK. It has also arrived in my current home of Australia. I won't bore you with a re-run of the rights and wrongs of it all but when you have it rammed down your throat while shopping for tea bags and toilet rolls something is wrong.

But the real eye opener was the huge boom in charity shops (op shops as they're called Down Under). They are one of the few growth areas in the small retail sector. They were everywhere. I counted nine in the centre of Bridgend. NINE. Small shopkeepers are deserting town centres, victims of the out of town superstores. When commerce moves out charity moves in. It's either that or empty shops or 'pound shops' which are also surging.

I have mixed feelings about the charity shops. On the plus side they're supporting many hugely worthwhile causes, hospices, sick kids, the blind. But on the other hand they reflect the change and decay of high streets. It's debatable whether they attract shoppers to the town centre. However, for a rather selfish reason they earned a tick in the box from me.

My 50 litre BlackWolf backpack contained only gear for hot weather and jungles. You'll find precious little of either in Wales, particularly the hot weather. So now I was in cooler climes I needed warmer gear. A shame really as it wouldn't get much use, I already had hotter climates on my mind.

As I hunted around Bridgend for cheap new clothes the penny dropped. I should get my clothes from a charity shop. This was kind of a new experience for me, they'd never had my custom before. However, this trip is about travelling cheap so to hell with my foolish pride, I went looking.

I was burdened and bolstered by the experience. The burdening was that you can find the odd character in these shops and I do mean odd. It can leave you burdened by aloofness and that's not a worthwhile feeling. Of course the vast percentages of customers are just ordinary, decent people and slowly I relaxed into the environment. The volunteers usually personified the simplicity of Welsh people that I'd mentioned and had hearts of gold.

In one shop I noticed a rail of men's clothes. On it was a handwritten sign, "Today. Everything One Pound!!!". I flicked through the rail. The offerings were on the cheap rack for a reason and most weren't my size but I did find a long sleeved shirt that passed muster. I tried it on, wasn't offended by what I saw and went to the counter to pay the little old lady my one pound. I brandished the coin at her but she wouldn't take it.

"We have a sale on today, my love," she said.

"Yes, I know, I saw the sign. It's my lucky day. Here's my pound."

"No, no, it's a special sale." She beamed at me. "Everything is two for one today. You can have something else off the rail as well for your pound."

"Oh no, it's OK thanks. This one is fine," I replied. There was seriously nothing else worth taking.

But she was insistent. "Two for one, love. Go on. I'll keep this for you. I won't let anybody else have it."

I could tell she meant it. My sister's opening words replayed in my head. The old lady was obviously of the same opinion, I must have still looked a little down on my luck. Disappointing really as this was several showers, a number of shaves and some brand new clothing later. Could people smell the solo backpacker about me?

I was about to refuse again but my charitable new friend had a determined look on her face. I'd better get something else for my pound. So I did. When I returned to the counter the old lady was clearly thrilled for me. Out I walked moments later with a perfectly fine long sleeved shirt and a hopelessly large Motorhead T-shirt from a tallish, fat bloke who'd obviously been to a gig sometime circa 1985.

Some weeks later it got donated on. But only after having travelled half way across the world from Wales, to America and finally to Burma, where I handed it to a small, thin destitute old man. Lemmy's new number one fan I suspect. I'm sure the little old lady would have approved.

I had an altogether different charity shop experience a few days later in another part of the UK. I had gone to stay with my friend Max in her place at Richmond. For those of you who don't know it this is a seriously wealthy and well-heeled area. It's stockbroker territory right on the edge of west London and bordered by the River Thames and Richmond Park.

Like Bridgend this place also has charity shops, although they are fewer in number and the town's High Street is thriving. Before I'd arrived back in London I'd decided the next leg of my travels would be to northeast USA. I'd probably be there for late summer and early fall (autumn in old currency) so I'd need a few more warm clothes.

I mentioned my new NONY charity clothes philosophy to Max and she happily pointed out what the area had to offer. There were a couple of fairly standard shops but there was another which dripped with pedigree. It was as far removed from the Bridgend shops as you can get without leaving the planet. The inside was laid out with a touch of style and the three ladies at the counter were clearly from the upper bracket of local society. Padded jackets and pearls were their idea of shop uniform. The three of them happily ignored me as I intruded into their domain.

I went in to a rear room and thumbed through the rail. Nice gear. Shirts, jackets, trousers all sporting Hugo Boss, YSL and other seriously quality brands. The city gents who donated them clearly had a need to keep up with the Farquahars next door, so clothes were replaced at very short intervals.

"Are you looking for anything in particular?" One of the ladies had appeared in the back room.

"How about a warm welcome instead of that frosty attitude which strongly suggests I'm some downtrodden oik interrupting your precious day."

It would have been a killer line to say but it stayed in my head. Something entirely different came out of my mouth. The lady had a strong whiff of good breeding and bad condescension about her. Her radar had obviously picked up my own particular odour of cheap backpacker.

I thanked her for her 'help' and said I'd call her if I needed assistance. She left, mentally counting all the clothes in the room so she could tell if I tried to nick any.

I thumbed through the prices, 30 pounds for a shirt, 150 pounds for a jacket. Second-hand it was but cheap it was not. I made my excuses and left. Further up the road at one of the more down at heel shops designer labels were fewer in number but still to be found and at much reduced rates. My travelling wardrobe increased in size again and quality, second-hand or not.

It really is possible to travel the world with a very small backpack. You can replace clothes for next to nothing as you go; new and cheap in Southeast Asia, second hand and cheap in parts of Europe and the USA; lightly used and designer in cities.

I suppose it boils down to mindset. I'd never have bought clothes from charity shops before this trip. But the necessity of travelling light meant I wasn't geared up for different climates. Buying new probably meant a reluctance to leave the clothes behind. Restocking at charity shops was a great way around this plus I got to re-donate everything back.... in theory. I'm actually sat here writing wearing the shirt from the Bridgend shop. And no, it's not the 1985 Motorhead top.

#

29

DOWN AND OUT IN LONDON

One morning I was using the free wifi in a London library. A local pensioners' group had gathered for a weekly outing of poems, prose, coffee and company. The librarian started proceedings by playing 'The Streets Of London', the song which had reduced me to tears after my cough medicine overdose. She followed it with an announcement.

"I'm very sorry to tell you all that local character Anne Naysmith has been killed. She was struck by a lorry in the early hours and died. For those of you who don't know the name she was the homeless lady who used to push her trolley around the local area for years."

There was a collective chorus of tempered sighs. The librarian pressed on and began to share some of the details of the old lady's life.

Miss Naysmith, it turned out, could have been a poster girl for 'The Streets Of London' song with a story of a life gone wrong and the spiral down into a wretched existence.

In her earlier years she was a classically trained concert pianist who had attended the prestigious Royal Academy of Music. After completing her education she performed in public at some impressive London concert halls. One of her performances was even reviewed by The Times newspaper. But in the early 1970s things began to go sadly wrong. Her heart was broken by a love affair which ended badly, she lost her job, her finances deteriorated and when she couldn't pay her rent the landlord ordered her to leave her apartment.

The loss of the home apparently hit her very hard. With nowhere else to turn the desperate musician began sleeping in her car, a Ford Consul, which was parked outside her former home.

And there she lived for the next 30 years.

The local council offered to house her as the vehicle became dilapidated but she always declined. She used a nearby doctors' surgery for her ablutions but all other offers of help were rejected. She became the archetypal bag lady wearing grotty old clothes with newspapers and cardboard wrapped around her feet for shoes. Nobody ever really understood her motivation for refusing help but she remained resolutely independent and non-dependent.

Most residents took her to their hearts over the three decades she spent living out of her car. But in 2002 a new neighbour complained to the council of rats living under the vehicle. The authorities finally decided to act and the vehicle was removed. As the dilapidated Ford was hoisted onto a transporter not a single rodent was seen.

Miss Naysmith was offered council housing once more but again she refused. Instead she fashioned a shelter out of bushes and trees on a nearby railway embankment and this became her new home. A decade on even this grim existence was denied to her. She was moved on so a new fence could be erected. Her final home was on the fringes of a nearby car park. There she lived until the early hours of a cold winter's morning when she was killed crossing a road. She was in her late 70s.

Her life was a lesson in how tenuous all our lives can be and how we often judge the homeless people of the street. 'Scroungers' is typically how they're labelled, parasites who live off handouts. Miss Naysmith proved the lie of that generalisation. The truth is, like all of us, they have their life stories, their successes and their sorrows. But their time on earth has often simply been less fortunate than our own.

My week of a low level chest infection, medicine-induced sluggishness and a little loneliness had reduced me to a couple of tears. Compared to the wretched, uncomplaining life of Miss Naysmith it was pathetically insignificant.

#

30

TRAVELLING THE WORLD FOR FREE

If you had to put a price on travelling the world what would it be? I suppose the answer depends on how much you've earned, how well you've invested and how much you've hidden from the taxman. In case you missed it that's a cheap jibe at HSBC which has just been forced to come clean that its private Swiss bank helped clients dodge their tax responsibilities. Tut, tut.

At the top end of the scale it is actually possible to guess a price for travelling 'The World'. This is the name of what's billed as 'the largest, private, residential ship on the planet.' On board are 165 privately owned apartments. They range in size from studios to a six bedroom penthouse. Ownership costs are estimated from $1 million in the cheap seats up to a whopping $13 million at the top end. There's everything on board from a library with 25,000 books to a 12,000 bottle wine cellar (sounds impressive but I bet you can't get the $7 cleanskin I'm rather partial to).

The vessel constantly sails the world and guests/owners get to pick the itinerary themselves, three years in advance. They go to amazing places but given I often don't know what I'm doing three hours in advance it appears I'm not cut out for 'The World'. This will come as a mighty relief to the ship's owners who probably don't view unkempt middle-aged backpackers as their target clientele.

At the polar opposite end of the scale I can tell you how much it costs to travel the world on the cheap. The answer is next to nothing. For many people the idea of cheap travel is loaded with horrible connotations. Admittedly I've seen my fair share of horrible but I have to tell you that's not how it has to be.

The cheapest day on my travels cost me the grand total of $28 and you'd be surprised what you get for your money. I was staying in Ubud the spiritual, cultural and ancient centre of Bali. I was there in the off-season which as far as I could tell just meant not in school holidays. Personally I think they'd got it wrong. No kids equals quiet and should therefore also equate to higher costs. But I'm not complaining. As for weather, normally a prime factor in determining off-season, it was warm and dry. The place I found was going for the bargain basement price of $10 a night. For that I had a large, comfortable room with double bed; ensuite shower and bath, which is rare in these parts; an outside sitting area with a fish pond, a three course breakfast; unlimited tea and coffee through the day; and free wifi. The place was spotless. Incredibly it was only 200 metres from the heart of Ubud town. (There are a couple of pictures of it at the end of this chapter).

I dined at two perfectly acceptable cafes, lunch and dinner came to just $8, both were fine. One dollar was lavished on a large bottle of water for the day and a small bottle for the evening. The rest went on luxury items.... of a sort.

The biggest luxury was a moped for getting around and the second indulgence was a massage, tip included. I'll admit this particular massage didn't have more than a nodding acquaintance with the idea of luxury. In fact it had no discernible relationship at all. After being accosted by the masseuses on the streets, the standard method at Ubud's least well-heeled establishments, I was led up a narrow staircase into a dimly lit room. There was an overpowering smell of massage oil. I could have scraped it off the walls but I suspect that was all that was holding the flimsy room dividers together. The towel for modesty was probably not finest Egyptian cotton, there again, it looked so old Cleopatra herself might have used it for a rub down.

The massage was fine. It was 45 minutes of deep tissue delight. I was so happy that I gave a 25% tip. I know what you're thinking, this is a generous guy. I'm blushing as I write this but at the time instinct took over and I did what I thought was right. Besides, she probably needed the one dollar more than I did.

And that was that, day done and dusted and all for just $28 AUD. If I'd upgraded to a massage with a decent room and newish towels I would have had to fork out just an extra three or four dollars. Ubud seems to be the world spa and massage capital. The high end establishments have elaborate packages for hundreds of dollars a day, the bottom end ones don't. But they'll soothe your weary muscles for the price of a Starbucks coffee.

The fact is that in Southeast Asia travel can be incredibly cheap. And I can guarantee that not one dollar of mine that day went to a major corporation. The people who needed it most got a benefit, small as it was.

Now and again when I needed a little more comfort I'd lash out but this was still at the peanuts end of the scale. I had a deal in the Vietnamese town of Hue at a fabulous five star hotel surrounded by the trappings of luxury, the cost was $62 a day. That would have been halved if I'd been with a companion (memo to self - find one).

Talking of which, I did share rooms several times with fellow lone travellers. People who I'd met, got along with and who were interested in halving their nightly room bill. I never had a bad experience. There again my vetting system always started with the same question, do you snore? This applied to guys and gals and yes, there were platonic roomies of both kinds - I don't come across as very threatening. This is mostly a good thing but in some tight spots it would be nice to carry a tad more air of menace about me.

After transport the biggest cost by far is for accommodation. To reduce bills you need to get creative. Staying in low season or off the beaten track or sharing a room are some ways.

There is a mass of accommodation websites to book hotels and guesthouses. However, I'd also come across a site called Airbnb and it's revolutionising the industry.

For those of you who don't know, it's a lodgings website on which people advertise a bedroom or even their whole home to travellers, kind of B&B but usually without the second B. The site is an internet phenomenon with an estimated 1.4 million listings in 192 countries. Mind-blowing considering it only started business in late 2008. One recent valuation estimated it to be worth a whopping $24 billion. By 2020 its annual revenue could be as much as $10 billion a year. Not a bad little business for its founders Brian Chesky and Joe Gabbia.

Like all the best ideas it came from simplicity and necessity. The guys were a little tight on money and were searching around for ways of making life a touch easier. To help pay the bills they put down air mattresses on the living room floor of their San Francisco loft apartment and began taking in short-term lodgers struggling to find hotel rooms. They quickly realised they were on to something and along with another partner, Nathan Blecharczyk, they launched Airbedandbreakfast (its name was shortened early the following year).

The company quickly attracted major investors including the TV and film star Ashton Kutcher. The actor made his name as the loveable but hopelessly goofy Michael Kelso in the comedy series 'That '70s Show'. In real life Kutcher is a very shrewd and active businessman. He co-founded a venture capital business and his highly successful track record includes investments in Skype and Foursquare. His connection with Airbnb will have been massively profitable.

However, the company has not been to everybody's taste. There have been squeals of protest from the hotel industry which is potentially losing out on huge revenue.

Early on there were also some ugly stories about misuse of homes by renters. These have included prostitutes setting up shop and meth addicts vandalising property. In a high profile incident US comedian Ari Teman rented out his apartment to what he thought was a family only to find it was actually used for an orgy. He was also left with a repair bill for $87,000 worth of damage. Must have been quite a night, lots of broken chandeliers and headboards I'm guessing.

Using sites like Airbnb will reduce your costs and often get you much more space. However, there's another gem which can effectively reduce your lodgings bill to nothing. I used it in a couple of countries and plan to use it a whole lot more. It's house sitting or pet sitting and it's an idea which has really taken off.

While I was in London I stayed in a lovely apartment in St John's Wood, literally across the road from Regent's Park. For those of you who don't know it this is one of the capital's swankiest addresses. The US ambassador's residence is across the road. Apartments in the block started at about $3 million and went a whole lot higher. If I'd tried to rent one of these for a week it would have costs thousands. But here I was in the heart of London and it was costing me not one cent.

All I had to do was to look after Dexter, an even-tempered gun dog. His owners Nick and Susan were going off on a short holiday to Africa. Dexter got stressed when staying in kennels so they'd successfully advertised for sitters on a number of occasions. It was a win win situation, Dexter stayed in his home environment and the owners handily saved themselves about $50-$60 a day in kennel fees. I just had to walk the placid pooch three times a day, make sure he was fed, watered and generally given some reassuring TLC. Not difficult as he was an affable soul.

Apart from that I just had to kick back and enjoy being in the middle of London with all its attractions just outside the front door. I planned my day around walking Dexter which still gave me plenty of time to enjoy the capital. Cats are, of course, easier to look after and allow you more time out and about in the city. They don't need long walks and generally their other demands are, well, undemanding.

In Australia I've looked after cats and dogs up and down the Sunshine Coast and been a house-sitter up in the hills. Many home insurance policies are invalid if the house is unoccupied for more than a month, so having a sitter is crucial for people travelling for lengthy durations.

I use Trustedhousesitters.com and it's amazing what they offer. There are stays available all around the planet, from Belize to Botswana, Paris to Sydney, rural to city. Plan it right and you can literally travel the world and never pay a penny in accommodation costs.

All you need to do is get a police check certificate, luckily mine drew a blank, and pay around $60 to get your C.V. posted on the website. The more places you look after the more references you get the more homeowners will want and trust you. The hard part can be deciding where you fancy visiting. There are people using Trustedhousesitters to tour the planet, often staying in luxurious places and almost never paying for accommodation.

I wonder if any of those apartments on 'The World' need a sitter. I better check my diary to see what I'm doing three years from now.

\#

31

WELCOME TO AMERICA?

Week 24; New York, USA; 32,460 kms travelled; 12 countries visited;
3 long sleeved shirts new/old; 1 Motorhead T-shirt;
1 wonder sock - a new low, crisis time

The toughest place to describe is the country that has more written about it on a daily basis than anywhere else in the world, AMERICA, and yes it deserves the capitals.

It's easy to love but around the world it's often intensely disliked. Its people can be incredibly hospitable and it has a soft, schmaltzy, apple pie core. But the place is a contradiction. It can also be brusquely inhospitable, rude and aggressive as all hell. This was how it was to be for me for a while.

The first sense of what was to come was on my arrival in the country. Getting through immigration and customs in most places requires you to suspend your bonhomie. They are almost without exception doleful experiences. But this time I felt like turning around and getting back on the plane. I understand, to a degree, the country's paranoia post 9/11 but these days it feels like the welcome mat has been ripped to shreds and replaced with a loud, "WHAT THE HELL DO YOU WANT" attitude. It was an utterly charmless exercise, graceless and coldly unwelcoming. That was only the beginning.

After a couple of days in and around New York I decided to travel to Philadelphia and I was going by bus. The image of long distance travel across the USA in a Greyhound coach is still a little romanticised in my head. Or at least it was.

I arrived 45 minutes early just to be on the safe side. Early I was, safe was another matter entirely. The underground dungeon that doubled as the waiting area had an uneasy air. Despite lots of uninterested staff and plenty of TV information screens the process of understanding what left from where and when was a lottery. Travellers were constantly having to ask the staff questions. At the bus station on the border of Montenegro and Albania employees had been bored and clueless. Here they were both of those but with half a gallon of bad attitude smeared on top (everything here is super-sized). Each question was met with a snarl or sometimes almost nothing at all.

I was finally herded onto my bus deep in the station's bowels. For once I was glad nobody was sitting next to me. Most people appeared fine but a couple of hoodied guys looked surly, unkempt and short of brotherly love, not America's finest ambassadors. And then the driver mounted his ride. He was a seriously big, rotund guy and mounting anything looked like no easy task. I wondered if there was a lady in his life, but for decency's sake I'll leave that wobbly thought right there.

He delivered a perfunctory welcome on board which dripped with insincerity. There was a brief pause and then he launched into what was really on his mind. His message basically boiled down to 'this is my bus and I ain't gonna take no crap from anybody. So don't f**k around with me.'

I had a feeling we wouldn't be passing around the tip hat for him at journey's end.

He recited rules on noise, earphones, litter and lots more. Some he repeated. After each repetition he drew breath, looked in his mirror and in a long drawl said, "Ya understan' me?" No cinema villain has ever delivered their words with more menace. These, I presume, were his lines in the sand, never to be crossed. Although the rest of the rules hardly sounded negotiable.

I couldn't tell whether this was just standard New Yorker talk, company policy or somebody who's had way too many bad experiences driving people on a bus. By this point on my travels I had been on plenty of buses in a number of countries. Nowhere had come within spitting distance (one of the driver's absolute no no's) of this unfriendly lecture. However, on another level it worked a treat. I swear everybody on the bus slunk a little lower in their seats, the hoodies in particular. There would be no skulduggery on board.

The journey was cheap, comfortable, efficient and incident free. I was disgorged into downtown Philadelphia on a late Sunday afternoon. Unfortunately, somebody had sent the air of menace on ahead. The area around the bus station was mostly deserted. There was a ton of graffiti and a few boarded up premises. Here and there a couple of guys stood around brooding, dressed once more in regulation hoodies. Philly had forgotten to put out the welcome mat.

From the boys at the border to the big bloke on the bus America wasn't showing me its best side. Not to be outdone the guys in government were going one better, they weren't showing me any side at all. I'd arrived in the middle of a government shutdown.

It was 24 hours to default, the moment at which the country wouldn't be able to pay its bills. Agreement was needed between the two main political parties to borrow more money – raising the debt ceiling as it's known. However, the Democrats and Republicans were at each other's throats and couldn't or wouldn't agree on a deal. America was in a mess.

The Founding Fathers must have been spinning in their graves. Lincoln was probably shaking his head with an awful sense of deja vu. A little while ago the country marked the sesquicentennial (150th anniversary) of Gettysburg. The Civil War battle was the biggest ever fought on American soil. It was the awful embodiment of a country at war with itself. Prior to the hostilities Lincoln had famously warned politicians, "A house divided against itself cannot stand". All these years later his words must have echoed hauntingly around Washington DC's

Capitol building.

The federal government was effectively closed, division once again the order of the day. Politics and politicians ideologically at odds with each other. In the most powerful country in the world non-essential government employees had been temporarily laid off, furloughed as the Americans call it. Institutions, museums, parks, landmarks, all shut; medical laboratories unable to get their work approved. The list goes on and on.

The Lincoln Memorial is one of the finest monuments in the world, a triumphant tribute to a great American. To describe the memorial to you was beyond me. Actually, to be more precise, it was beyond a fence. On it was a sign: "Because of the federal government shutdown all national parks are closed."

That sign, or at least a variation of it, had been keeping me company down the North East coast of America. In New York the Statute of Liberty was closed. Philadelphia's Independence Hall and the Liberty Bell were also off-limits to me. In Washington the national monuments and the Smithsonian Museums were all closed. Visitors from all over the world gawked at the landmarks from behind the barricades.

Everywhere I'd been the angriest tourists were the Americans themselves, embarrassed and unhappy at the farce. At the World War Two memorial veterans and families decided it was an insult they would not tolerate and they brushed aside the fences. They were in no mood to be told they couldn't pay their respects to those who died while wearing the uniform of the United States.

Putting the politics aside what upsets many people is the absurdity that closes some facilities. In Philadelphia one man told me of a dog park in the middle of Philadelphia which had been closed down.

"It's really tiny," he said. "Get a couple of dogs in there and it's full. No rangers ever go there and the gate is never shut. But because it's federal property the gate was locked and entry was impossible. Crazy."

Wealthy private citizens stepped in to fund veterans groups who provide crucial services. Mount Rushmore reopened courtesy of money from corporations. Ford's Theatre, where Lincoln was assassinated, was about to reopen thanks to a private donor. The Grand Canyon was being temporarily funded by the state government in an effort to bring the tourists back.

To be honest, life for most people continued as normal. As a tourist there was plenty to see and do. But the reality was that America might, just might, be about to tip itself over the edge.

Foreign governments and financial institutions warned that shutdown could become financial meltdown if the debt ceiling wasn't raised. America's credit rating was in danger and it would start to default on its worldwide debts.

If you or I default on our mortgages our home can be repossessed. I wondered if that could happen to the USA. Perhaps it would be divided up between China, its biggest creditor, and Britain its former owner/occupier. The "shutdown" signs at the Lincoln Memorial are bad enough, imagine if they have to be rewritten in the language of the new owners, "由于联邦政府关闭所有国家公园被关闭"

Absurd I know. But no more ridiculous than the world's only superpower laying off its own public servants over a budget feud.

\#

32

FIGHTING AND FORNICATION

Week 25; Harrisburg, New York State, USA; 33,180 kms travelled;
4 wonder socks - a modern day miracle;
1 commitment to pack better

With several of Philadelphia's star attractions closed I decided to cast my net a little further afield. I mentioned this to a family I was lodging with. One of their suggestions was Harrisburg. My blank face obviously gave away the fact I'd never heard of the place. After gently gliding over my ignorance the family informed me it was actually the state capital of Pennsylvania.

You're never more than a few moments away from an American quirk and state capitals do their bit in this department. We're all well acquainted with the names of the country's major cities but most capitals are a source of mystery if you don't happen to come from the US.

Take a look down the list and there are some corkers. In California I suspect most people would guess at Los Angeles or San Francisco but the capital is actually Sacramento. Further up the west coast in Washington state I'd have put my money on Seattle. Wrong, it's actually Olympia. Who knew? Clearly not me, another to put on the list of places I'd never heard of. In New York state the Big Apple plays second fiddle to Albany. I can't believe this sits well with the notoriously combative residents of 'the city that never sleeps'.

In Pennsylvania I really shouldn't have been surprised that Philadelphia would miss out to Harrisburg. The city lies 200 sleepy miles away so I hired a car and headed out to take a look. I have to say it was a big surprise and that surprise was unsurprising really as I'd not known of its existence.

The Harrisburg metropolitan area is credited with around 600,000 residents, peanuts compared with their big city cousins down the road in Philadelphia. Its metro area has roughly ten times that number. However, the place has no whiff of inferiority. In 2010 Forbes magazine named it America's second best city to raise a family. Impressive stuff even if the 'top 100' list is full of unexciting places. The survey was based on education, affordability, commuting time and a few dull factors which will have you yawning (yawning more?) if I mention them here.

Driving through Harrisburg on a Sunday morning it did seem rather listless and lifeless. There wasn't a soul about. I could have raced stark naked through its main streets without causing a stir. Mind you, I'm not sure I'm equipped with a body that would cause a stir on any day of the week. I had the distinct impression that even die-hard criminals couldn't be bothered to get off their backsides to do what they do best.

But slowly I began to see its attraction. The area around the Susquehanna River is very attractive. But the Capitol building, home of the Philadelphia's government and Supreme Court is the clincher. It is one of the finest in America. The giant dome is visible for miles around, grand in scale and design. President Theodore Roosevelt called it, "the handsomest building I ever saw."

Incidentally, did you know Roosevelt was the inspiration for the Teddy Bear. If you know the reason why feel free to skip ahead one paragraph, for the rest of you here's a little bit of toy history.

Roosevelt was commonly known as Teddy, a name he supposedly loathed. One day in 1902 he was out hunting with friends in Mississippi and, unlike most in the party, he had been singularly unsuccessful. Some other hunters had chased and eventually captured a black bear and tied the exhausted beast to a tree. Roosevelt was invited to finish if off but declined saying this would be unsportsmanlike. When the story got out a cartoonist for the Washington Post drew a sketch showing a disgusted President Roosevelt refusing to shoot the bear. Subsequent reproductions of the cartoon made the animal smaller and by degrees cuddly and cute. A man called Morris Michtom was inspired to create a toy based on the sketch. He contacted the White House and asked for permission to call it the Teddy Bear. Approval was surprisingly given and the rest is history.

The Harrisburg Capitol Building Roosevelt admired so much is on an epic scale. When constructed it had 55 more rooms than the federal government's Capitol Building in Washington DC, home to the US Congress.

It's as impressive on the inside as the outside and testament to its designer's stated ambition to be a 'Palace of Art'. The marbled entrance rotunda leads to a magnificent, sweeping white marble staircase based on the Paris Opera House. The domed roof was inspired by Michelangelo's design for St. Peter's Basilica in Rome. European influence is everywhere, as is opulence. The rooms are full of stained glass, gold leaf and crystal chandeliers. There's marble from Ireland and wood from Belize.

Violet Oakley was commissioned to paint some murals, the first woman in the US ever to be so honoured. She got the taste for it. In all she painted 43, a project that took up around two decades of her life. The building also took some of the life of its architect Addison Huston but not in a positive way.

The total bill for his project came in at a whopping $13 million. Huston's original budget was around the $4 million mark. But hey ho, what can you do, buildings always cost more than initial estimates.

The Republicans, who dominated state politics, happily turned a blind eye to the excess. Unfortunately for Huston the only Democrat elected to statewide office for 39 years took it upon himself to investigate. He began a forensic analysis of the spending. Item after item was checked and soon huge discrepancies were discovered. A mahogany desk for the senators' barber shop should have cost $325. It was charged at ten times the amount. A $150 flagpole came in at nearly six times the amount. The list went on and on. The investigations uncovered graft and corruption on a massive scale and eventually five people were jailed. One of them was Addison Huston. His building now stands as both a grandiose symbol of man's ability to transcend his environment and also his love of a dodgy quid or two.

After my morning of art and architecture I discovered Harrisburg's more sombre side. The city is host to the National Civil War Museum. The war ran from 1861 to 1865 and was pivotal in preserving the union. There are a few museums that deal with the war and its causes, this one was highly informative, pretty well-balanced and had many interesting displays. Two hours are recommended for a visit – I took three.

The reason Harrisburg hosts the museum is that it's just down the road from Gettysburg. The country's most famous battle site is seared into the American conscience. The engagement is often cited as being the event which turned the course of the war. In all 51,000 men were killed, injured or listed as missing during three days of fighting.

Four months later President Lincoln made a visit to inaugurate the Soldiers' National Cemetery on the site. His Gettysburg address is without doubt one of the finest pieces of oratory in the country's history. It's made all the more remarkable by being just two minutes in duration. Its content and its brevity should have been short enough to hold anyone's attention. However, I'll confidently wager that some of his audience slept through every single word. This was no fault of Lincoln's but entirely down to the Honourable Edward Everett.

The former Governor of Massachusetts was given the honour of presenting the main address of the day. He wasn't a man to miss out on his moment in the sun. Some of the 15,000-strong audience must have had a terrible, sinking feeling from the outset as he launched himself into his floral opening sentence.

"Standing beneath this serene sky, overlooking these broad fields now reposing from the labors of the waning year, the mighty Alleghenies dimly towering before us...."

On and on the opening sentence went. I have decided to take pity on you by stopping here. His audience had no such kindly benefactor. Everett was merciless and it was only after two exhausting hours that he decided to call it a day and shut up. His 13,607 words would have numbed any audience.

After a brief hymn by the inappropriately named Baltimore Glee Club it was Lincoln's time to speak. As he rose to his feet the president probably made a mental note to get himself a better warm-up act for his next address. History has looked favourably on his two minute speech. His audience, if they were awake, would have been unspeakably grateful.

Gratitude wasn't something I was feeling myself. Deep frustration was much nearer the mark. As much as I wanted to jump in the car and drive the short distance to Gettysburg it was pointless. The place was closed, yet another victim of the government shutdown. America was still getting my blood pumping for all the wrong reasons.

#

I needed something else to stimulate me and as I sat and thought about it a smile leaked from my lips. I had the answer - Intercourse!

We're all consenting adults here, so let me share with you a few pearls of wisdom. Pay attention now, this could be useful.

ARTHUR'S GUIDE TO INTERCOURSE

1) You need to take it slowly. Guys, this one is mostly aimed at you. Intercourse can be over in a few unfulfilling moments if you rush it.

2) Intercourse is best done in the daylight. You really need to see

what you're doing. Intercourse in the dark can be a little difficult.

3) Taking photos can be a highly sensitive matter. Pictures of bodies are acceptable but showing a face in Intercourse is definitely bad form.

4) If Intercourse is going well you might want to go all the way and try and reach Paradise. If so here's what you need to do; go to your left, then right, left again and then really hard right. Bingo, you're now in Paradise.

There are two obvious questions about Intercourse that come to mind. Firstly, how on earth the Pennsylvania town got its name to begin with. Secondly, why did it then become the centre for one of the largest Amish communities in the USA.

How the settlement got its name is a little uncertain. There are a couple of versions, neither of them smutty. What is known is that the place was originally called Cross Keys until the name change to Intercourse in 1814.

Whatever the reason, Intercourse has a large Amish community. When I arrived in the small town the light was fading. However, there were plenty of horse and traps about. Some of the Amish were still out working in the fields, others just walking along the road.

The Amish believe in the literal word of the Bible. Life is about devotion to God, family and community. Anything that distracts from these is frowned upon. They live a life of simplicity and eschew most modern technology. Cars and TV are off limits. The Amish mostly wear black and white, fashionable clothes are banned, they're thought to lead to pride and vanity.

I'd always had the impression the Amish lived together in remote areas, contact with outsiders a rarity. However, that's not how it is. Many live next door to non-Amish. The sloth, envy, and temptations of modern society are all around. To put it another way, they constantly see and hear modern day Intercourse.

#

33

ICE CREAM WITH AVA GARDNER

Week 26; Katonah, USA; 33,510 kms travelled;
buildings shut, shops open, splash out on 3 new undies

The most beautiful woman in the world is sitting just across the table and she's smiling right at me. For an hour or so I have been putty in her hands as she tells me tales of Hollywood. The stars, the glamour, the gossip and of course the tantrums. She knows it all, she is part of the legend.

I lapped it up with boyish enthusiasm and asked a thousand questions. Patiently she answered until my well ran dry. As we paused an impish smile broke across her face. "Do you like ice cream?" she asked. My day kept getting better.

We moved to the freezer and with a theatrical flourish the beauty pulled open the door to reveal a treasure trove of a dozen flavours.

Two minutes later I was eating ice cream with Ava Gardner.

Ava was a Hollywood superstar, the most beautiful woman of her time, a silver screen siren. She was a hard drinking, wise cracking vamp. Sex scandals, profanity and bad behaviour were her hallmarks.

Sadly she passed away in London in 1990. But a part of her lives on. That part is Rosemary Mankiewicz. Her story is remarkable and her home is testament to an extraordinary life.

On a wall are two framed letters, both handwritten. They are thank you notes to her father from the Duke of York, later King George VI (given the Hollywood treatment as the stammering monarch in 'The King's Speech'). Rosemary's father was the Duke's chaplain in the navy during the First World War.

The royal connection opened doors for the young Rosemary and she was invited to parties with the Duke's daughters, Margaret and Elizabeth, now Queen Elizabeth. "It was great fun," recalls Rosemary, "They were lovely and it was just a wonderful time."

As a teenager Rosemary dreamt of the stage and studied at the Central School of Speech and Drama. This, of course, was no ordinary school. It was based inside the Royal Albert Hall, one of the most iconic theatres in the world. "Quite something really," said Rosemary with great understatement.

It was all going fine and taking Rosemary on towards her chosen career of acting. But after three years she suddenly quit. "My sister married an Italian count and moved to Rome so I packed it in and went and stayed with them."

"It sounds a brave move," I said to her.

"I was young and it was exciting," she explained. "And, of course, it was Rome. It felt too much like fun to worry about leaving the school."

Rosemary quickly mastered Italian and soon crossed paths with the cinema. She was offered work helping Italian actors with their English for a film being shot in the country. The film's star was Errol Flynn, the greatest male sex symbol in Hollywood history. Some introduction to the movies.

However, the picture ran into financial problems and production stopped. Rosemary headed back to Rome and while she was kicking her heels another offer of work came along. This one would change her life for ever. The film was the 'Barefoot Contessa', directed by Joseph Mankiewicz, her future husband. Its star was Ava Gardner. She was wildly unpredictable, enigmatic, ferocious of temper and above all stunningly attractive. Ava and Rosemary hit it off and became friends.

"She was fun and we got on very well together. But she could be extremely difficult and would drive poor old Joe nuts," said Rosemary. "She'd be late on set, she'd make demands and she never hid her opinions," said Rosemary.

"One day they were filming a scene in which Ava drives her car into the square in Portofino. But she'd gone missing again. Joe had had enough and after a few discussions it was decided they would use me instead. I had the same curly hair and some other similarities. In those days you could get away with it."

And so Rosemary doubled for the most beautiful woman in the world.

I wondered whether the film trailer might be on YouTube, everything else is. We sat down in her study and set to work. To her great delight we found not just one but several versions of it.

In the first a booming, manly American voice, accompanied by giant blood-red text, introduced Ava as the 'Most Beautiful Animal' in the World".

Rosemary looked at me, smiled broadly and said, "You couldn't get away with saying that now, could you?"

I agreed, but I suspect Rosemary is amused at the idea of having been a 'beautiful animal'. She doesn't lack a sense of humour.

We passed half an hour or so looking at various extracts from the movie. Rosemary's face switched between amusement and nostalgia.

A little later she asked me if I'd like to see the toilet. Now, this is not normally the kind of offer to get my juices running but this time I was desperately keen.

The walls were covered in photos. Rosemary featured in a number but most were of her husband Joe either working or out on the town with the Hollywood greats he wrote for and directed. There was Marlon Brando, Humphrey Bogart, Michael Caine, Bette Davis, Cary Grant, Frank Sinatra, Elizabeth Taylor and Richard Burton.

They are the stuff of legends and they formed the backdrop to a large part of Rosemary's life. But she plays it down. "People get the impression that these people are constantly having dinner at your home. It's not as glamorous as you think."

But she did know many of them and I asked for her thoughts on Taylor and Burton.

"Elizabeth was lovely but Richard would screw anything that moved," she told me.

It's five star Hollywood gossip from yesteryear and I cannot resist asking the obvious question. "Did he ever try it on with you?"

After a little reticence she nodded and said, "Yes he did but I just pushed him away. He couldn't help himself."

Many stories later we departed the loo and headed to a sitting room. There were original movie posters and other pieces of wonderful film paraphernalia. Above the fire-place was a mantelpiece, upon it was the jaw-dropping sight of four Oscars. Her husband was the only man in Hollywood history to win both Best Director and Best Original Screenplay in back to back years. The awards were for 'All About Eve' and 'A Letter To Three Wives'.

I asked politely and a little pleadingly if I could pick one up. The beauty happily agreed. It was surprisingly heavy. Rosemary snapped away on my camera to capture my brush with cinema glamour. As I posed I was briefly lost in a fantasy where I was clutching the award delivering my acceptance speech before an admiring movie industry and billions of TV admirers.

Rosemary read me like a book. "I'll count them before you leave," she said. I suspected she was joking but I'm not certain. Rosemary can certainly act. She appeared on stage and the silver screen in her own right.

She showed me a black and white photo of herself in her role as a mermaid. But she didn't pursue it.

"Any regrets?" I asked her.

"None," she told me.

"The first reviews weren't great. And then I married Joe. Life was wonderful."

#

34

AMERICA – THE POSH PART OF WALES

Week 27; Philadelphia, Pennsylvania, USA; 33,960 kms travelled;
5th pair of thongs lost; I now believe in fairies, bad ones

I never thought I'd ever be able to say this but there is actually a posh part of Wales. It's taken me more than half a century to find but exist it does. I have seen it with my own eyes.

I stumbled across it quite by accident while doing some on-the-spot research for the planned crime book I mentioned previously. I had a checklist of places in Philadelphia I needed to visit. First on the list was a slightly dodgy area which would be the setting for some low-life crime action.

After asking around I'd been steered in the direction of Kensington, a few commuter stops outside the city centre on the Market-Frankford line. After a little bit of online effort I found a place to stay as a paying guest in the home of a young couple. From the station to their home was only about eight blocks. My walk didn't exactly take me past slums but it sure as hell didn't take me through middle class suburbia either. Every home had metal bars on the windows, many featured solid metal entry doors, several were abandoned and derelict.

There were discarded sofas and chairs on the street and others used for lazing. Several guys hung around but very few people were walking. I strode purposefully to my destination dressed in my jungle gear, backpack securely strapped to my body. I was feeling a little incongruous, to put it mildly. To put it more strongly I stood out like a lamb chop at a vegetarian wedding reception. Carrying a backpack and wearing my jungle khakis was tantamount to carrying a sign announcing, 'tourist in town, muggers please form an orderly queue'.

I had a few appraising looks and in my paranoia a few cars appeared to slow as they passed by, their occupants sizing me up. At five feet eight and a half inches there's not a whole heap of appraising or sizing to be done. Fortunately, I made it to the house and navigated through the security - a keypad, double locks, grills, a chain and a killer dog. All that was missing was a Dementor from Harry Potter and the place would have been impregnable. If my young hosts ever forget their keys getting back in will be impossible.

Stan and Joanne had bought in at the very earliest stages of what they were hoping would be a gentrification of the area. Both told me they felt comfortable, interestingly neither used the word 'safe'. Despite this vote of confidence they gave me a stern rundown of do's and don'ts. Most of it boiled down to be very careful in the day and be seriously bloody careful in the night.

There was a push bike they kept in their garage which I was welcome to use. It came with more do's and don'ts. None were about rules of the road, all were about the rules of the jungle, the urban jungle that was their neighbourhood. Perhaps my khakis would fit in here after all.

The most alarming advice was to watch out for cars attempting to sideswipe me. Apparently stunned victims are left lying helpless on the road as muggers rush from their vehicle, steal bags and wallets then drive off. Warning heard and heeded, my small daypack would stay in the house and I'd dress rough. That wasn't going to be too difficult, looking tough was a different matter.

My short time in Kensington was enough to give me a sense of the area. This and other parts of inner city Philly are struggling with issues of crime, decay, unemployment, drugs and neglect. It's a horrible cliché but police and ambulance sirens really were the soundtrack to my stay there. I cycled around to get a flavour of the area. Some of it actually was on the up but my antennae were always sharply tuned for trouble. This kind of constant looking over your shoulder lifestyle must be incredibly wearing for the residents.

After surviving four days it was thankfully time to research some affluence. The main character of my book would live with her family somewhere in the city's wealthier suburbs. Finding a place to stay in the semi-rural commuter belt was easier and way more relaxing.

My next hosts kindly filled me in on Philadelphia's smarter addresses. Among the places they mentioned was Bala Cynwyd, a name which could only be Welsh. It was, they said, very upmarket, home to some seriously wealthy and powerful people and part of Main Line. I could tell this last part was supposed to mean something to me. After pleading ignorance they explained that Main Line is one of the most prosperous parts of the whole of the USA. It rivals Westchester County and Fairfax County as a bastion of 'old money' and is incredibly well-heeled.

The unofficial sub-region took its name from the railroad built between Philadelphia, Pittsburgh and Harrisburg in the mid-19th century. Its construction allowed the rich to flee the inner city and set up home in the rolling hills and meadows bordered by the Schuylkill River, yet be within comfortable travel times to their businesses. They were pioneers of commuting.

My B&B owners also mentioned other areas of the Main Line, again with Welsh names. So the next morning I set off for a look. The towns are affluent but the surrounding country homes and estates are palatial. Long, leafy driveways lead to opulent mansions, many with huge parcels of land attached. The country roads hum with the sound of beautiful people driving even more beautiful cars. Everywhere is refinement, privilege and wealth.

When Philadelphia's elite originally pitched up in this rural idyll sitting on much of it were the Welsh. In the late 17th century William Penn, who established the Province of Pennsylvania, undertook to hand over 40,000 acres (160kms sq) of land west of the city to Welsh Quakers. Rather decent of him, there again Penn had just become the single largest private landholder in the world. King Charles II had given him a charter for 120,000kms sq of land to satisfy a debt to his father. The Welsh Tract or Welsh Barony, as it was also known, would be its own separate county with Welsh the official language of its local government. It would be a little bit of Wales in America.

The Welsh headed out there in large numbers and began to set up communities. But Penn's promise of self-governance never came to fruition. Parcels of nearby land had already been divvied up and a county structure put in place. It didn't include a separate Welsh entity. Despite the setback hamlets, villages and towns began to spring up and the Welsh Quakers gave them names from the old country including Bala Cynwyd, Lower Merion and Radnor. Penn favoured calling the whole state North Wales before being convinced to change his mind and name it Pennsylvania.

Another township with Welsh origins is Bryn Mawr, in English it means big hill. Fair to say it loses a little something in translation, a touch less poetic. Since 1885 it has been home to Bryn Mawr Arts College, one of the finest women's liberal arts establishments in the country. I came across it quite by accident, stopped my car and got out for a closer look at its breathtaking gothic buildings. There was also some post-modern rubbish but I ignored it.

The original constructions were based on the principles of Oxford and Cambridge Universities, Collegiate Gothic as it's known. Nine have been added to the National Register of Historic Buildings. It's the kind of old America you rarely glimpse. Magnificent, old and without a hint of the commercial edifices which scar so much of the country. It was grand, inspiring architecture and I could happily have stayed sitting there for hours taking it all in. But this being a women's only establishment I thought I might look like some kind of midde-aged pervert, so I got up and left.

Later I did some digging into the college's history. It turned out Katherine Hepburn was one of Bryn Mawr's most famous alumni. She later starred in the academy award-winning movie 'Philadelphia Story', quite apt for somebody educated in the city's suburbs. The movie was produced by Joseph Mankiewicz. Life is all joined up connections.

Before leaving Main Line I had a final idea. I opened up my iPad and punched in the words 'Main Line' and 'Rhyl' – the name of my old home town in north Wales. It was an unpretentious seaside resort which attracted working class families for beach holidays. I loved growing up there but through the 70s and 80s it was blighted by fighting between visiting mods, rockers, skinheads, hell's angels and any bad-ass looking for a dust-up. Those grim days were followed by a boom in cheap foreign holidays to exotic places with guaranteed sunshine. The tourists stopped going to Rhyl. Deprived of its key source of income, it went into free fall. For six years in a row one part of the town was officially classed as the most deprived area of Wales. In 2014 it finally managed to rise one place in the depressing league table.

In Main Line I was really hoping the old town had got some kind of foothold in this area of outstanding affluence. Disappointingly, my internet search found no town of that name. But there was a street. So off I excitedly went to gawp at an American road sign. Strange what our heritage does to us.

It didn't take long to find Rhyl Lane and even less time to walk its entire length. It occupies a small part of Bala Cynwyd, small but not insignificant. Its half dozen homes were grandly designed, most in Georgian style. Several were hidden behind imposing trees but one which was visible had immense, two-storey, colonnaded porticos for entrances. There weren't too many of those in my old street. This was a seriously wealthy little lane, it seemed thousands of miles and many light years away from my home town. I contemplated ringing a few doorbells to ask if they knew anything of their street name's heritage. But I decided unsolicited knocking followed by random questions was a stupid thing to do. There again, that pretty much sums up my early career as a journalist.

There are two more little gems that unquestionably confirm America in its status as a colony of Wales. Firstly, there are claims the Welsh warrior Madoc or Madog actually discovered America as far back as the late 12th century, that's 300 years before Columbus pitched up. Madoc and 100 followers supposedly set off in his boat to escape warfare raging in Wales – early Hell's Angels issues, I suspect. The settlers are said to have married Native Americans from which a separate tribe of "Welsh Indians" developed. The Mandan tribe has been named as the most likely candidate as they differed from their neighbours in appearance, language and culture.

Allegedly, one of the supporters of the theory was none other than Thomas Jefferson, the man who drew up the American Declaration of Independence. He was one of 16 signatories who claimed Welsh heritage, that's almost a third of all the men who signed.

Jefferson is often credited with encouraging research into the notion of 'Welsh Indians' but I have to say the evidence I've seen is open to interpretation.

The final gem I have for you is the 'fact' that a Welshman is currently in the White House. That's right, Barack Obama is another to have his ancestry traced back to the 'Land of Song'. Genealogists claim to have the 44th president nailed down as the great, great, great, great, great, great grandson of Margaret and Henry Perry from Anglesey in north Wales. Welcome to the clan Mr President. If you have a few million dollars of spare subsidies floating around there is a small seaside town in the land of your forefathers which would benefit from a hand out.

In the interest of accuracy I should point out genealogists have also traced Obama's roots back to Irish, Scottish, English, German and Kenyan ancestry. He is also linked to America's first recorded slave and allegedly on the other side to slave owners. This is the problem with the six degrees of separation rule. We're all linked together. There again it's comforting to think there might be some obscure, wealthy relative of mine out there potentially tittering their head off at this book and thinking about sending me a large cheque in appreciation. Go on, titter and send.

Footnote: Philly's original 'old money' Main Line elite have prospered but it's a different story for the Pennsylvania Railroad company which built the track.

From its foundation in 1846 the company grew massively into a corporate behemoth. By the first half of the 20th century it was the largest railroad in the country. The company acquired or merged with more than 800 other rail lines and controlled more than 10,500 miles of track.

At its peak it employed more than 250,000 workers and its budget was bigger than that of the American government. It reached its financial zenith by becoming the largest publicly traded corporation in the world. The business was the first to pay annual dividends to its stockholders for 100 consecutive years.

In 1968 it merged with rival New York Central Railroad to form the Penn Central Transportation Company. The new entity held a position of invincibility in the American railroad business. It was a monster of a corporation with no serious competitor and its assets were estimated at a staggering $4.5 billion. It was an unstoppable colossus.

Two years later it filed for bankruptcy.

The company's spectacular demise was the biggest corporate failure in American history. An estimated 100,000 creditors and an even bigger number of stockholders were affected when the company went belly-up. Management infighting, the growth of airlines, unprofitable routes, inflation and a whole lot of reasons were put forward for its implosion.

#

35

STARING DEATH IN THE FACE (PART 2)

Week 28; Swarthmore, Pennsylvania, USA; 34,120 kms travelled;
laundry $9 - 10 times the cost of Bali;
1 new undies missing ☹

There are some things in life which almost defy description. The driving of Emma Sulx (not quite her real name) is right at the top of the list.

The octogenarian is the mother of a friend of mine and had kindly invited me to stay for a few days. When I told my friend her mum had offered to pick me up from the railway station there were hints of motoring misdemeanours. When I asked for details all I got back was "you'll see", followed immediately by "good luck".

I'd dismissed it all as a little gentle mischief-making to put the wind up me. But as I walked out of the railway station I knew I might have underestimated what lay ahead.

A car was slewed diagonally across the road rendering the narrow street completely impassable. Puzzled drivers were queued up behind with surprising patience. They probably assumed there was some kind of problem. Nobody would just stop their car in the middle of the road at a crazy angle unless there was a serious issue. Would they?

I knew instinctively that this was my ride. I strode over, opened the back door, threw in my pack and climbed quickly into the front passenger seat. As I got in I took a nostalgic look around like an astronaut entering a space rocket, unsure whether this was their last living moment on earth.

"Hello Arthur. Lovely to see you."

"Hello Emma. Thank you so much for picking me up." Shameful really, my first words were a lie. I wasn't grateful in the least; fearful, tearful or reluctant would have all been nearer the truth.

"We'd better get going," I said to my kindly old friend. "There's traffic waiting."

"Oh, is there?"

She was blissfully ignorant. This, I was to discover, was her natural state behind the wheel of a car. Her natural position was even more alarming. She was low-slung in the seat with her face tilted up, her nose in the air and her hands almost up above her head to grip the steering wheel. Visibility over the dashboard would have been somewhere between impaired and non-existent.

Just down the road we stopped at a junction and the left indicator was flicked on. Emma looked around, took a hard turn on the wheel and off we went.

"How was your journey?"

I couldn't immediately answer. I had a vague feeling that something wasn't quite right.

"Er, um, fine, thank you.... fine," I eventually replied. I couldn't put my finger on it but something a little troubling was gnawing away.

I looked ahead into the distance at the oncoming traffic. Something just didn't make sense.

"Did you have any problem finding the right train?"

"Er, no. It was um, um.... "

Still the nagging feeling wouldn't go away.

Then in an awful rush my brain's self-preservation finally kicked in. It had frantically solved the problem - cars drive on the right in America. We were on the left! Seventy five metres ahead there was a vehicle coming straight at us.

"We need to be on the other side of the road Emma." It was said with a calm assurance which actually masked blind terror.

We moved to the right as the oncoming vehicle flashed and honked away.

"What was his problem?" Emma was completely unfazed.

I let out a low whine as a horrible thought struck me. I'd be staying with her for five long days. We were only in minute two and death had already been staring me right between my eyes.

A few miles later along mostly quiet roads we arrived at Emma's home, a lovely building in a tranquil, rural location. We pulled up outside her garage, the wooden doors wide open.

The right hand frame looked like it had been used as target practice by the American military. It was battered to hell, the telltale markings of a car's wing. A baton dangled limply from the main frame. I would repair it twice before I left.

Cautiously Emma turned the vehicle in and avoided contact with the door. A good start. A little ahead a rubber ball on a string was hanging from the rafters. It was there as a parking aid. Emma just had to drive up to the spot where her windscreen touched the ball and stop. That would leave her a couple of feet away from a small staircase which led up into the house.

We moved at a steady crawl, Emma's head even more angled as she peered over the steering wheel at the oncoming ball. Slowly, slowly she went, inch by careful inch. Mere fractions from the dangling aid, the car lurched violently forward, swiped the ball nonchalantly aside and smacked hard into the staircase. We'd arrived!

Over the next few days Emma, ever the generous hostess, showed me around the area. Her enthusiasm made a lie of her 80 something years. Her driving didn't. Near her home was a particularly notorious blind junction.

Moving out was an act of faith for every driver. The only technique to employ was to put the pedal to the metal and race off at ultimate acceleration. If anything came around the bend this was the best chance of avoiding being consigned to history. Emma, however, had a different approach. She felt that a dangerous bend required extreme caution. Each and every time we drove out we moved at snail pace. Anything coming around the corner would be on top of us in an instant. I tried repeatedly to encourage her to rev it up but the advice never sank in. My only resort was to turn my head in the opposite direction to the bend. That way I wouldn't be a witness to my own death.

"I hate this turning," she said with feeling.

"I hate it too." I replied. It was said with even greater passion.

Miraculously we kept getting away with it. But on the other side of town was a much busier road we had to turn across. Cars doing 50 miles an hour were charging past us from both directions. We waited and waited for a break in the traffic, low-slung Emma missed a couple of opportunities and waited some more. She looked to her left, then to her right and back intently left. There her eyes remained until eventually a very decent gap appeared. This time she went for it, floored the accelerator and out across the road we went.

Unfortunately, somewhere in this process it had slipped her mind that traffic was coming from the left AND the right. I screamed "STOP" and she hit the brakes just as a speeding vehicle raced past, its horn blaring.

"Where did he come from?" asked Emma. Excellent question.

The next day she took me for lunch at her golf club. Somehow she managed to avoid the car park altogether and we ended up on rough ground used by the greenkeepers.

"Can we park here do you think?" I diplomatically asked.

She eventually got us back to the car park and peeping over the dashboard spotted a space. After an unsuccessful 25 point manoeuvre there was a knock on the window. A young guy had been dispatched from the golf shop to offer a valet service they didn't normally provide. Emma gratefully accepted.

A pleasant lunch followed and as we contemplated leaving she had an idea, she would take me to see her old home. We drove out along manicured country lanes and past some fabulous houses.

"There it is," she said with delight.

I expected her to pull over onto the grass verge from where there was a perfectly good view. But Emma motored on and shortly turned into a drive. The first 30 metres were shared with another home before dividing into two separate entrances. We thankfully stopped short of large electric gates and from her sunken seat she told me of the house and her family's happy times there. A large group of Hispanic gardeners worked away in the grounds while looking suspiciously in our direction.

When her tales had all been told Emma began to reverse the car. We needed to go back ten metres, wheel left into the driveway of the neighbouring property and then head out to the road. It didn't go to plan. For some unfathomable reason after a few metres in reverse she turned to the right. There was a loud crunch and we came to a stop.

I got out to see the damage. Emma had clobbered into a temporary wooden fence which was now leaning at a perilous 45 degrees but just about still upright. It was impossible to know what it had done to the car as the vehicle already carried 101 previous scratches and scrapes. I went to Emma's window, told her to go forward and then back up but this time turn to the other side. All went well until I shouted to turn the wheel. Once more she opted for the wrong direction. Before words of warning could escape my lips she ploughed into the battered fence. This time she took no prisoners and the thing crumpled to the ground.

The gardeners decided it was time not to get involved in anything and they immediately averted their eyes and began frantically working away.

"You've hit the fence again," I told Emma.

"Oh dear," she said. "We better get out of here. You drive."

Thanks. If the cops turned up I'd look like the culprit. They'd never believe the innocent-looking old lady in the passenger seat was the crim. I'd been set up.

Fortunately we got out in a hurry and we were soon back on the road. Emma told me she was happy to resume driving but her offer fell on deaf ears.

On my final night she arranged for us to have dinner with an old friend of hers, a mover and shaker in the world of theatre. I made plenty of overtures about taking the wheel but all were declined and once again Emma was our pilot.

All went surprisingly well until we reached her friend's property. We turned into a long driveway, running along the left was immaculate hedgerow and to the right an impressive grass lawn. It was 30 metres wide and ran the entire length of the drive. It looked newly laid.

Her friend's house was a fabulous mansion with a huge gravelled turning and parking area in front. It would comfortably accommodate 20 vehicles. Somehow, Emma contrived to miss it, instead we veered off to the right and onto the lawn. Within moments her friend was out of the house and at the car. Breathlessly she confirmed the grass had recently been laid and she'd be grateful if we could get off it NOW. A slightly frazzled Emma duly obliged and we reached the safety of the parking area.

After an initially cool reception the incident was put aside. The three of us headed out for a pleasant restaurant meal and a lovely evening was had. At night's end we headed back to the house to drop off the old friend. Emma masterfully headed us up the driveway and as we said our farewells we were urged to exercise care on the return trip. Apparently the turfing had cost thousands and only recently settled in. Emma told her not to worry and down the driveway we headed. Unfortunately it was now pitch dark. The car headlights were plenty powerful but from deep down in her Formula One driving position Emma was having problems seeing anything other than blackness.

The sudden bumpiness of the ride should have told her we'd strayed off the drive and on to the hallowed turf but she was oblivious. When I informed her that her navigation was out she raised her head a little, still saw nothing and nonchalantly decided against any avoiding action, literally ploughing on across the new lawn. For the next 100 metres we churned up the gleaming greenery until reaching a tree line from where Emma expertly tacked to the right and eventually back to the drive.

All was quiet in the car as we reached the open gates. Emma eventually turned her head towards me. There was a slight look of guilt on her face.

"She sounded a little precious about that grass. Do you think she'll know it was us?"

I couldn't miss the word 'us', blame was clearly to be shared. I was once more an accessory to her crime.

She gave a little shrug, the merest hint of a naughty schoolgirl smile appeared on her lips, and out we turned onto the road.

#

36

KINDLER, GENTLER AMERICA

Week 29; Somewhere in the USA; 34,490 kms travelled;
nerves wrecked – nothing else matters

Emma's driving had been seared into my consciousness for its dazzlingly erratic quality but her kindness was equally memorable. She had been very generous, putting me up and showing me around. She'd also introduced me to interesting friends, including one of the country's former top ranked CIA officials. He was a fascinating man but unfortunately no state secrets escaped his lips.

Trying to pay for anything when out with Emma was tantamount to a declaration of war. She was by no means the first nor the last person in America to be so hospitable. A few weeks earlier when I was back in the UK visiting old friends, Andy and Sharon Riley, I'd mentioned my plan to spend a few days in Philly researching my book. By coincidence, Sharon's parents had some friends living just outside the city. They offered to try and put me in touch.

Sure enough, through phone calls and emails, contact was made and I met up with total strangers, Kate and Joel, at their home north of the city. They fed me, chauffeured me, entertained me and patiently answered 101 questions about the city. They were warm, kind and generous people. When they heard that I was staying in Kensington, the dodgy part of town, they insisted on driving me home. It was a long way from the suburbs but they were adamant. Joel, it turned out, was originally from the area and was all too aware of its subsequent decline and reputation. Wandering the streets at night was not something they were keen for me to do.

A few days later different people, same kindness. Courtesy of Airbnb I'd found a room at a home owned by Rebecca and Tim. Rebecca was headmistress of a school she founded for youngsters with substance abuse issues. Tim taught music and was a singer with the Opera Company of Philadelphia. They were fascinating people. I mentioned I was on the lookout for a swish ballroom as a setting for another scene from my crime book and they began to wrack their brains. The following morning they went off to work but continued making phone calls. Through a friend of a friend I was put in contact with the Union League of Philadelphia.

The League is a seriously prestigious private club. To quote its own website, the Union League 'is a shining jewel of history in a city defined by such treasure. The League has hosted US presidents, heads of state, industrialists, entertainers and dignitaries from around the globe and has proudly supported the American military in each conflict since the Civil War'.

Despite its private status I was invited to go and take a look. The League House is in the heart of the city occupying an entire block. Built in 1865, it's now listed on the National Historic Register. The elegant brick and brownstone facade is in French Renaissance style and gives a clue as to what awaits inside.

I was met by Jim Mundy, the Director of Education and Programming. When I explained what I was after he happily agreed to show me around.

The place is sumptuous, an elegant mix of leather, wood and polished marble. The carpets are deep and the air of refinement even deeper. There are fabulous artefacts and pieces of art at every turn. Its members, drawn from the city's movers and shakers, enjoy access to a 25,000 volume library, three restaurants, lounges, cigar room, gymnasium, ballroom and sleeping rooms. Services include a barber shop, personal trainers and a massage parlour.

I have to admit I wouldn't have been looking my best. After months of living out of a backpack something well short of smart casual was the best I could manage. When I say 'well short' it is a rare case of understatement. The League's dress code essentially boiled down to jacket and tie. Nobody there, neither staff nor member, had a hair out of place. Despite my lack of grooming Jim showed me around for a good hour. He was generous with his time and his expertise and even presented me with a hardback book on the club's history.

A few days later I went to Washington and met up with Mark, an old friend from BBC days. He mentioned a dinner invitation at a friend of a friend's place near Middleburg, Virginia. It's horse country a couple of hours outside the capital. He made a quick phone call and I was soon added to the guest list.

I'm not sure if socialite was the right label for the hostess, Cathy, but it wouldn't be too far off the mark. Highly successful in her own right she and her wealthy husband owned a four story home in Georgetown, historic Washington, in addition to the sprawling place near Middleburg. Cathy was clearly au fait with the upper echelons of American society. But once again, dressed in a second hand charity shop shirt and some un-ironed trousers, I was welcomed with warmth and generosity. The house was fabulous, the food and wine flowed and there was an insistence that we stay the night. It was a kind gesture, although to be honest Cathy wasn't exactly short of a few beds. I could have happily slept in the fireplace, it dwarfed many rooms I'd stayed in on my travels.

These are just snapshots of a few of the kind and friendly people I met. It was all so far removed from the unwelcoming and aggressive introduction to the country. However, this schism in attitudes is nothing new. It was one of the main issues on the mind of George Bush Snr in his presidential nomination acceptance speech back in 1988. Addressing the Republican convention he told the American people he wanted them to be '… a kinder and gentler nation'. It was a theme he later revisited when he urged the country's families to be '… a lot more like the Waltons and a lot less like the Simpsons'.

A host of political and business leaders from Dick Cheney to Donald Trump publicly lampooned the ideas at one time or another. Trump famously declared, 'I think if this country gets any kinder or gentler it's literally going to cease to exist'.

The extremes between the soft-centred, schmaltzy, mom's Apple pie America and the tough as hell, win at all costs America is just one of a mass of complex contradictions which define the place.

As a country it is more patriotically devoted to itself and its ideals than anywhere else I've been. At the same time it's in the middle of an ugly, internecine war. Politically it's tearing itself apart. There is visible hatred and contempt in politics and society. Consensus is breaking down.

Abroad, its place in the world has been diminished, its reputation post Iraq War often down in the gutter as an aggressive bully throwing its weight around. But that now appears to be changing. According to polling analysis from the non-partisan Pew Centre the view of the US across much of the world is generally improving. Its stance against ISIS is generally very favourably received as a defence against extremism. It's often the case that when the world gets scared it usually looks to the USA. From bully to a benevolent and reliable big brother.

It all kind of sums up the country. It's full of incongruities and pretty much unfathomable because in reality there really is no one America. So don't try and put it or its people in a pigeonhole, they just don't fit. And for all of its faults when the world's policeman finally fades from its sole superpower status we will miss it. The next lot will be way worse.

#

37

THE WORLD'S MOST BIZARRE CAPITAL?

Week 31; Naypidaw, Myanmar (Burma);
49,110 kms travelled - equivalent to one and a quarter times around the globe;
wonder socks not even worn out

I didn't need to toss a coin at the end of my American jaunt, I knew where I wanted to go. As unplanned and spontaneous as most of my travel was I'd picked up lots of stories about destinations that I 'mustn't miss'. One place that other travellers kept frothing over was Myanmar - Burma in old currency. It was a long, long way away but Southeast Asia also had the advantage of still being hot. And so I took a deep breath and steeled myself for an epic journey.

From the US capital Washington DC I headed back to London. After several days meeting up again with friends and family I flew on to Bangkok, my third capital city in a week. I spent a short time there reprocessing my brain to cope with the 11 hour time difference and did the paperwork for my onward visa. A short break for R&R and I was heading to my fourth capital in ten days, the Burmese city of....

If your geography isn't quite up to scratch you're probably wondering where the hell I was. If you paid attention in class you're probably thinking Rangoon, or Yangon, as it's now known. However, if your international politics is one step ahead of your geography you are a very well informed rarity, take a deserved bow.

Who's ever heard of Naypidaw? But if you need confirmation just search down Wikipedia's list of world capitals and there it takes its place. That's about the last connection it has with most major metropolises. This place is different.

Three thirty pm is typically about 60 minutes before the start of the dreaded rush hour in most major cities around the world. Gridlock time would be fast approaching. In Myanmar's capital Naypidaw things are.... a little different.

I stood at the edge of a monster highway, glanced to my left, sauntered out to the third lane and casually sat down. Death would be certain in most cities. Here, the biggest risk was scorch marks on my bottom from the baking hot road surface.

After sixty traffic-free seconds I got up and wandered across seven more lanes to the central reservation. I poked my head through the bushes and saw the exactly the same thing on the other side.... nothing.

I exaggerate, but only a little. For a mile or so I could see five or six motorbikes. And that's all. Twenty lanes of emptiness. And this in the very heart of the capital city. But to be honest Naypidaw doesn't have a heart. And it has absolutely no soul either. In fact, there's not much that it does have. There are few people, a sprinkling of shops, no tourists nor taxis. The only way to get around was to pay for a ride on the back of a motorbike.

Oddly, it's not short of hotels. There are lots of them, all shiny and new. Each and every one situated in the dedicated hotel zone. That's how it works here. Everything in its own area. There's a commercial zone, although it's woefully short of businesses and offices, a ministries zone, a military zone and a zone where the generals live. Civilians, mostly government workers, live in the residential zone. The rooftops of their apartment blocks are colour coordinated depending on which ministry employs them. It is very Orwellian, 1984 come to life.

The zones are spread over a huge area, nothing is within walking distance. They are linked by excellent roads, the only decent ones in the country. They cross every few miles and at each intersection is an imposing security box and armed policemen. Nobody moves in

Naypidaw without being noticed. But that's not such a big deal, there's nobody to notice anyway.

The city didn't even exist until 2005. Yangon was the country's pre-eminent city, no doubt about it. But after years of secrecy the people woke one day to an announcement that a new capital city had been built. It was called Nay Pi Taw, or Naypidaw, which translates grandiosely as Royal Capital. Situated half way between Yangon and Mandalay it cost an estimated four BILLION dollars to construct. In such a dirt poor country this money would have transformed the country's desperate health, education and transport infrastructure. Here it transformed the life of the military, or at least its upper echelons.

The exact reasons the generals built the new city are unknown. But rumours are rife, just take your pick. It's easier to defend against foreign invasion; it's designed to prevent a popular uprising; an astrologer told the generals it would be the smart thing to do.

Whatever the real reason it's clear Naypidaw is an act of self-love and self-preservation on an epic scale. A monument to the madness of military men who became rich and paranoid on the broken backs of their countrymen.

After decades of abusive control reform is slowly being introduced. If the people ever truly wrest power from the army this will be a safe haven for the men in uniform. It is in essence their folly of fear.

Naypidaw does have two or three tourist sites - an average of about one attraction for every tourist. There's a zoo and a safari park, I went to neither.

The Uppatasanti Pagoda is the pick of the tourism spots. It dominates the skylines for miles. It is just 30 centimetres shorter than Shwedagon, Yangon's sacred and world-renowned Buddhist monument. Lifts and staircases are needed to reach the hollowed out entrance. It is immense. Amazingly, it was said to have been personally paid for by Than Shwe, the country's former military dictator. Quite how he could have afforded it on the pay of a humble general, I really don't know. Perhaps he came up on the horses.

In December 2013 the city did have a moment in the international spotlight when it hosted the Southeast Asian games. New stadia and sports halls were built, foreign media and tourists came to town. However, the hotels are now back to empty, the streets deserted and the Uppatasanti Pagoda is once again quiet.

Across the road from the complex is another 'tourist attraction'. Several white elephants are brought out each day to amuse a handful of spectators. In Myanmar they are considered lucky and a sign of justice and power. When the British were here they came up with an alternative definition of a white elephant - something that is excessively expensive in proportion to its usefulness. That's as close to an accurate definition of Naypidaw as you can possibly get.

#

38

THE SEARCH FOR THE SOUND OF SILENCE

Week 32; Bagan, Myanmar; 49,620 kms travelled;
16 countries visited; first electro-bike;

Silence, solitude and sunset. A rare and elusive alchemy. In the wondrous and mystical setting of ancient Bagan, they formed a soothing balm for my soul.

The world's largest collection of stupas and pagodas sprinkled the skyline below and beyond me. Tiny honeycombs and vast temples stood side by side and took their silent and timeless place.

All around the light was being gently smothered by the slow, smooth sinking of the sun. Colours changed from moment to moment and for as far as the eye could see and the ear could hear stillness and silence reigned.

It was a time and a place to feel a deep calm and peace. A moment to glimpse deep within myself.

And then I heard them. Moments later I saw them. From nowhere a coach had arrived, disgorged its tourists and they were hurriedly rampaging towards me.

My perfect peace was shattered as they huffed and puffed into the temple. Their guide led them through the darkness and up the narrow stone staircase. Within seconds a tidal wave of tourism smashed through my wall of solitude. They were a mass of loud, excited chatter, whirling cameras, coughs and splutters. "It's amazing," they screamed to themselves and each other. "Stunning. Wonderful".

For me it was close to heartbreaking. I couldn't stop there knowing what a rare and elusive moment had been lost. I had just 25 minutes or so until the sun finally settled. But this was a place that offered choices.

Bagan is one of the world's great architectural sites. A treasure trove of around 2,200 monuments spread over 26 square miles. They stand, lean and in many cases decay, on a vast, dry plain framed by a bend in the fabled Irrawaddy River.

Serious building work began in the eleventh century. It continued for 250 years by when 11,000 stupas and temples had been constructed. All part of the Buddhist belief that such devotion on earth builds credit for what follows.

But the marauding hordes of Kubla Khan's army wrought havoc in the area and thousands were obliterated. Earthquakes great and small have continued the destruction ever since. Today Bagan is awe-inspiring, eight centuries ago it would have been utterly beyond words.

A few days are needed to tour the sites. Many people go by horse and trap, plenty more cycle. Others, like me, go on electro bikes. Stately but a little faster so more ground could be covered.

I spent three days armed with a vague map of the 'highlights'. There were some vast and hugely impressive structures that towered up to the sky. But often it was the small, intimate temples that surprised. Inside each was a Buddha but sometimes there were also fabulous frescos and carvings. Tourists always visit the big pagodas but with so many monuments to choose from the smaller sites are mostly your very own to explore.

I was now in a race against time to recover my alone time. I set off, desperate to rediscover peace and quiet, to watch the sun set in silence. I passed many small stupas but they were only single storey. Height is crucial to really appreciate Bagan's vast scope.

I was getting a little desperate as the light deserted me.... and then I spied it. A large pagoda several storeys high stood surrounded by fields, its access marred by overgrown scrub. It would be enough to deter most people but on I ploughed. The electro bike was buffeted by the hard, dried clay surface. It made loud, complaining and discouraging noises but it got me through.

The temple's interior was a still, murky darkness. I searched for steps and after one and a half full circuits my torch illuminated the entrance of a stone staircase. It was raised a few feet above the ground. I made the narrow climb under a low ceiling and two storeys later I emerged into the fading light.

A vast panorama of stupas and temples stretched for as far as I could see. And minutes later, when the sun's rays left the day behind, I sat alone. Just me, the beauty of planet Earth and a warm, comforting blanket of silence.

#

Evenings in Bagan were also a fairly sedate affair. I trawled quietly up and down the main street on my electro bike looking for a place to eat dinner. There were a fair few choices but then I had a thought. I headed for the banks of the Irrawaddy River, one of the most fabled waterways in Southeast Asia. Its name is forever linked with Rudyard Kipling who wrote the poem 'Mandalay'. Three verses were later set to music and the piece renamed 'The Road To Mandalay'. The road in question was actually the Irrawaddy River. British soldiers gave it the nickname as it was the quickest transport route through the country.

I soon found a restaurant, most tables were outside, situated to take in the views of the river. A waiter asked where I wanted to sit and then escorted me to a prime spot. I had the run of the place, there was only one group of four people, the other 30 tables were completely empty. I was given a menu and placed my drinks order. A gin and tonic quickly arrived and was followed a few minutes later by a light starter.

Half an hour after I'd arrived I was contemplating my main course. But when the waiter next turned up he wasn't carrying any food.

"Would you mind changing tables please?"

"Sorry. Change tables?"

I'd heard him perfectly but didn't quite believe my ears.

"Yes. Please let us take you to another table."

"Why?"

"This table is reserved."

"Reserved? The restaurant is empty apart from the table over there. Anyway, you showed me to this table. You brought my drink here and my salad. Didn't you know it was reserved?"

"Sorry but it's reserved. We have another table for you. I'll take your drink for you."

I wasn't overly happy but I'd been travelling many months by now and it took a lot to rile me. I assumed somebody had booked the table for its plum view across the Irrawaddy.

I got out of the seat and followed the waiter. Two footsteps later I'd arrived. It was the very next table, an exact replica. I could almost touch the seat I'd just vacated.

The rest of the evening passed in mild disbelief but without further incident. I ate my dinner and paid my bill. As I left I looked around the restaurant. Nobody else had arrived during the course of the night and my original table stood empty.

What I haven't mentioned was that it was pitch black, and it had been even before I'd arrived. The Irrawaddy was out there somewhere but neither I nor anybody else would have any kind of view. It was impossible to see the near riverbank never mind the far one. Whoever had reserved my table would have a vision of total blackness.

The following evening brought more quirkiness. It was a Sunday evening, which meant there was a good chance of an English Premier League football match on TV. Throughout Southeast Asia the EPL is followed with fanatical devotion. If I wasn't with people or travelling I'd seek out a bar to watch a game, it was a good way to pass the time and entertaining to watch the fans. I fired up the electro bike and once again headed for the main street. I spotted a coffee shop cum cafe with seats inside and out and a fair size television. Nobody spoke any English but they managed to work out I was after coffee and footie.

After 15 minutes the staff called everybody inside and about 60 of us crammed around the TV. Temporary screens were put up behind us so nobody passing by could see what was happening. In Myanmar there are government restrictions on late night entertainment. This was to be my first ever night-time coffee shop lock-in. Oddly, the owner didn't even try and sell any drinks to his captive audience.

During the game the fans were glued to the TV but fairly muted. Gentle murmurs were the stock reaction to major incidents. Half an hour in a goal was scored and I jumped up in my seat and let out a hearty "Yesssss". All around was the sound of silence. It was as quiet as the temple at sunset. Noise, it turned out, was not welcome as it would draw attention to our 'lock-in' and we shouldn't have been out so late.

For the rest of the game I reverted to a few very muted "yups" or the locals' preference for whispered "ooohs". They were clearly happy I'd grasped the need for quiet and wasn't going to get them all jailed for late night exuberance. My downplayed enthusiasm at big moments in the game was greeted by vigorous nods of their heads in my direction. It was their attempt at saying 'belter of a game and thanks for not being such an idiot foreigner anymore'.

At half time I stood up and cast an eye over my fellow spectators. I was the only non-Burmese, 50 or so locals made up the majority. Off to one side, dressed in maroon coloured robes, were eight or nine monks. They ranged from young to ancient. It was hard to discern any great enthusiasm for proceedings but they stayed to the end.

At the conclusion the crowd got what it wanted, a Manchester United win. On the final whistle there were lots of smiles and a surge of supporters towards me. Almost every man and boy in the cafe seemed to want to shake my hand. I was so carried away with my new iconic soccer status that I shared a few incisive comments on the game. They were all wasted, of course, nobody spoke my language. The locals were spared my pompous post match analysis.

After the handshakes the screens were removed and we piled quietly onto the streets, my first ever coffee shop lock-in was over and I didn't even have so much as a caffeine high.

#

39

SORE BUMS AND SOARING ROCKETS

Week 33; Taunggyi, Myanmar; 50,020 kms travelled;
20 flights — why oh why wasn't it 21?

I was in need of a little help from my trusty coin. For once the destination was decided but I couldn't make up my mind on transport. I was heading from Mandalay to Inle Lake and there were a couple of options. The two alternatives were a simple 40 minute flight or a seven or eight hour road trip. The lazy side of my brain (pretty much most of it, I suspect) was all for taking it easy. My heart was pretty much on board with the idea as well. But some small part of me felt the need to see more of Myanmar's spectacular scenery. Despite my best instincts up spun the coin and, predictably, out went the flight.

I was tempted to change the rules to best of three, a sure sign that a large chunk of me was decidedly unenthusiastic about a lengthy road journey. However, I grudgingly accepted the decision.

I asked around and soon found a couple of guys interested in sharing a taxi. Their plan was to travel to Inle, drop off their backpacks then head a further hour into the hills to see the Taunggyi balloon fireworks festival. I'd never heard of it and fireworks and balloons sounded an insane and incendiary cocktail to me. I told them to count me in. Despite the unappetising eight hour journey ahead I let them know I was eager to hit the road.

This turned out to be a very poor choice of words. One of the guy's mates had hit the road a few days earlier, literally and painfully. The pair had hired powerful motorbikes in Mandalay and set out for Inle. A few miles out of town his machine had seized up at high speed catapulting him over the handlebars. He had broken bones and would be holed up in the city for weeks. His travel insurance was invalidated as he'd been motorbiking so he'd have to wait around until he'd regained some mobility. Only then would he be able to get out of the country and off to better medical facilities. His companion had done the decent thing by him but after a few days nursing and waiting-on he'd been keen to get moving again. This time he was happy to be in a car.

The mountains of Myanmar are poetically dramatic and the lowlands a lush mixture of jungled exoticism. But a sore arse is a sore arse and after six hours in the back of a car battered buttocks leave a much bigger impression than nature's beauty. Oh how I salivated over the 40 minute flight my coin toss had rejected. Not for the first time I threatened to chuck it away.

When we finally arrived at Inle Lake my companions and I went our separate ways to check in to our respective guesthouses. We all met up an hour later for the second part of the journey to the Taunggyi Festival. At least three of us did, the driver had disappeared. It took another hour to track him down and then some hard-bargaining and extra cash was needed to get him to carry on. All too soon his reluctance became understandable. He'd obviously known what to expect.

The one hour journey took four times that. The road up the 4,712 feet mountain was entirely gridlocked, we seemed to stop at each and every foot of elevation. We were all running low on reserves of patience but the driver's finally hit empty and he mutinied. As we sat stuck solid in the jam he hailed some nearby locals. When he found one of them spoke English he told him to inform us that he wasn't going another inch. We had a revolt on our hands and there was nothing we could do about it. In the end we got out, walked, thumbed when the traffic moved and immediately sat idle again the moment somebody picked us up.

It was a nightmare. Our taxi ride from Mandalay took us 13 hours, thank heavens it wasn't metered. But it turned out to be worth every second of the journey to witness the unique event that is the Taunggyi festival.

When we arrived 100,000 people were already cocooned in chaos. The number could have been even greater, the chaos couldn't. However, high above, an elegant 15-metre giant balloon decorated with a smiling Buddha was rising at a stately pace towards the heavens. It was a majestic sight. When it reached a couple of hundred metres off the ground Buddha suddenly unleashed a battery of fireworks. The night sky was lost in a violent storm of light and sound. Rockets raced outwards and upwards from a trailing basket. Flashes flared and died in its wake and piercing explosions echoed around us.

Down on the ground dozens of young men from the launch team began a frenzied celebration. They chanted and jumped and banged drums as if their very lives depended on it. This was the highlight of their year and it had gone flawlessly.

Taunggyi Balloon Festival is unique, there really is nothing else quite like it in Myanmar. The festival is a week-long visual spectacular seemingly almost entirely liberated from rules and regulations. Foreign tourists are also conspicuously absent. I counted two dozen at most. For those who made the journey there was a massive outpouring of goodwill. My two friends and I were feted like rock stars. There were dozens of handshakes and countless requests to pose for photographs. My younger friends may have been the centre of attraction for those below a certain age but I was holding up the George Clooney end of the spectrum pretty damn well.

Put the festival on your bucket list. But perhaps not too high. It can get a little hairy, things do go wrong. On the final night (I wasn't there) a balloon climbed fifty metres into the air, caught fire, stalled and plunged to the ground. Its cargo of fireworks spitting out lethal spears of rockets into the fleeing crowd. There were injuries, I don't know how many or how serious. A few years ago 200 people were reportedly hurt when a balloon showered them with falling fire debris.

Despite the hazards the festival is massively popular. People travel from across Myanmar to Taunggyi, capital of the Shan state. The event takes place around full moon in October or November. It marks the Buddhist celebration of Tazaungdaing.

The daytime festival is a fun and comparatively sedate affair. Towns and villages compete for the best designed balloon which mostly take the shape of cartoon animals. At night the flavour changes. Bars get louder, young men rowdier, huge conga lines cut through the throng. Gambling gets serious. Guys roaming around with mobile tattooing machines do good, if unhygienic business. Ancient funfair rides thrill adolescents and the aged alike. The Ferris wheel is powered by brave, fit, young guys who run on the giant spokes like mice in a wheel.

Then there is the main event. Villages and towns compete to build and launch the best balloon. People can often spend several months creating and crafting their dirigibles. They're judged on design, fireworks and height achieved. Balloons are built to soar extremely high.

Small candles in colourful lanterns are often painstakingly attached to the exterior skin or attached by ropes to swing under the balloons. As they rise some jettison scores of colourful little candles with tiny parachutes. It is mesmerising to watch them fill the night sky as they gently sway to and fro while falling to earth.

Most dramatic of all are the fireworks balloons. A team is divided into three groups. One brings in the folded canopy, another is responsible for a huge basket laced with rockets and thunder flashes. The third, the fire-starters, enter with huge flaming wooden torches. It is chaotic and in the confusion it's easy to get past the ropes and right into the thick of it. I easily skipped the ropes and even helped launch one.

The canopies are made of cloth and paper and supported by bamboo frames. Flameproof they most certainly are not. To get them airborne the fire-starters crawl under the canopies which are held aloft by their friends. The flames are inches away from turning the balloon into a fireball. When they finally struggle to the centre hot air from their torches inflates the canopy. Another team then attaches the firework basket to the frame. A fuse is lit and the balloon launched.

There are false starts but mostly they make slow and steady ascents. A few hundred feet off the ground the spectacle really begins. As the fuse burns to its critical point rockets race into the dark. The night skies explode with showers of bright and colourful light. It is completely low tech, there's not a computer in sight, yet it is fabulously choreographed. As the balloons climb the pyrotechnics continue for 15 to 20 minutes.

However, things do go wrong. Launch teams are mostly young men loaded with enthusiasm and testosterone. However, what they have in bravado they lack in fire safety. It is entirely absent from the whole affair.

Fortunately on my night it was chaotic but it went well enough. We finally caved in to exhaustion at 1.30 in the morning. The show would continue for another hour or two. We had a weary walk of 25 minutes to get to a minibus we'd seconded and traffic was yet again at a standstill. Fortunately our driver took us a different route and we were soon moving well.

All the more disappointing when we had a puncture a mere 500 metres later. The spare, of course, was flat. It added another torturous 30 minutes to an impossibly long day. We arrived back at our Inle Lake guesthouses at 3.15 am.

Sometimes the world makes you work to see its wonders. But the balloon festival really did put a rocket up my enthusiasm.

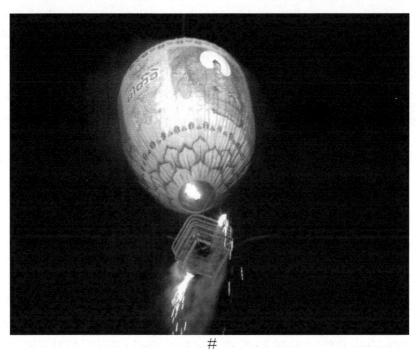

#

40

THE ROAD TO HELL (PART 1)

Week 34; Kyaikto, Myanmar; 50,560 kms travelled;
1st food poisoning - last food poisoning?
1 month-old thongs broken, now using 6th pair

We were being tossed around in a tempest, rag dolls in a storm. Myself and 50 pilgrims clinging on for dear life. I looked at the young boy next to me, his head was bowed low. My heart went out to him, 'Hang on, be strong, this will soon be over. Just don't throw up.'

As if he heard my thoughts he flicked his head up and there on his face was a smile. He was fine. I, on the other hand, was most definitely not. My stomach was churning and the colour in my cheeks was draining. My discomfort levels were off the charts and my self-pity registered even higher.

Just at that point we were thrown violently to our left and up in the air, moments later we were whipped back to the right. For the umpteenth time in 20 minutes I wondered what the hell I was doing there. The answer brought me no comfort. I was on my way to look at a rock!

Of course it was a little grander than that. This rock was special. The Golden Rock, or Kyaikto Pagoda as it's properly known, is one of Myanmar's most sacred sites, an absolute must for Buddhist pilgrims. It is a small pagoda built on a colossal rock perched at a precarious angle on a solid granite cliff. A lock of Buddha's hair is said to be all that holds it in place.

Right now the only thing holding my breakfast in place was the worry of projectile vomiting over half a dozen pilgrims sat tightly around me.

The Golden Rock sits atop a high, steep hill. There are two ways up. Walking is estimated to take five hours, the other option 45 minutes. I choose the path of least resistance, which is a fancy way of saying I took the easy way out. Or so I thought.

The 'bus station' was overflowing with pilgrims. 'Bus' is of course a misnomer. What they were all clamouring to board were small open-backed trucks. I joined a queue and climbed several steps to take my place on one of half a dozen benches. I was in the centre and packed in tighter than a winter Olympian's lunchbox.

I expected a gentle ascent. It didn't happen. The truck raced up the rough mountain track. It twisted and turned at breakneck speed. Mostly we headed uphill but now and then we plunged perilously fast downhill. Sat in the middle of the truck I could see nothing. After 45 minutes and at the point of reacquainting myself with my breakfast we arrived.

The rock was mesmerizing. It's about 7.6 metres in height (25ft) and the pagoda on top of it the same again. Over the years they've been decorated in gold leaf and pilgrims are constantly adding more and more layers. Monks and men pray at the rock face, women aren't allowed across the gantry.

How the rock defies gravity and stays where it does is beyond me. The tiniest sliver sits at a precarious angle on the cliff face. It has an overhang of half of its length.

The rock is said to have come from the bottom of the ocean through the combination of a hermit, a king and a serpent dragon princess. The boat used to transport it turned to stone and is situated 300 metres away - it too is revered.

There were thousands of people at the summit. Pilgrims massively outnumbered tourists, many make the trip annually. The elderly are carried in litters, there are no roads on the mountain top.

There are, however, a couple of hotels and dozens of restaurants and shops. There is some crass commercialism up there but more to my liking were some fabulous walks and views.

It was all blissfully distracting from what lay ahead, the return journey down the mountain. Catastrophe awaited as I had by now rediscovered my appetite and was weighed down by a heavy Myanmar lunch. The country is undisputedly bottom of the league for food in Southeast Asia. Everything is saturated in oil, flavour is even less in evidence than democracy.

Fortunately, I'd heard that foreigners could pay $3US to ride in the truck's cab. But an equal measure of bargaining and begging didn't do the trick. The cab was full I was told ad nauseum.... which sounded uncannily like where my stomach would soon be heading.

Luckily I had been in the region long enough to understand that "No" means "Absolutely No".... until a bribe is paid. I handed the driver an extra dollar and was welcomed into the truck's VIP area, along with seven Singaporeans. It was potentially a world record for a small truck cab.

In the tiny space arms and legs were flailing around but I concentrated on the road ahead and sucked on some delicious sugary sweets. My lunch stayed comfortably where it belonged. Comfort being a relative term, obviously.

The following day was lunch free and in fact food free. I'd eaten something on the mountain which didn't meet with my stomach's approval nor probably any food hygiene inspector's. It was, thankfully, a comparatively mild dose of poisoning and within 36 hours I was fine.

Not eating was actually something to put down in the plus column, Myanmar's food was the worst I came across on my travels so I didn't feel like I was missing out.

There was another unexpected plus. My visa was running out and having been holed up while heaving up I was running out of time to head further south. I aborted my plan and turned north back to Yangon and an unexpected piece of magic.

#

41

DRIVING A TRAIN IN MYANMAR

Week 35; Yangon, Myanmar; on an early lookout for Santa;
Miracle On 35th Week

CHRISTMAS PROLOGUE

When I was a little boy my sister, Avril, and I would write letters to Santa Claus. They were really just lists of the sackful of toys and games we feverishly hoped to receive as presents. A week or so before Christmas Day we'd send them up the chimney to ride a hot air trail all the way to the North Pole.

Father Christmas never failed us.

But some years I had special requests for Santa. These were secrets between the two of us and were never written down. They were about much more than mere toys. These were dreams.

For a couple of years or so I silently pleaded with Santa to fix it so I could drive a train. It didn't happen. The closest I got was when the real life Santa, my dad, a railwayman, got me on to the footplate of a steam engine as it stood at the station. It was good enough.

As I grew up I also grew out of my secret conversations with the man in the bright red tunic. But now and again, in an idle moment, the wishes still return and fill a quiet daydream.

And then in mid-December Father Christmas showed up. Was he a little early this year or was he about 45 years late? I'm not quite sure. Either way it's not important. All that matters is that the magical man from the North Pole finally made a little boy's silent wish come true.

The following story is dedicated to the memory of my dad, the real life Santa, who passed away just before Christmas 1998. He gave me a passion for life.... and trains.

DRIVING A TRAIN IN MYANMAR

With a sharp tug on the wheel and an easing of the brakes the driver sends the train inching away from the station. Slowly, with concentrated deliberation, he takes the engine up through the gears. First, second, third and fourth all quickly gone with short clicks of the wheel.

He has one eye on the gauges, pressure and revs are both fine. The other eye intently surveys the track ahead. The engine strains a little, it's getting on in years and its days of top speed are long gone. But it's still a sturdy and reliable workhorse and today it comfortably pulls seven carriages with 400 or so passengers. From the rear they hear excited and repeated bursts from the horn, otherwise they are blissfully ignorant of what is going on up front. They are unaware that a boyhood dream is being realized. They don't know that I am DRIVING THE TRAIN.

Lifelong dreams, if they're met at all, rarely come cost-free. Mine certainly didn't. But I have to say, it was probably the best one dollar I ever spent. That's the fee foreigners pay for riding the Circular Train around Yangon, formerly Rangoon. It doesn't feature in the world's great railway journeys but it's a wonderful ringside seat into the city, its rhythms and the people who call it home.

The railway, built by the British in 1954, does a full circle around the sprawling city and its surrounds. The journey is almost 46 kilometres and the train stops at 39 stations.

Foreigners are usually directed to the rear carriage - quite often a cut above the others. Hard plastic or wooden benches run down either side. Outside, the city is there for all to see. The first section of the anti-clockwise trip is voyeurism on poverty, grim shanties and slums hustle in close to the line. People live right on the trackside. They even put their washing out to dry between the rails. But the worst of Yangon soon gives way to a more rural backdrop.

After 20 minutes, when the train made one of its frequent stops, I jumped off and headed for another compartment where the locals sat and stood. I was welcomed as a rare surprise and was met by huge smiles. People made room for me or came over to try some English. Girls giggled, old ladies smiled. Young boys followed me as I got off and on at different stations to move further up the train.

The circular train is the cheapest way for the people to move around the city. It's also the most convenient, Yangon's roads are often gridlocked. They use it for travel, transport, trading, business and a whole lot more. On board people carry furniture, huge sacks of vegetables, electrical equipment, bundles of brushes, live chickens. When it comes to cargo nothing is off-limits. It's also grocer cum restaurant. People get off and on with huge trays of food to sell. One man was cooking in the middle of one compartment.

In another, without a word exchanged, the man next to me put his hand on my leg and gently pressed. After a moment he started stroking it. I was a little concerned. Was this a local custom on the circular train?

When his hand moved to my thigh I was startled and on the point of violent self-defence. But the smiling faces of other passengers suggested there was no ill intent. I finally worked out he was a masseur and this is where he worked. This was his salon. I paid him a dollar and moved on.

In every carriage it was the same, more amazement on my arrival, immediately followed by beaming faces. Finally I ran out of compartments and on the spur of the moment made a bold decision.

At the next stop I jumped off and ran alongside the engine. I shouted at the engineer as he leant out of the window.

He was clearly stunned by the sight of a shouting foreigner and he couldn't grasp what I was after. The train began to move and as the big wheels turned I resorted to sign language. It did the trick and he realized I wanted to come on board. He made frantic 'hurry, hurry' gestures as I tried to haul myself up the enormous gaps between the steps. As the train gathered speed I finally managed to scramble on. The rest of the crew was equally amazed at the foreigner in their midst but they made me instantly at home.

It was incredibly exciting to be up front after all these years. I joyfully lapped it all up. After 20 minutes of close study I took a deep breath and went for broke on my boyhood dream. In exaggerated sign language I asked if I could drive. There was a hesitant look of doubt on the driver's face, we were clearly in unchartered waters here. But then amazingly he got up, stood back and waved me into his seat. A few quick lessons later I found myself in control of a railway engine.

Like a naughty schoolboy I fulfilled another dream and flogged the horn to death. The crew smiled widely. Top speed was pretty relaxed, the track wasn't up to breakneck. Ahead of me it buckled and bent alarmingly. But the sheer thrill of it all wasn't dependent on speed.

As a station approached the driver gave me more voice and sign commands. With his prompting I managed to slow the engine down. The people lining the track and the platform suddenly noticed the new driver. All my Christmases and all of theirs seemed to have come at once and there was delirium inside and outside the cab. Wisely they scattered off the rails ahead.

I admit to taking us in a little fast but the driver gripped my hand on the air brakes and we came to a stop. With times at stations kept to a bare minimum I was quickly prepped on the starting procedure and seconds later I inched the train slowly out and up through the gears.

I drove the engine to the next station and, exhausted by exhilaration, made my grateful leave of the driver's seat. My dream had moved from fantasy to fact and I spent the rest of the ride in a Burmese daze.

The little boy inside of me contentedly relinquished a dream and on the gentle breeze I'm sure I caught the sound of laughter from a dearly missed old railwayman.

#

42

CHRISTMAS WITH THE SISTERS OF MERCY

Week 36; Khao Lak, Thailand; 55,470 kms travelled;
29 flights; too many minibus journeys; 100 beds

For the next few weeks it was a case of tossing coins and dodging storms - or at least forecast storms - they never actually arrived. I headed from Yangon to Bangkok. There, with various options available, my trusty Bali coin sent me on a lengthy trip down to Koh Mak - a lovely little island off the east coast.

I would have kept tossing the coin but my soon-to-be-expiring Thai visa took the decision out of my hands. I made a circuitous journey back to Bangkok, had a close encounter with death in a minibus, and flew straight down to Singapore on a visa run. After one night I planned to head back to somewhere in Thailand. With a newly minted visa in my hand I looked down a list of flights, sent the coin on its way and next thing I was on my way to Krabi.

It was a hectic few days and although there were some beautiful places around it was a little too loud for my taste - not least the endless cacophony of long-tail boats. Time to keep moving.

And so it was three days before Christmas I arrived at a small hotel in Khao Lak on the west cost of Thailand. For several reasons I'd been looking forward to my arrival. Firstly, the direct minibus journey from Krabi didn't quite go as advertised. It involved three changes of vehicle and driver, one of whom redefined the concept of 'death wish' (you are probably aware by now that minibus rides in much of Southeast Asia can be a little hairy). Secondly, the hotel had excellent TripAdvisor reviews and I was in need of some comfort. I was fortunate to have found a room in the peak holiday season, especially as I'd made yet another last minute booking. So, despite a harrowing journey, I breezed up to the small reception in high hopes.

"Hello, I have a reservation," I said quite jauntily.

"Sorry, we have no room. There was a problem with the booking."

Oh dear, no room at the inn at Christmas. I was tempted to ask if they had a stable but this being a Buddhist country they might not have got the joke. Truth be told humour was not on my mind. I wasn't overly happy at the bad news I'd been given. Yao, who ran the place, was also a little stressed at being confronted by an unhappy foreigner.

"My sister is coming. She has another hotel. You can stay there."

With that we retreated into a Mexican stand-off. Me looking all huffy, Yao sat with her arms defensively folded. We were both very keen for her peacemaker sister to appear.

Ten minutes later Wandee arrived, she brought with her lots of smiles and a relaxed attitude.

"Sorry about the problem. Overbooking."

It was a word I heard a lot during the Christmas period. Wandee explained that she ran another hotel and she had a vacant room if I'd like that. Yes, probably I would, but I wasn't saying yes until I'd seen it.

When I saw it I said no. The room was basic but fine, I wouldn't lose any sleep over not having a trouser press or spa bath. What I would lose sleep over was the noise. The room overlooked the busy main road which cut through the town. I can pretty much sleep on any kind of bed but traffic noise is a guarantee of no shut eye. Staying there would mean a sleepless Christmas. Wandee had sensed my grumpiness even before I rejected the room.

"Don't worry, my friend has a hotel," she said.

"Is it quiet?"

"Yes, it is. You'll sleep very well there."

Hotel number three was acceptable. Quieter, if not absolutely silent. I knew that there wouldn't be too many options this being Christmas so I took it and was just relieved to have a place to stay. Wandee made a final apology and began to leave. But then she turned to me and asked me what I was doing in the evening. I had zero plans, knew nothing about the place really and didn't know a soul there.

"I'm not sure, I haven't made any definite arrangements yet." I said it in an implausible attempt to appear cool. I was still nursing a feeling-a-little-put-out attitude.

"My sister and I are going out for dinner. You're welcome to join us. It's on us because of the overbooking."

I went, of course, and we had a fabulous night. The sisters were a lot of fun and told me about life running two hotels. It's not for the faint-hearted, that's for sure. They were smart, educated people, Yao had a Masters degree and mostly lived in Europe with her Austrian husband, Wandee was an ex-journalist and the driving force behind the two hotels.

They overflowed with kindness and humour. They told me overbooking is a real curse at busy times of the year. They used a couple of the Internet booking agencies and communication wasn't always instant. It meant dual bookings happened on a not infrequent basis. My anticipated grumpiness had apparently been discussed before my arrival. When I'd duly appeared Yao had quickly sized me up and told her sister there wasn't a cat in hell's chance that I would take the room overlooking the busy road. I asked her how she could tell that. She smiled, kept her innkeeper secrets close to her chest and said simply that she knew. Am I that easy to read? Clearly the answer was yes.

After dinner we said our goodbyes but not before the sisters told me there was a room available at the hotel the next day. Unfortunately it was just for one night. By now we were on great terms so I said I'd be delighted. The next morning I arrived with my backpack at the appointed hour and there was Yao to greet me.

"Sorry, I don't know how this happened but we are overbooked again."

Conflicting emotions began racing through my head. Yao clearly recognised this.

"Don't worry, Wandee has a room in her hotel. It has a view of the road."

She gave me a wicked smile, she'd been winding me up. Very funny.

The next day was Christmas Eve. Christians make up less than one per cent of Thailand's 67 million population but Christmas is happily acknowledged. Ninety five per cent of Thais are Buddhists. There is no official state religion, however, one quirk is that the king is legally obliged to be Buddhist. The present incumbent, Bhumibol Adulyadej, also known as Rama IX, is the world's longest serving head of state. He became king in June 1946. If you're ever in Thailand you'll notice his portrait everywhere. He is held in very high esteem and his people revere him, literally. Since 1908 there has been a clause in the country's constitution which states:

"The King shall be enthroned in a position of revered worship and shall not be violated."

It's known as lèse majesté, which translates as 'injured majesty'. Criticism and defamation of the king is absolutely forbidden. Lèse majesté was sparingly used between 1990 and 2005 when there were only four or five prosecutions a year. However, since 2006 there's been a 15-fold increase in the number of cases brought.

It's claimed the law has been hijacked for political purposes and is stifling criticism not of the monarchy but of the wider establishment in general. In a 2013 Supreme Court ruling the law's interpretation was widened to include previous monarchs. In other words you can't speak ill of the dead. One scholar taking part in an academic debate was charged for questioning the details of an elephant battle between a Thai king and a Burmese prince. It took place 400 years ago.

Simply calling for the principle of lèse majesté to be overhauled has led to people being charged. Tens of thousands of internet pages have also been blocked because they contain criticism of the king or show a lack of respect. This can simply be for not having the king's photo above all others on the page.

Although it's mostly Thais who are tried for lèse majesté foreigners are not exempt. A Swiss man was sentenced to 10 years in jail in 2007 for daubing paint over portraits of the king. Fortunately the head of state was in a forgiving mood and gave the man a royal pardon after less than a month.

In Thai cinemas the royal anthem (different to the national anthem) is played before every film and a picture of the king is screened. Not standing for this is deemed to be an insult and a breach of lèse majesté laws. If you're ever in a Thai cinema you best get to your feet, this particular convention applies to Thais and foreigners.

Back in Khao Lak I was also on my feet preparing to leave the sisters' hotel after one very comfortable night's stay. I was heading for my third bed in as many days and inevitably a Christmas spent on my own. But before I left Wandee invited me to return for a Christmas dinner that evening at their hotel. They don't serve food other than at breakfast, this would just be me, the sisters and two friends. Definitely not formal and could I bring a little something to contribute to the night. It was agreed I'd bring wine and chocolate. I was also roped in to be Wandee's bag carrier in the afternoon as she toured local markets for the best ingredients.

By the time we met up the shopping list had grown massively. Wandee and Yao had taken pity on their other guests and invited anybody without plans to join the Christmas feast. It was a general invitation to pitch up and pitch in.

And so on Christmas Eve night we gathered. There was a family of four from Finland, one person from France, two Germans, one Swiss, a Swede, one Algerian, two Thais and an Australian. We sang carols in Finnish, Christmas pop songs in English and hummed along to a little Thai music, I don't think it was Christmas in flavour but that didn't matter. Traditions and Christmas tales from our respective countries were swapped as were bucket loads of bonhomie.

The German couple told us about their morning dive off the coast. This was no mere "we saw amazing fish" kind of tale. Gottfried told us that at an appropriate depth underwater he'd whipped out a ring and through the universal language of signing had proposed to his girlfriend. Amazingly he didn't drop the ring and she didn't have palpitations before giving an enthusiastic nod of the head. Their story sent the Yuletide party into a new height of happiness. We finished the night with big hugs, huge smiles on our faces and goodwill in our hearts.

The next day was Christmas. It was a much quieter affair. Santa had somehow missed me in the night but as I'd moved hotels so often I wasn't pointing fingers. My quiet day gave me a chance to pause, think and reflect. It was a time for thoughts of family and friends across the globe. Of loved ones no longer here. Of Christmases past.

The party from the night before kept coming back to mind. We had been Christians, Buddhists, a Muslim and a couple of atheists all happily celebrating together. It may sound ridiculous given that this was a Christian festival but our multi-faith and faithless gathering reflected much of the 'spirit of Christmas'. Togetherness, peacefulness, respect, differences enjoyed and celebrated.

And all of this made possible by two sisters who initially had no room at the inn. The brightest day in the Christian calendar had been made memorable by the Buddhist sisters of mercy.

#

43

CURRY MANOEUVRES AT THE MOVIES

Week 42; Luang Prabang, Laos; 56,990 kms travelled;
2 undies discarded – health hazard avoided…for now

It was whispered but the question was only just about audible.

"Green curry and hot chocolate?"

I raised my hand slightly and in a hushed tone answered back through the gloom.

"Over here."

But I was thwarted, one of the upright people had beaten me too it. Damn, I'd have to wait.

As I lay there I wondered if there might have been a mix up. Surely nobody else would have ordered such a ridiculous combination of food and drink. It took a leap of faith even for me, a confirmed chocoholic. To think I had a doppelgänger was a little unnerving.

But it was only another five minutes before the waiter was back whispering again. It was exactly the same question. This time I pushed myself up onto my elbows and rotated my head 90 degrees to make myself more visible.

"Yes please, over here."

It was still said quietly but I'd added some deeper manliness to the tone and it did the trick.

He nodded in acknowledgement and began to pick his way gingerly towards me. He went past the uprights in their seats, carefully skirted around the sofa for two on which four people were intimately entwined and then entered the minefield around me.

The first hurdle was easily cleared and both his feet were soon firmly planted back on the floor. His next move involved the cunning and calculation of a chess grandmaster. There were only a few feet between us but there were also six arms, half a dozen legs and three torsos. Two of the bodies belonged to guys clearly more concerned about other body parts which were at risk of being trampled. They both instinctively performed protective twists on the floor but wriggle room was severely limited. After a brief time out to survey his options the waiter boldly took one hand off the tray and shimmied audaciously to his side, the free arm out at a right angle to act as a counterbalance. The bowl and the cup slid perilously and there was nervous squirming on the floor but amazingly nothing was spilt. Next he circled to the side of me, paused once more before raising his right knee high to step over my neighbour. His left leg expertly followed and he brought my food down on to the low level table next to me with aplomb.

"Green curry and hot chocolate."

He said it with the pride of a Michelin chef theatrically revealing some gastronomic masterpiece. The devil in me contemplated apologising and telling him it wasn't my order after all. It would have been fascinating to see him try to reverse out with his loaded tray. But I resisted.

Next came the really tricky part. How do you eat green curry lying down? I'd eaten one a couple of days earlier downstairs at the cafe in the bookstore. It was absolutely delicious but had rather a lot of liquid sloshing about in the bowl. The obvious solution tonight would be to sit up but I was very near the front and the 20 or so people behind me wouldn't be able to see the screen. I say screen but in reality it was a rather old and not very large TV. But in Laos it is what passes for a screen. Cinema choice is limited. Actually, from what I'm led to believe, there isn't a choice at all. Nobody I talked to knew of any other place in the country where movies are shown on a nightly basis.

At first I just ferried the curry spoon by spoon from the table, over my prostrate body and into my mouth. My head was already raised a little by a headrest on the floor. But even in the semi-dark I knew I was missing and spilling juice all over myself.

Next, I tried holding the bowl over my chest. The spoonful of food would have very little distance to travel and might actually still be a spoonful when it reached my mouth. But with limited space, getting my elbow out far enough was difficult. It meant some of the soup was wide of its target and trickled down my chin and on to my chest. Thank God for the dark.

Five minutes later, after further trial and error, I finally worked out the best way to eat my rapidly cooling curry. I turned on to my side, tucked the bowl into the crook of my supporting arm and brought the spoon vertically into my mouth. Bingo. Except I was now facing away from the screen.

Missing five minutes of the visuals wouldn't normally be a huge issue in a Woody Allen film, dialogue is way more important. But here in the Lauang Prabang 'cinema' there was a problem. The premises next door hosted a regular fashion show, also a novelty in Laos, and the music was thumping. Cate Blanchett was in mid monologue on the screen but I could only make out every fourth or fifth word. She was losing out to some seriously loud hip hop. When the Luang Prabang fashion show fires up lip reading becomes an essential part of the Laos movie experience. So I quickly slurped up and slid back on to my back to rejoin the film.

This was Oscars week so all the selected movies had been contenders in the Best Picture category. There was no projector just imported DVDs, straight from the markets of Bangkok in Thailand, no questions asked.

Movies are shown every night, about 35 people is maximum capacity but there are plenty of evenings when the numbers are as low as three or four. In the afternoon it's movies on demand. Whether you're solo or in a group you turn up at the bookshop put in your request and the cinema is all yours. Just buy a book, order a drink or some food and you get the movie house for nothing.

Since I was a boy I've always loved going to the flicks, as we used to call them, and on my travels I sought out different types of viewing experiences. This was actually my third attempt to see Blue Jasmine and the second actual viewing.

In the Albanian city of Shkodra half a dozen of us staying at a local hostel had gone en masse to watch it in a nearby cinema. The place was very old and looked way past its prime. It's exactly the kind of movie experience I love. We arrived fifteen minutes before the advertised show time and waited outside. As the minutes ticked by it was clear the film wasn't very popular with the locals. Nobody else was there and the doors to the cinema remained firmly shut.

Eventually a passing Albanian stopped and in excellent English told us that we were unlikely to see the movie. Apparently management only go ahead with a screening if they see enough people waiting outside. If there aren't enough bodies they simply don't bother. Tonight was clearly one of those nights. We waited another few minutes, saw no life inside or outside the theatre so we trudged off in search of a bar.

I did get to see Blue Jasmine in Belgium. It was in a plush, modern cinema in Brussels right by Atomium, the city's most popular tourist attraction. Built for the 1958 World Fair Atomium once had the dubious pleasure of being named by CNN as Europe's most bizarre building. It is 102 metres high (335ft) and made up of nine huge, metal-clad, interconnected spheres. The concept is based on the cell of a crystal and is allegedly magnified 165 billion times. Not something you can easily verify unless you have a very good ruler and a lot of spare time on your hands.

In the nearby cinema I settled in for a night of stimulating fun. It wasn't long before laughter was ringing around the auditorium. However, it was some way in to the movie before I realised it was only my laughter that was doing the ringing. Nobody else was joining in save for a kind of half-hearted belly laugh now and then from a lady several rows back.

I asked my Belgian friend, Leela, if she was enjoying the film. Yes she was, very enjoyable thank you. After the film finished I pressed her a little more and she told me loud, raucous laughter isn't really something most Belgians go in for. She kept a straight face when she told me this so I assume she wasn't winding me up.

Therefore, if you plan to watch a movie in Belgium my advice is don't go to a comedy. You might feel a bit self-conscious if you start belly laughing. Perhaps you'd be on safer ground going to a weepie instead. There again, that might not necessarily be good advice either. I have absolutely no idea if the Belgians blubber in cinemas. Probably best you just err on the side of caution and ignore the movies altogether. I really can't be sure what Belgians get up to when the lights go down. You'll be more comfortable just going to the pub or a restaurant.

However, a word of warning. If you take up the restaurant option, make sure you have some change with you. I had an embarrassing moment in a cafe on the beautiful Grand Place. After a lovely lunch taking in views of the amazing 17th century architecture I excused myself and went to the cafe's loo. Up two flights of the twisting, narrow, creaky staircase I went. In a short corridor outside the toilet door there was a man sitting at a table with a box of coins. It turned out there was a charge. I told the man I was dining in the cafe. It made no difference. Patrons pay for peeing. I only had a 50 Euro note on me, which he couldn't change, so I asked if I could tinkle first and then come back with the money. No I couldn't. My credit wasn't good enough in a toilet! It was a new low point in my life. Unable to urinate I huffily descended the stairs and told my friend of the dual shock of having to pay to pass water and of being declined credit. She smiled in sympathy but informed me this was fairly standard practice in Brussels.

What a city, no laughing out loud and now no free peeing, the place was surely taking the....

#

44

ANGKOR – HENRI AND THE HORDES

Week 39; Siem Reap, Cambodia; 57,740 kms travelled;
18 countries visited; 2nd prescription sunglasses lost

There's a whole lot more to Luang Prabang than simply providing the country's premier cinema experience. The town has become a major draw for Nony types, the young are definitely in the minority here. It's become 'the must see place' in Laos.

In part that's down to its geography. Luang is situated at the confluence of two rivers and they frame it perfectly. To one side is the Nam Khan, on another flows the mighty Mekong. The town sits sedately perched above and beside the region's mystical waterway. All around and for as far as the eye can see is a seductive necklace of dense, green, forested hills.

The town itself adds to the sense of picture perfection. It is home to a beguiling and exotic fusion of gilded Buddhist temples, traditional Laos wooden houses and French colonial architecture, much of it beautifully restored. Most views of Luang are also filtered by tableaux of exotic flowers which create walkways of perfumed air. The mix is a blend of sophistication and charm. UNESCO gave it world heritage status in 1995 which also means strict traffic rules.

Many of the revived buildings are home to restaurants. The place has burgeoned into the country's capital of dining. Every budget is catered for. There's plenty of great street food at one end and some high quality French at the other. Luang Prabang has also firmly established itself as a centre for cooking classes. It's become a very popular pastime for tourists.

However, it wasn't always such an easy destination. In the mid-19th century an intrepid French explorer, Henri Mouhot, arrived in what was at the time the Laotian capital. Just getting there was no mean feat, getting out was something else entirely. No westerner had successfully made the return trip in the previous 25 years. A combination of wild animals and deadly disease was more than a match for most outsiders.

For Mouhot the struggle to get there was entirely worth it, or almost entirely anyway. He was hugely impressed with the place but greatly underwhelmed by its inhabitants, who he dismissed as "…dull and apathetic and full of small vices."

"But for the people," he wrote, "Luang Prabang would be one of the most charming places in the world."

I suspect some of that charm may have worn off a little when he came down with a fever. And I'm fairly certain it lost all of its appeal as he soon succumbed to the illness and died.

However, Mouhot left his mark on history for something a little grander than his snootiness towards a people he didn't understand. He is generally cited as being the man who 'discovered' the temples of Angkor in neighbouring Cambodia. It's quite something to have had on his lifetime C.V. although it's not quite correct.

'Discovered' implies nobody knew they were there. The Khmer had abandoned Angkor four centuries earlier through a combination of wars, food shortages and the king's desire to move to Phnom Penh. However, they were well aware the temples were there but neither had the will nor the means to reclaim them after centuries of neglect. Other Europeans are also known to have visited the site prior to the Frenchman. But in January 1860 he hacked his way through the jungle and set to work on detailed accounts and sketches of the temples he found. In his journals Mouhot made comparisons to Solomon's temple and the works of Michelangelo. The history books did the rest.

What Henri found must have been almost beyond comprehension, it still is today. The Temples of Angkor formed what was effectively a megacity built over 400 sq. kms (250 sq. miles). Work began around 900 AD and was still ongoing at the time of its abandonment. Temples, terraces, moats, waterways and defensive fortifications seem almost endless. Work to uncover other lost shrines continues in what is one of the world's most important archaeological sites. Each year brings new discoveries. In 2012 an airborne laser camera search mapped an entire city deep in the jungle.

The centrepiece of the region is undoubtedly Angkor Wat, the world's largest religious building. It pretty much features on every bucket list in the world. However, I was still in freewheeling mode up in Luang Prabang so was quite prepared to make a coin toss on my next destination. Just because everybody else went didn't mean I had to go there, I pompously informed several fellow travellers one night at dinner. This was greeted as a heresy. I would be insane not to go, they said. Actually, what they really said can't be printed here but enough to note they thought I was an idiot. Enough said, my sanity and wounded pride boarded a plane for a short flight to Siem Reap, Angkor's nearest airport.

Monsieur Mouhot's monuments were initially a monumental let-down. Nothing to do with the architecture or the temples, all to do with the experience. While Henri had hacked his way through the jungle to get a view I had to hack through hordes of people. Not literally, although at times it was very tempting. There were people here, there and everywhere. The queues to get to the second level of Angkor Wat snaked forever.

At sunset a tidal wave of thousands were walking up Bakhneg Hill. It was impossible to reach the viewing platform. I couldn't believe that this is what the Angkor experience served up on a daily basis. The good news, as it turns out, is that this wasn't typical. I had managed to arrive during the Chinese New Year holiday, literally the busiest few days of the year.

Somehow, in my complacency, I had forgotten to check the dates for public holidays in the region. And this was the big one. Chinese New Year, or Spring Festival, officially lasts a week. It is the world's largest human migration. Many Chinese head from the cities to their hometowns. This year they'd had a change of plan and all 1.4 billion of them had come to Angkor. Much of the rest of the world had come along for the ride.

I had screwed up and made a rookie mistake. During my travels I had learned to check dates so as not to be anywhere particularly 'touristy' during public holidays. Everything is more expensive and busier. From what I later heard from other travellers a week either side of the Chinese New Year would have meant a very different Angkor experience.

The main season is comparatively short. November to March is prime time. Outside of that is often either blisteringly hot or monsoonal. However, it's all perfectly doable even within peak season as long as CNY is avoided.

Having suffered from the crowds at Angkor Wat and the nearby Ta Phrom and Bayon Temples on day one I did a little bit of homework in preparation for day two. I read a couple of travel blogs and took the key advice to travel further afield. It might be a little time consuming but there are still plenty of temples to see and they are much quieter.

The experience was all the better for it. Some of the better preserved temples are magnificent showcases for the beautiful architecture and intricate carvings of the Khmer people. Others have a hauntingly lost-world feel to them. They stand strangled by the clasping, choking roots of huge trees which have insinuated themselves into the very fabric of the buildings.

Mother Nature has run riot since Angkor was abandoned in 1431. On one level it is a terrible pity to see the destruction. However, this deadly and intimate slow dance between the natural and the man-made worlds has created a bewitching and enchanting fantasy. The ravaged temples exude a magical and mysterious aura.

In a piece of historical irony Henri Mouhot was himself lost to the jungle. A tomb erected at his grave outside Luang Prabang by a French expedition was eventually forgotten. Over time it too was swallowed up by creepers and trees. Only a century later was it accidentally rediscovered and the jungle cleared back. Now Mouhot's resting place has itself become an attraction for tourists who have heard of his Angkor 'discovery'. However, while the temples he popularised now draw a global audience I suspect that even if you want to pay your respects during Chinese New Year you'll probably have his own monument to yourself.

#

45

HUNTING WITH THE HEADHUNTERS

Week 45; Rajang River, Borneo: 63,090 kms travelled —
one and a half times around the planet;
2 jungle shirts now crop tops after dodgy laundry

The still, silent, dead of night, deep in the Borneo jungle. The full moon cast a silvery, dreamlike trance over the primal rainforest. Gently, two paddles sank into the inky water, the surface broke and we moved in a gentle and soundless glide downstream. The moonlight added a sheen to the edges of the virgin forest but beyond the riverbank was impenetrable darkness. Only the rattling chirp of the cicadas and the mooted calls of owls tainted the silence. It was a canvas of calm and the night was achingly and hauntingly beautiful.

The silence was finally broken by a low murmur from behind. Two beams of light flashed onto the bank to our right. There in the rays of death stood a mouse deer.

With a few rapid strokes we reached the riverbank. Two tribesmen raced from the canoe and scrambled up the muddy rise. Their torch beams slashed through the trees and undergrowth in a frantic search for their prey. It was to no avail and one of the hunters gave up and returned empty handed to the boat.

As we waited we caught fleeting glimpses of torchlight off in the distance but silence had settled once more on the jungle. It seemed the deer had escaped with its life.

Fifteen minutes later the peace was shattered by the grave, echoing sound of gunshot. A few minutes passed before Jangolin reappeared at the riverbank. He carried a rifle in one hand and from the other dangled the bloody, still and lifeless mouse deer.

Seventy years ago the Kayan were a feared headhunter tribe living in the remote upper Rajang River area of Borneo. Nowadays they hunt only for food. Their lives depend upon it.

Lower down the river at Kapit, only accessible by boat, many of the traditional Iban longhouses have gone. The majority of people now live in modernised concrete versions, often with electricity and TVs. The slow creep of the 21st century is progressing further into Borneo.

But in the older wooden longhouses the past still lurks and in some the skulls of headhunting victims hang in baskets. The practice is remembered by some of the elderly, it's not ancient history. The trophies are reminders that not too long ago these were dangerous places.

Belaga, which is mainly Kayan territory, is a further five or six hours upstream through the Pelagus rapids. I was told the boats didn't run there anymore. However, by this stage of my journey I knew not to necessarily believe everything I was told and sure enough, the next day, a boat was available.

Belaga is a small, isolated place. But that physical isolation is slowly disappearing as the loggers make inroads deeper and deeper into the rain forests. I asked around, firstly for anybody who spoke English and then for somebody who could guide me. Eventually I met Buro. His English was excellent. I told him I wanted to visit an authentic wooden longhouse away from tourists and the trappings of modern civilisation.

Buro knew a place and agreed to be my guide for a few days. Early the next morning we set off. Our journey began with lifts along logging trails and some hiking. After Belaga we saw no villages and no tourists. The lack of travellers was hardly a surprise, there hadn't been any in Belaga so we weren't really going to see any out here. Our journey was taking us into primary rain forest.

After an arduous journey the longhouse appeared through the trees. It was a few paces away from a wide river and set high above the ground. The wooden building was probably 70 metres in length and a wide communal area ran down its entire length. Off that was a warren of small rooms. There was no furniture nor any obvious signs of 21st century life. Every room was dark and dismal, there was neither electricity nor running water. What there was though was the smell of smoke and it infiltrated everything.

The people were distant but not unfriendly and although dirt poor they were generous. Buro handed them some tuak, the local rice wine, as a gift. In return, small pieces of smoked fish were brought out by the women. They were dried, crumbly and crusty - the fish that is.

Five of the men sat on the floor to eat and Buro and I joined them. The tuak was opened and shared in small glasses. I am not much of a drinker and Borneo's notoriously strong rice wine was definitely not to my taste. It had a sharp, warm bite to it and I had no choice but to drink it. Forty minutes later another bottle was produced. I had an awful sinking feeling as Buro explained that today was a rest day so drinking would be heavier than normal. I began wandering around to study the longhouse and more importantly to discreetly chuck my glass of firewater.

The women mostly kept their silent distance. Some of the older ones had fully inked lower arms and long, drooping earlobes from days when this was considered fashionable. The practice is no longer en vogue and is dying out.

As the drinking and talking session continued more food arrived. There was a selection of meat the men had hunted. Wild boar, rich and quite sweet; mouse deer, which looks and tastes a little like pork; and 'wild cat', civet, I think. Its meat was gnarled and gristly and I found it almost impossible to chew. Rice and tapioca were also brought out by the women who joined us for the meal.

Everything they ate was the result of their self-sufficiency. They either grew it, caught it or shot it. Even their cigarettes came from their own tobacco.

After the food the men and I headed off for a wash and scrub up. A nearby stream was the bathroom. They sat on rocks in the water and began cleaning their teeth. Next they headed to deeper hollows where they submerged themselves before beginning a thorough soaping.

The easy chatter began to get a little louder and they would sneak looks at me and laugh. No wonder really. I was sat on a rock, my legs partially in the cold water and the rest of me lily white, covered in goose pimples and ingloriously naked. Compared to their tanned, lean, muscled, fat free bodies I cut a pathetic sight and it amused them no end.

The jungle is the Kayan's toilet. But only in daylight. Bruno warned me the night can be dangerous so I should just stand on the longhouse verandah and do what I needed to do over the side. I was on a steep learning curve here.

Late in the afternoon, after several more bottles of tuak, we headed to the river, boarded a canoe and set off fishing. A catfish was quickly caught and we pulled over to a stony outcrop for an impromptu barbecue. Dried grass and wood were soon collected and a fire started. An old metal pot was hung between two broken branches and cooking was quickly underway.

But we never got to eat there. Buro soon wandered over to me and explained that we had to return to the longhouse as one of the men was feeling 'unwell'. What he really meant was the guy was completely off his trolley on tuak. Several of the others were also sporting the leery smiles of excess drinking.

We returned to the longhouse where the women once again took over the feeding responsibilities. By now it was pitch black and a single, small, portable gas lamp was all that we had to eat by. This may have been a good thing.

The drinking continued into the night while the drunk tribesman lay off to one side muttering, moaning and occasionally laughing to himself. The night appeared to be heading towards sleep time so I was a little taken aback when two homemade guns were produced in readiness for hunting.

However, as the Kayan were about to show, they are expert hunters, drink or no drink. When the mouse deer was taken only a single shot was required.

On our return Buro showed me our 'bedroom'. There were no blankets, no pillows and, of course, no bed. The floor is where the Kayan sleep and as you'll remember this was not a single room. I would be sharing with three others. I knew it would be a snug fit but I didn't realise at the time quite how close one of them was about to get. I placed my trusty BlackWolf backpack under my head, put on an extra top for warmth and settled down hoping some sleep would come my way. But as you already know, what did come my way was a seemingly randy tribesman.

After a night full of turmoil and empty of sleep dawn finally arrived. I was first up. Only hours after I fled the room did the rest of the human debris emerge. The longhouse was a slow scene of inactive men with heavy heads. The women went off early to do chores.

Buro and I eventually set off back towards Belaga. The Kayan gave us the mouse deer as a gift, we gave them tuak. When we arrived at a logging trail we waited to hitch a ride. Huge logging trucks rumbled past, they never stop for passengers. The monster lorries coated us in thick, blankets of dust. My face was caked and my hair thick and matted with grit. Eventually a battered old ute came along and stopped.

Buro and I climbed onto the open back of the vehicle and crammed ourselves in between boxes, tools and bags. For the next 90 minutes the only thing moving in the back was the dead mouse deer. As we sped along at breakneck speed it slid from side to side, slowly edging closer to me. Its body was stiff but its head flopped around in constant motion. Its haunted, accusing eyes seemed to stare at me. I wanted to say don't blame me I didn't shoot you, instead I turned and looked at Borneo. As our ute traversed a ridgeline the panorama was an endless forest of green. Lush, isolated and breathtaking.

I was still in my reverie when the brakes were thrust hard to the floor and the driver lurched us to the edge of the track. An oncoming truck tore past and carried on down the hillside, stopping had never been an option for the logging lout behind the wheel. For thirty seconds we sat motionless, our driver unable to move until the dust cloud disappeared. The first thing I saw was the mouse deer, its congealed blood mixed with dust. It lay against my backpack now discoloured brown by a thick layer of grit. But here and there some splashes of red, all that remained from the poor animal's life-force. Removing it from my pack would be almost impossible and I began to rehearse some plausible excuses for unhappy customs officials across the world.

"I was out in the Borneo jungle one night with some drunken headhunters and.... "

It wouldn't wash, literally, I'd need to work on something a touch more believable.

Finally the ute reached another track, this was my cue to get out. I was told to wait and hitch, a vehicle would be along sometime. It would take me to a sealed road close by and from there I'd be able to thumb a lift back to the modern world. With those instructions filed away in my head I said goodbye to Buro who was heading back to Belaga with the mouse deer.

It wasn't too long before a big 4x4 came along and stopped. Inside were two engineers who'd been measuring water quality in the area. They were a little surprised to find me but they spoke excellent English and offered me a ride. They were heading north to Miri and asked me where I was going. I asked them if Miri was a city. They said it was. It sounded good to me.

Four hours later they dropped me in the city's centre. Once there I immediately began hunting again. I had clear targets in my sights; a hot shower; clean clothes; a wire brush to scrub my bag and, most importantly, a bed that I would share with nobody.

#

46

THE SEARCH FOR DUMBO

Week 48; Kintabatangan River, Borneo; 63,940 kms travelled;
42 flights; 6 hats; 2 boardies; 7 shampoos - all left in showers
(pack better or shower less?)

It's amazing who you bump into in the jungle. I kept coming face to face with a relative, admittedly of the distant kind but we were definitely related.

When I saw him for the first time I could see the resemblance straight away. The facial expressions and the way he stood. But truth be known we've grown apart, like many modern families, I suppose. It had been a while since we'd got together, fourteen million years apparently. That was the last time we were thought to have had a common ancestor. But Pongo Pygmaeus, better known to you and me as orangutan, shares 97% of human DNA. And it shows.

The great ape is only found in Sumatra and Borneo and they are seriously endangered. It's estimated their numbers could have fallen to as low as 20,000. Huge scale logging, both legal and illegal, is destroying their habitat. Flying over Borneo I saw huge tracts of cleared forest ripped from the landscape. At ground level some of these areas look apocalyptic. Scenes of utter destruction where once stood rainforests dating back 140 million years.

Evolution moves at a barely perceptible pace. It was 550 million years ago the flatworms became the first animals to have a brain. The fully anatomical modern human being didn't finally emerge until 200,000 years ago after millions of years in the making. And it was just 10-20,000 years ago Europeans developed light skin. These are huge evolutionary numbers. But Borneo is living, or dying, proof of man's awesome power to radically impose permanent change in the blink of an evolutionary eye. To see it is to believe it and it is frightening.

In the Indonesian part of Borneo satellite analysis showed more than half of protected lowland tropical rainforests were cut down between 1985 and 2001. That's almost the size of Belgium - something else for Belgians not to laugh at. It has been estimated that illegal logging is worth a staggering $10 billion a year. With such massive amounts of money at stake the practice isn't about to stop or be stopped any time soon.

Much of the deforested land is turned into palm oil plantations. Between them Malaysia and Indonesia make up 90% of the world's palm oil production area. It's the cheapest vegetable oil in the world and demand is growing. It means more and more of the orangutans' habitat has been lost forever.

There are still places you can see the apes. Two of the best close-up experiences are in Semmengoh, in the southwest, and Sepilok in the northeast. Both are rehabilitation centres for orphaned orangutans and the aim is to release them back into the forest. They are very successful.

After release, some orangutans turn up at the centres for fruit, which is provided twice a day. The food is deliberately monotonous so as to encourage them to stay away and forage for themselves in the forests. Feeding time is hit and miss for viewing, there are no guarantees. If the primates have successfully found food they will stay away.

At Sepilok I hit the jackpot. I was the first person on to the viewing platform, well in advance of the official feeding time. As I and half a dozen people stood around there was a loud crashing sound from the trees. A minute later an orangutan climbed boldly through the wooden fencing and on to the platform. He had no fear of humans and walked straight towards me. He was probably a fairly mature adult, his long, wispy, reddish-brown hair covered a strong muscular body. He walked with the knuckles of his hands on the floor, unusual as orangutans usually use their palms. Knuckles are the reserve of chimpanzees and gorillas.

At a distance of about six feet I decided not to test either his strength or his friendliness and sidestepped out of his way. The primate kept walking and after a few more paces climbed onto a sign reading 'beware of falling branches'. I admired his bravado. Only as he went to climb the sign did he stand up tall. At about five feet four in height and with a straight back he appeared uncannily human.

Twenty minutes later he was joined by another nine or ten orangutans. The dominant male was a serious beast but the rest were mostly contentedly playful. It was thrilling to see them at such close quarters and it made their decline all the more bitter.

Sepilok was a stopping off point on the way to the Kintabatangan River, home to many other species of Borneo's renowned wildlife. There was one in particular that I wanted to see, the pygmy elephant. It's an animal which has captured my imagination since I was a young boy. It's as close to Walt Disney's Dumbo as an elephant gets. Roughly 20% smaller than Asian elephants, they have smaller, rounder faces, proportionately bigger ears and long, dragging tails. This would almost certainly be the best chance in my life to see one in the flesh.

I spent three days at a chalet camp on the banks of the river, the second longest in Borneo. Morning, afternoon and night I joined a group of about eight others in guided motorized canoes up and down the wide waterway. Everywhere teemed with wildlife. Orangutans roamed freely in the trees, although a fair distance from our boat. There were macaques, gibbons, crocodiles, eagles and the utterly weird proboscis monkey. These are the unloved rejects of nature's master plan and found only in Borneo, I doubt anywhere else would have them.

They have several alternative names including orang belanda, meaning Dutchman, as they were thought to have some unflattering physical similarities to Dutch colonisers. The male's nose grows to about 10 cms in length and hangs down over the mouth. The snout hardly lacks width either, making it one hell of a hooter. The female nose is a little less bonkers but still large compared to other primates. Both also have bizarrely big pot bellies giving them a slobbish characteristic. In case this wasn't quite attractive enough the males also live in a state of permanent arousal (no schoolboy humour required).

I liked the monkeys, they had another-world kind of look about them but I was set on pygmy elephants. I knew they were rare, only 1500 survive. Like the orangutans their habitat is getting more and more squeezed by the loggers.

On the afternoon of the second day a call was radioed to our boat. A small herd of small elephants had been spotted upriver. We were a long way away but off we charged. It took an age but finally we headed into a narrow tributary.

Five hundred metres along we knew we had struck gold, half a dozen other small boats lay motionless in the water, every pair of eyes glued to the riverbank. We could see trampled grass, the unmistakable sign of elephants. We craned our heads and sat and waited. From the other boats there was low level but ecstatic chatter as people relived what they'd just witnessed, one of the rarest animal sightings on earth. In my canoe my 50 years of patience was being tested. And then from a few metres away there was the sound of animals moving through thick vegetation. The excitement on our boat charged the damp air.

But they never came. They were heading off. We'd missed them by moments. The other boats left the scene, their human cargo buoyed by the euphoria of a once in a lifetime experience. Our guide looked, strained and listened but the elephants had gone. Several times he went to start his outboard motor, each time he faced a mutiny. We pleaded for more time. After a further 20 minutes of silence our spirits were crushed and the boatman headed for home.

On the journey back he did his best, pointing out orangutans, hawks and monkeys in the high trees. But travel makes you a hypocrite. What two days ago had been thrilling now barely merited a glance.

Then came the crackle of the radio, our guide's tone suggested something out of the ordinary.

"More elephants," he said excitedly. "Mother and baby. Five minutes away."

We begged and beseeched him to spare not an ounce of the engine. Large tips were promised if he could get us there in time. And he did.

The boats which had already feasted on one herd were in the middle of the river gorging on another. Cameras whirred and fingers pointed at a bush. The mother and calf had just moved behind it. This time we would have our reward. Binoculars which earlier had been shared around the boat were now held on to with base selfishness. All requests for a look were ignored. The mother and child on land were also ignoring us and our desperate pleadings. By now the light was retreating rapidly and the bush was losing its form. Behind it we could hear the sound of elephants. If they moved left or right we'd see them. Backwards would be the only way for them to spoil the party.

Just as an awful sense of deja vu settled on my shoulders the mother moved. Cameras clicked and whirred. Mine stayed silent, I'd left it in the room. Its 20-times zoom would have given me a close-up view, instead all I could make out through the gloom was the top of her back. I might have caught sight of the baby's trunk but in good conscience I can't say for sure. The pair then retreated into the bush and were swallowed up by the dark.

On our return to the lodge two German friends showed me their photos shot through a long lens camera. They'd captured the mother fairly well but no sign of the baby. They gave me a copy which was very kind of them. However, it was no consolation for the fact that twice I'd come within moments of seeing this rare animal and twice I'd been thwarted. The best my gravestone inscription will state is that I once saw the arse end of a pygmy elephant.

Little did I know how close I'd be to requiring this memorial the very next day. Seven of us were picked up by minivan to be taken three hours or so back to Sandakan. Just 20 minutes into the journey, along a heavily rutted surface, the vehicle had a puncture. The usual lack of equipment in these parts meant it took 30 minutes to sort out. When we got back on the road our driver was intent on making up time. Her speed was borderline madness for a while and then she squeezed the accelerator harder and crossed into insanity. She launched into a crazy overtake with a car coming straight at us. Undaunted she didn't give an inch and only ferocious last moment braking by the other vehicle avoided calamity. We told her quite firmly we were not yet ready to meet our maker.

Fifteen minutes later she repeated the manoeuvre but this time the other vehicle didn't slow. All of us shouted to her but she ploughed on. Two girls in our minivan screamed and the other driver realising death was imminent swerved off the road into a shallow ditch. We were literally inches or one second from death.

Through all the shouting and some tears I climbed from the back of the van to the front. In my calmest voice I told her she had almost killed me, the other passengers and herself. She wouldn't get the chance to do it again. If she tried anything crazy like that I solemnly promised I would grab the wheel from her.

For the rest of the journey I sat inches away from her and every time she contemplated overtaking I would firmly tell her no. Eventually we arrived and as I got out she told me I talked too much. She had a point, I had talked at her for more than 90 minutes. But I smiled, she smiled back, we shook hands and I walked away. I made a strong mental picture of her face. When the grim reaper comes looking for me I will know what she looks like.

#

47

THE ROAD TO HELL (PART 2)

Week 50; Port Barton, Palawan, Philippines; 64,820 kms travelled;
food poisoning - 2; will to live - gone, probably never coming back

Borneo had been a hard slog and I felt myself in need of some chill
out time. It had been a couple of months since I'd been to a beach so I
was ready to put that right. The island has plenty to choose from but I
ignored them all.

In my first month travelling I'd met a Dutch couple, Claudia and
Philip, who lived in Bali. They'd spent several years travelling
throughout the region and knew it well. They gave me a bunch of
suggestions for beautiful beaches off the beaten track - most were in
The Philippines. I hadn't realised how close the country was to Borneo
but a quick check of the map showed they were almost kissing cousins.

Out came the coin again. It was time to toss once more, heads for
Borneo, tails for The Ps. My head wanted Borneo, I was weary and an
easy journey would be really welcome. My heart, on the other hand,
fancied The Philippines, a new country and a different culture. Up went
the coin spinning in the air. On every previous toss I'd caught it in my
right palm then clapped it over on to the back of my other hand. I'd
pause for a moment or two before seeing what the fates had in store.
But this time I simply stood and watched as it fell to the ground. My

body may have been a little on the tired side but my heart was still up for adventure.

In the brief time the coin spent in the air my head had been outflanked and overruled. It was a completely unconscious act, quite inexplicable after more than 11 months. I glanced down at the floor, momentarily nonplussed, then smiled to myself, said a quiet thanks to the coin for all its help and walked away.

There were no flights from Sandakan to The Philippines but a short flight would get me to Kota Kinabalu. From there I quickly found an onwards connection to Puerto Princesa on Palawan Island. It was all falling into line. Claudia and Philip had told me about a place called Port Barton on the east coast, slightly difficult to get to, short on travellers but big on beauty. I had a vision of myself swinging lightly in a hammock between two palm trees, the lethargic lap of the waves folding gently on the soft, bleached sand beneath me. Tranquillity all around with stunning views out over the amazing aquamarine sea to uninhabited islands. I hoped the reality matched the fantasy.

The flight to Palawan confirmed I was heading somewhere special. We flew over a dozen or two atolls, all picture perfect. The sea was shaded from the faintest blue through the entire spectrum to dark navy. These mosaics ringed the islands, green in the middle and fringed by white, powdery sand, all seemingly deserted paradises.

I spent a day and a half in Puerto Princesa, the capital city of Palawan. It's not got anything particularly going for it so I rented a 75cc moped and headed off north for Port Barton. I decided to break the journey on the way and spend a night at some beach chalets travellers had raved about in TripAdvisor reviews. The food was all cooked by the owner and apparently a treat.

The two storey chalets were basic but comfortable and right on the deserted beach. The owner was a lovely old lady who cheerfully looked after me and one other couple, the only guests. The three of us enjoyed a delicious meal and chatted late into the warm night.

The Philippines has more than 7,000 islands and the closest to us was privately owned and lay just offshore. It was home to Dos Palmas

Island Resort. The name immediately rang a bell.

In May 2001 around 20 masked gunmen had stormed the island by speed boat. During the breakfast time raid they took 20 hostages, including four staff and three Americans. The men, from the Abu Sayyaf terrorist group, fled hundreds of kilometres back to their stronghold of Mindanao. During a year-long pursuit by the army up to 100 hostages were taken from various places, 20 of them were killed. Two of the Americans died in a final shootout with troops.

It was strange to sit in total peacefulness looking out to Dos Palmas, scene of so much terror. Apparently the resort stills retains its name, life and leisure there carry on as normal.

The next morning I took a stroll along the shoreline then headed for breakfast. My first mouthful sent a shockwave of nausea through me. I'd woken with a slightly odd feeling in my stomach, now I had proof that something wasn't right. I quickly retreated to my room, debated staying and considered leaving. I tossed the issue around in my head, a substitute for my abandoned Bali coin. Quickly my verdict was in, I was going. I moved as fast as I dared, got on my bike and headed for Port Barton. Remember what I said previously, we get older but not necessarily wiser. It was clearly a bonkers decision but I didn't particularly want to hang around in a place that had poisoned me.

Fifteen minutes into my journey I was regretting the decision. My stomach was churning and I was struggling to keep everything in. The road wasn't bad but there were plenty of potholes and rough sections where I was bouncing around way outside my comfort levels.

I'd made a rough calculation that my odyssey would take about three hours. After half an hour I stopped, bought some water and cooled off. This seemed to do the trick and I managed to continue to the Port Barton turnoff without incident. But this was the cue for my troubles to really begin. I had read about 'the road' to Port Barton. And what I'd read was that there wasn't a road, not really. There was a track cut through the jungle which the government had been promising for years to turn into a sealed road. At times it was either an impenetrable, muddy quagmire or sun baked and as hard as hell, depending on the season. I was on the solid stuff, unlike everything inside of me.

My speed was about 15kph which felt to my stomach like food blender level nine. Every bump, sent bad tastes up to my mouth. The track was a constant bone-rattling rodeo ride. It wasn't helped by some unsettling knowledge - there were 20 kilometres of it between me and my destination.

I was desperately close to throwing up. However, I knew these were only the early stages of whatever I was suffering from, almost certainly food poisoning. It was only going to get worse. If I'd stopped and got off my bike I might not have the strength to get back on. There were no towns between me and my destination, just a rough, wide track through the jungle.

I tried to stare at fixed points on the horizon and to focus on a spot. It was impossible, my ride was about as stable as a bucking bronco with a crack cocaine addiction. I counted every kilometre as they turned over on my odometer. It was painfully slow. By now my stomach was making gurgling and fizzing sounds loud enough to almost drown out the noise of my motorbike. I felt dreadful and I knew I couldn't hang on much longer.

Finally, at the top of a rise, I saw the ocean in the distance. Port Barton had to be close. A couple of kilometres later I rolled slowly into civilisation. I had no accommodation booked, my original plan had been to take a look around and find something fairly decent perched by the water. However, I now determined to take a room in the very first place I came across.

I reached the beach and saw several small wooden chalets. A sign proudly proclaimed 'German owned'. Perfect. I brought my motorbike to a halt and could see the tiny open-air reception area a mere fifteen paces away. I carefully climbed off the bike and began to walk. The reception proved to be five paces too many. A wave of nausea overwhelmed me and I just had time to turn to face a small bush before violently throwing up. God only knows what the receptionist was thinking because he was sitting on a balcony almost within touching distance. There was a chance he couldn't see me but he sure as hell must have heard me.

After several minutes I managed to haul myself to his desk.

"Do you have a room please?" I was raised to be polite.

"How many people is it for?"

"Just me."

"How many nights would you be staying?"

"Four please."

I knew I'd be going nowhere for a few days.

He looked diligently down his small reservation sheet.

"We have one chalet left but it is not immediately on the beach."

"I'll take it thanks."

"Would you like to have a look first?" In no other place in Southeast Asia had this offer been made. In several dodgy establishments I'd been the one demanding an inspection. This was different.

"No thank you. I'm feeling quite ill and just need to get in the room."

With that he walked to the edge of his balcony and peered around the corner. After 15 precious seconds which I really couldn't afford I got a little firmer.

"Excuse me but I really need to get in the room NOW. I'm not well."

"I need to find the cleaner to see if she has done the floor. The bedding was changed this morning but she may not have finished." His efficient German training was obvious. Anywhere else I'd have been grateful for it but not here.

"I don't care. I need to get in the room IMMEDIATELY."

This hit home and he went to his board of keys. He slowly plucked one from its hook.

"I will show you to your room and I can see if the cleaner has finished."

"Fine but we must go NOW."

He broke into a dawdle, twice the speed you normally get in these laid-back kind of places but literally painful to me. He'd no sooner half turned the key in the lock when I shoulder-charged him mercilessly out of my way. Actually, it probably was a mercy, it spared him from a vision of deep unpleasantness.

I barged into the room in a full-on SAS assault. The door almost flew off its hinges. In mid-stride my daypack was hurled to the floor and two steps later my full backpack was unbuckled and crashed into a table. I rushed towards an interior door, my trousers already at half mast. I had a momentary fear that it could be the linen cupboard not the loo but I was now at the point of no return. Whatever was inside would have to do. I bulldozed it open and just had a split second to elbow the door shut, crash land onto the toilet seat before....

You don't need much imagination to picture the Armageddon which was playing out in the bathroom. Seven or eight minutes later I just had time to flush and fall to my knees before I reverted to throwing up again.

It was a full quarter of an hour of indescribable noises and even worse odours before I struggled out of the bathroom to get water. But as I opened the door another wave ran over me. This one was pure embarrassment. There, politely standing in the middle of the room, was the receptionist. He hadn't seen but in every other sense he'd been a first-hand witness to the total collapse of my bodily functions. Of all the hideous things I was going through this felt the worst. However, he gave me not even the merest hint of any unease. Instead he ploughed straight into what had been on his mind for the past 15 minutes.

"I'll just explain how the switches work."

He flicked one switch up and down for the light, then another for the fan. That was it, briefing over. An unwavering commitment to the requirements of his job had clearly been drilled into him. He carried out his task to the letter and left.

For two whole days and nights I festered in my room. I ventured out just once to a nearby shop that sold water and dried biscuits. It was all I could keep inside me. However, by day three I was able to walk the short distance to the beach and sit myself up on an old wooden lounger. I wasn't going anywhere near the empty hammocks, swaying would have to wait.

By day four I was fine and I began to appreciate what a rare beauty I'd found. To say Port Barton is gorgeous is an understatement. The crescent bay is lined with palms bent lazily over a sliver of honeysuckled sand. The shallow water is a mesmerising dream of pure azure. A kilometre or two offshore are lush, tropical islands.

And there I could leave it, a picture of somewhere fully deserving of the word 'spectacular'. However, after months of travel in Southeast Asia I was aware that paradise isn't always all it's cracked up to be.

Port Barton was close but it had a couple of niggling flaws. The dreamy waters close in to the beach were home to many stinging jellyfish. And along the beach there were too many occasions when I heard the rattling motors of long-tail boats. Compared to the cacophony of Thai beach meccas like Krabi they were fairly insignificant. But hey, if you're seeking paradise you really need to set the bar a little high.

Accordingly on day five I decided to move on. I'd spotted some cottages on the hillside on the northern side of the bay. There were four of them and it turned out none were occupied. I quickly tracked down the owner and after agreeing a price of $25 a night I hauled myself up there. It was a walking track only, the motorbike stayed in the village.

Port Barton was beautiful at ground level, now it left me in a state of utter reverence. I sat for hours just taking in the beauty and dreaminess of the view. And then the most amazing thing happened. The sun began to set and the place took on an intoxicating, trance-like serenity. The fresh, bright colours of the day surrendered graciously to the dusk, leaving behind a deep red tinge to the cotton wool clouds. All around was a soothing, enchanting calm.

Later that night I went to bed in a state of deep contentment. I was set on a long night of sleep. After several days of illness I felt dog-tired. Unfortunately the dogs didn't feel tired at all. They began to tune up for a night of barking and howling. It is a scene repeated throughout the region, dogs will do their damnedest to keep you from shut eye whether you're in cities, countryside or by the beach. And they are not alone.

They have formed a bizarre and unholy alliance with cockerels. The dogs have clearly agreed to take the first watch and cockerels the second. So what you have is barking until about two in the morning and as they clock off the cockerels clock on and there is a seamless transition into crowing. The price of paradise is regularly interrupted sleep. I've tried everything from earplugs to dreamy music but the canines and cocks will not be silenced.

One way or another it had been a tough week. It was time to act.

#

47

HEADING HOME TO HOMELESSNESS

Week 51; 73,770 kms destination to destination + approx 5,000kms wandering/ biking = twice around the world; wonder socks - 4 ; Oboz shoes - fab; weariness - small; happiness - huge; gratitude - immense

Numbers, like words, can paint a picture, tell their own story. They can give you insight and understanding. The numbers on my journey were all telling me the same thing. And with the howling dogs of paradise giving me a final nudge, I knew it was time to go home.

I packed my trusty BlackWolf backpack and made one final, thorough check of my room. Better late than never I suppose. I climbed a little wearily onto a motorbike for the last time and began the long journey back to Queensland.

I'd left Australia 51 weeks earlier. In essence a full year, unless you're the Aussie tax man, in which case definitely only 51 weeks - apparently there are rules. But in everybody else's language an entire calendar had flipped over since I boarded a plane at Brisbane with what turned out to be an illegal ticket.

I'd visited 19 countries, admittedly Singapore was just a single night on a visa run from Thailand. I'd taken 47 flights, which is a hell of a lot of time at airports. Air travel itself can get a little tiring but at least it serves a purpose. By contrast the hours sitting in airport terminals always seemed a total waste of time. I started doing some calculations to work out how much of my life had disappeared there. Fortunately I realised the answer would be really depressing so I stopped. My worst delay was three days but thankfully very little of that was spent at the airport.

During the trip I got through seven pairs of thongs (flip flops), some broken, others lost. Seven was also the magic number for hats, not all were worn out. If you change rooms as much as I did you need a good system for packing. Shame I never got around to having one.

Hats and thongs were left and lost in rooms across the globe. I also got through two pairs of prescription sunglasses which is really not clever. I lost one, bought a replacement in Vietnam then lost them in Cambodia.

Amazingly, the two pairs of socks bought in a hurry on the morning of my departure were still with me. On so many parts of the journey one or other would be missing, presumed lost, and then they'd miraculously turn up again. Often they were pounded for days without washing, remarkably they were never uncomfortable and there were far worse odours on my travels. They really had fitted their billing as 'wonder socks'.

And then we come to the big number. I slept in 142 different beds. They ranged from tiny to huge, saggy to solid. Sometimes the bedding lacked a little cleanliness, other times it was non-existent. I slept on my own towel in a couple of places for fear of bed bugs.

There were some really big numbers as well. I swapped hundreds of stories and had thousands of laughs. At the other end of the numerical scale I had two marriage offers on the same day, admittedly my potential father-in-laws may have been keener than their daughters.

I'll confess to two tears, one, from self-pity in Penang, which you know about, the other was from pure happiness. A perfect day in Bonn had finished with a free concert at the Beethoven Theatre. Massenet's sorrowful violin piece Meditation was immediately followed by the heartache of Puccini's Vissi D'Arte from Tosca. If you don't know either of them search them out, they are wrenchingly beautiful. As I sat and listened in total rapture a single tear rolled gently down my cheek. It wasn't sorrow but something close to a feeling of total contentment.

Apart from the numbers there were many pearls of wisdom I picked up on my travels. For instance I now know the best time to commit a driving offence in Mandalay. The answer is after 5.30pm. All the traffic cops quit work then so the country's strict motorbike helmet rules are immediately ignored. But in Thailand and Bali you want to leave it a little later. From four o'clock to six o'clock is often tea time for the cops. In other words the time they're looking to fine you so they can go and buy some food for tea.

I now also know the best method for eating green curry while lying down in a cinema. These are the kind of gems they never teach you in school.

I saw the wonder of the natural world and the genius of man's creativity. I met a gigolo and the most beautiful woman in the world; spent time with the headhunters, a nuclear physicist and a former CIA chief; came across people with almost literally nothing, and a couple whose wealth could probably be counted in tens of millions.

I drove a train, became a Hindu for a day and witnessed ancient rituals. I was enchanted by great company, loved the solitude of lone travelling and at other times felt the heavy hand of loneliness.

Sunsets were the best and the worst of times. At moments, alone in perfect silence, deep in contemplation, the sinking of the sun could be almost mystical. On other days it brought on a heightened sense of isolation. A number of times in breathtaking cliff top Greek tavernas I sat alone, the only person at a table set for two.

But I was never far from the kindness and caring of wonderful people. The generosity of complete strangers was incredibly uplifting throughout the year. One simple scene from my final day in Borneo summed it all up. I'd spent a month on the island and some of it was tough going. On my last day I'd been to visit an Australian War

Memorial in Sandakan and was walking with my backpack to the airport. It was hot and humid and the hike had become a trudge. A car stopped alongside me, the window came down and in perfect English the Malaysian driver asked if I would like a lift.

I gratefully got in and the lady explained that her young niece had spotted me passing her home and asked her aunt to give me a lift. Without hesitation she'd gone to the car and rode to my rescue. These random acts of kindness from strangers can reaffirm your faith in humanity.

The same went for old friends and new, family and relations. Their friendship, kindness and help journeyed with me across the globe. In a time of great unease around much of the world it's important to put our lives in context. The reality is the good people of all faiths and creeds around the world outnumber the bad by a massive margin. Despite all that I saw and did it was the people who made it a year like no other.

As for travelling as a Nony without a plan, I'd highly recommend it. Being unrestrained and freed of enslavement by a guidebook really does open up the world. It led me to amazing places and people I'd never otherwise have found. I'm not saying you should throw away your 'Lonely Planets', just don't let them be your bible. Flexibility and a willingness to follow your own instincts can find you unscripted treasures.

You don't need limitless time, as I had, just an inquisitive mindset that allows unplanned possibilities whether over a week or a month.

As a middle age backpacker very little is off-limits and what is, well the young are mostly welcome to it. But you will find your energy and enthusiasm for life rebooted. It might also be a reminder that the world is fundamentally a safe place. It won't all be plain sailing but you'll feel the wind in your hair, the sun on your back and the liberating feeling of your mind being prised a little open. As we mature we can forget how amazing this all feels.

And so I reached the end of the road. My journey was over. It was time to go home.

There was just one tiny, little problem I hadn't factored in. I didn't have a home. I'd sold it. Oh dear, time to add to the statistics. I wondered if any friends might have a bed for a couple of nights. Ah well, something would turn up. I'd learned not to sweat the small stuff.

#

ACKNOWLEDGEMENTS

My thanks to Alex Mankiewicz for all the hours and inspiration
designing the book cover.
Roger and Suellen Petrie who went through the manuscript line by line
catching untold errors.
Satomi Mohr who was a rock of encouragement.
Arlene Penlington who read the book several times and came up with
numerous improvements.
Last and not least to my family and all friends, old and new, who
showed me incredible kindness on my journey. There are far too many
to mention by name but their generosity, support and great company
made it a year like no other.
My heartfelt thanks to them all.

AUTHOR NOTE

Arthur Penlington was born in Rhyl in north Wales. He moved to
Australia in 2005 and home is the Sunshine Coast in Queensland.
He spent 17 years working for BBC TV News, his final post was Senior
Editor of the news channel. He worked extensively in the field and
covered three wars, a coup, the aftermath of the Rwanda genocide and
elections in three continents.
He now spends his time travelling and writing

www.arthurpenlington.com

Printed in Great Britain
by Amazon.co.uk, Ltd.,
Marston Gate.